THE WAY

of the

WALL STREET
WARRIOR

THE WAY

of the

WALL STREET
WARRIOR

THE WAY
OF THE
WALL STREET
WARRIOR

THE WAY

of the

WALL STREET WARRIOR

CONQUER THE CORPORATE GAME
USING TIPS, TRICKS, AND SMARTCUTS

DAVE LIU

WITH **ADAM SNYDER**

WILEY

Library of Congress Cataloging-in-Publication Data
Names: Liu, Dave, author. | Snyder, Adam, author.
Title: The way of the Wall Street warrior : conquer the corporate game
  using tips, tricks, and smartcuts / Dave Liu, Adam Snyder.
Description: Hoboken, New Jersey : John Wiley & Sons, Inc., [2022] |
  Includes index.
Identifiers: LCCN 2021037401 (print) | LCCN 2021037402 (ebook) | ISBN
  9781119811909 (Hardcover) | ISBN 9781119811916 (ePDF) | ISBN
  9781119811923 (ePub)
Subjects: LCSH: Success in business. | Executive ability.
Classification: LCC HF5386 .L739 2022 (print) | LCC HF5386 (ebook) | DDC
  650.1—dc23
LC record available at https://lccn.loc.gov/2021037401
LC ebook record available at https://lccn.loc.gov/2021037402

COVER DESIGN: DAVE LIU
COVER ART: PAUL MCCARTHY
SKY10029982_092321

This book is dedicated to my mother, Vicki Liu, who showed me through hard work and determination that anything is possible. She also taught me not to take crap from anyone—from jerk customers at Safeway to narcissistic CEOs. Thanks, Mom!

Contents

Acknowledgments

This book would not have happened if it were not for the heroic efforts of me, myself, and I. So first, I'd like to thank myself for a job well done and pat myself on the back. I honestly thought I wouldn't be able to write enough to fill a postcard, but it looks like I have plenty to say!

I'd like to thank those people who allowed me to waste an hour or more of their precious Netflix time by sharing their stories. Extra kudos for letting me use their real identities. That includes Juan Alva, Frank Baxter, Herald Chen, Joanne Chen, Paul Clausing, Edward Fu, Eric Heglie, Michael Henkin, Gina King, Chris McGowan, Harry Nelis, Bret Pearlman, Sreene Ranganathan, Jon Seiffer, Spencer Wang, Dave Wargo, and Lauren Wu.

The feedback from those who read early manuscripts of this book was also tremendously helpful. Thanks for helping me eliminate the mindless drivel that would have sent this book straight into the discount pile. In particular, I'd like to thank Gad Allon, Bing Chen, Shubhan Dua, Brian Flynn, Tomoko Fortune, Bjorn Hovland, Eric Hu, James Liu, Tina Longfield, Leda Nelis, Mas Siddiqui, and Katherine Stevenson.

I'd like to thank the team at Wiley for their support and making me change the title more times than my underwear. And to my agent, Kevin Anderson, and his team, for taking a chance on me—a first-time author who was more anonymous than Bitcoin founder Satoshi Nakamoto.

I'd like to give a big high-five to my co-writing partner, Adam Snyder. Thanks for keeping me on track, fixing all the mistakes, and making this book readable. Without your help, my Mom would've been the only one to read it.

Last, but certainly not least, I'd like to thank my family. To my wife, Lauren Wu, for encouraging me to write a book to share my love of storytelling. To my older son, Logan, who convinced me that it was time to press the eject button out of the Wall Street rat race and devote my life to being a great dad. And finally to my younger son, Lucian, who's convinced I'm writing a book about working at Wal-Mart and managing my way out of paper bags. Thanks to all of you for constantly reminding me that there's much more to life than making a ton of money!

Dave Liu

About the Author

Dave Liu is a seasoned veteran of Wall Street where he worked for almost 25 years. He started his investment banking career working for Goldman Sachs and then joined the fledgling investment bank Jefferies when it had less than 200 employees. Today, Jefferies is a multi-billion-dollar public company and one of the world's leading investment banks. During his 25-year career at Jefferies, Dave progressed from the proverbial janitor level of analyst to managing director, co-running all digital media and Internet investment banking activities.

As one of the firm's only managing directors of color, and among its youngest, Dave successfully rose the ranks by not only working his ass off, but also playing the corporate game. He has managed, mentored, and trained hundreds of bankers, many of whom have gone on to some of the best business schools in the world or achieved great career success on Main Street and Wall Street. He has completed over $15 billion of transactions for hundreds of companies, including IBM, Google, Microsoft, Sony, Yahoo!, and Yelp.

After retiring from Wall Street in his early 40s, Dave became an entrepreneur, starting four companies, and an active investor. He has helped many multi-billion-dollar companies, including Internet Brands/WebMD, a technology company; Vobile, a video software company; and MobilityWare, one of the world's largest mobile gaming companies. He is involved with Capacity, an artificial intelligence platform; Stampede, a film production company; TEG Live, a Grammy Award–winning and Tony Award–winning live production company; and Philz Coffee, an iconic coffee retailer. He was also CEO advisor to ProSiebenSat.1 Media, one of the largest media companies in Europe.

Dave is also a perspiring artist and writer who is learning how to draw and write "funny." He studied creative writing at the University of Pennsylvania, Sundance Institute, and The Second City. He publishes a career advice column called *Breaking Bamboo* and a cartoon series called *The ABC Life*.

Dave completed the Management & Technology Program at the University of Pennsylvania where he received a bachelor of science in systems science and engineering (with concentrations in manufacturing and robotics) and a bachelor of science in economics (with a concentration in finance) from the Wharton School. He graduated with great honors and was inducted into the national engineering honor society, Tau Beta Pi. Dave also attended Harvard Business School where he received his master's degree in business administration.

Dave is active in philanthropy and nonprofit organizations. He currently serves on the Executive Board of the Management & Technology Program at the University of Pennsylvania and on the Trust Advisory Committee of Tau Beta Pi. His family supports many charitable initiatives helping women of color, children with disabilities, and other disadvantaged communities. Net proceeds from this book will go toward charities helping children born with clefts, Asian Americans, and other disadvantaged groups.

Follow Dave on his website, **www.liucrative.com**.

Adam Snyder, since working as a congressional press secretary, has been a freelance writer for decades, authoring or co-authoring more than a dozen nonfiction books focusing on such diverse topics as real estate, business leadership, and Buddhism. He is currently working on a novel revolving around the descendants of H. G. Wells. Adam is also the president of the Oscar-winning animation company Rembrandt Films and lives everywhere with his filmmaker wife, Pat. They have two children, a son-in-law, and a granddaughter.

Introduction

Game On

Congratulations! Whether you're just getting started in your nonexistent career or contemplating a switch from your current job, the smartest thing you've done to date is to buy this book. If you bummed it off your buddy, then kudos to you! You've already taken one small step toward proving you have the right mettle for earning a high salary in this dog-eat-dog world. The pearls included in these pages may not be the first career advice you've ever received, but I guarantee these tricks of the trade will be the most valuable.

As the title suggests, *The Way of the Wall Street Warrior* will show you how to use tips, tricks, and smartcuts to get hired, get ahead, survive, and excel on Wall Street, Main Street, or any other street where you're mining for gold. It comes from my experience as a 25-year investment banking veteran who did the unthinkable. I, an Asian American with a cleft lip and palate, rose up in the white, male-dominated world of high finance, becoming a managing director before the age of 33. I then left my high-profile job in my early 40s, on my own terms, while on top.

While my lessons were learned on Wall Street, they're applicable to *anyone, anywhere* working in *any* competitive corporate environment. If you can make it in the Machiavellian world of banking, you can make it anywhere. Wall Street is a jungle, the toughest jungle there is. I had a highly successful career because I learned how to game the system, and now I'm writing this book so you'll learn my tricks and avoid making the same mistakes as your peers.

Unrig Your Mind

If you care about money, this book is for you. If you want practical advice without the BS but don't mind some acerbic humor that goes along with it, you're in luck. If the do-nothing in the cubicle next to you is earning more than you, or you can no longer stomach hearing your mother's sighs and your father's *tsk-tsk*s, or you need a kick in the pants—read this book!

Here's what you'll gain: You'll learn how to survive and thrive by *not* relying on the skills you mastered in the warm confines of the classroom. Instead, you'll learn from me what it actually takes to get ahead.

Another reason to read this book is if you're stuck in a dead-end job. You might be severely disillusioned and filled with self-doubt. Perhaps you've been wondering if there is a secret handshake that will gain you entrance into the inner circle or a magic carpet that will carry you up to the executive suite. Maybe you're the person who buys every how-to book you can get your hands on, hoping one might unlock the secrets for getting that coveted raise or promotion. Even if you have yet to reach this level of angsty ambition, I can guarantee you've seen dropouts become billion-aires or buffoons become your bosses and asked yourself, "Why not me?" What's the answer? You already know because you feel it in your bones: THE SYSTEM IS RIGGED!

The Way of the Wall Street Warrior is going to *unrig* it for you. From a young age, we're pounded with the idea of meritocracy—that we're rewarded based on our talents. If we just study hard, keep our nose to the grindstone and follow the straight and narrow, we can achieve greatness. These rules of engagement were pounded into my brain during my Asian American upbringing. The tenets of respect, honor, and obedience are an integral part of our culture. We're taught that if we work hard and obey the rules, life will take care of itself, and that in business you'll get promoted and do great.

Horse manure!

I got ahead by ignoring these rules. Most of what we're taught in school and by our elders are just guardrails put there to keep us in check. We know that getting the right opportunity is less about *what* you know and more about *who* you know and that the easiest way to get filthy rich is to *start* rich. Of course that doesn't work for most of us, so if you, too, feel fooled, it's time to come up with a new mindset and a new game plan. If you take this book seriously (but not too seriously), the tricks and tactics revealed in the following pages will drop like dollars from heaven.

Built with Sweat, Backed by Science

I have more good news. The tactics in this book are not just something I made up out of thin air. In fact, they're based on scientific research in the fields of **cognitive bias** and **behavioral economics**. In get-rich-for-dummies terms, these disciplines use an understanding of human psychology to account for why people often don't act rationally, particularly in economic decision-making. Smarter people than I have won Nobel Prizes for their work in this field, and I'm here to summarize their most salient takeaways—to help you get that big promotion and salary you've always wanted. I got hooked on the field more than 20 years ago, read every book I could get my grubby hands on, and actually applied what I found to advance my career. So what are their conclusions? That human beings are imperfect and fundamentally irrational when making decisions. In my words, people can be *stupid*.

The interesting point here is that there are creative ways (that have scientific backing) for you to maneuver events and attitudes toward your advantage. But don't worry, there won't be any pedantic lessons, Excel spreadsheets, PowerPoint gibberish, or 15-letter acronyms in my explanations. You've had a lifetime of that already.

Instead, *The Way of the Wall Street Warrior* will put in plain English the scientific basis behind my practical advice. Terms like **affinity bias, signal-to-noise ratio, asymmetry of information, social proof**, and **Dunbar's Number** might seem like scientific gobbledygook, but a shorthand knowledge of each of them can give you the upper hand in any cutthroat business environment. And for those wanting a cheat sheet of the tips, tricks, and science covered in this book, you can sign up on my website[1] to get a copy of my Career Codex.

Lessons from the Elephant Boy

The first part of *The Way of the Wall Street Warrior* is where you'll learn how to edge your foot into the door and then how to dance the dance when you get there. It provides titillating tips about landing an interview (including scrubbing your social media accounts like leprotic calluses on gangrenous feet). This set of chapters will show you how to knock their socks off when you do get that one-on-one interview.

From there, we'll learn how to play well with others (suck up) and how to have the adaptability of a cockroach (always show how and why you belong). Then again, if you haven't made it past square one, I'll have some gems about using failure as fertilizer, hosting short self-pity parties, and then going out and crushing it.

The middle chapters of *The Way of the Wall Street Warrior* will focus on making your way up the **corporate ladder**. If you want to be showered with financial rewards and prestige, the name of the game is longevity, and that means making the best possible decisions to ensure your rise. Climbing the rungs motivates us because it promises more of everything—more compensation, more respect, more power.

This middle part is all about how to lead the pack, like choosing an office consigliere who will point out for you the potholes and political landmines. Remember, with each promotion, the higher you climb, the narrower the room, so ally yourself with the senior person who makes the most money and carries the most sway. Soon only one ass can sit on each rung. Make it yours!

The final chapters are where we discuss the "less critical" aspects of your life, like your health and well-being, significant other, and progeny. I'm being facetious, of course, but sometimes when you're simmering in the pressure cooker, what *should* be most important takes a back seat to what you *think* is important. I'll also share some insights on wealth creation and the afterlife (aka life after making piles of dough). This section will stress the importance of developing a personal brand— not the one on your LinkedIn profile, but the description given when someone asks about you when you're not in the room. You always want to manage the answer to the question, "What do you think of Dave Liu?"

---

[1]www.liucrative.com

One particular chapter close to my heart (yes, I have a heart) is Chapter 15, "Turn Liabilities into Assets." I haven't always been the cocky guy who comes across in this Introduction. In fact, at my ex-employer, Jefferies, I actually earned a reputation for having empathy for those who weren't making the grade or who were struggling to overcome personal issues. That's because growing up, and then when entering the workforce, I didn't have to be told I had two strikes against me.

First, I'm Asian, and how many persons of color do you see in the top echelons of Wall Street or on any well-heeled street for that matter? But wait, it gets better. I was born with a bilateral cleft lip and palate, a severe facial deformity that if left untreated, literally leaves children with a hole in their face. I was bullied and shamed, as kids thought nothing of gawking at me and referring to me as "Elephant Boy."

Ironically, being different—standing out in an obvious way before even opening your mouth—eventually had its advantages. As a junior player at Jefferies, at every meeting at which I was invited I made a point of trying to make at least one interesting point. The thing about having a scarred face is that you're going to be remembered, so if I succeeded in making just one comment that wasn't totally stupid, I usually ended up being remembered as "that smart Asian guy with the scars who spoke up."

My disability also gave me a superpower: rhino skin. In life, you'll run into many obstacles on your way to greatness, and I truly believe that not giving a hoot about what people think of you will make you a better businessperson. It worked for me.

It is my hope that this book will speak to my strategies for overcoming disadvantages and that my story will be inspirational for others dealing with their own challenges. I've worked on Wall Street, Silicon Valley, and even Hollywood, and I have to tell you, they're all corrupt regimes where white men rule the roost and will likely do so for some time. Unfortunately, I don't have a silver bullet (I'd definitely tell you if I did), and if you're a person of color, a woman in a man's world, a member of the LGBTQ+ community, or a person with physical disabilities, being different can really suck. Fortunately, the media is starting to show some of the cracks through the veneer, but as an insider, I can tell you, it's even worse than you think.

But all is not hopeless. Being different can actually be the recipe for being great. That might sound counterintuitive, but I'm going to show you how *I* did it; although pay heed to the fact that I'm not going to tell how *you* should do it. Nothing infuriated me more than a Caucasian person telling me what it's like to be Asian American, so I'm not going to pontificate about how I would do it in your shoes. How the hell would I know what walking in your shoes is like? I may be arrogant, but I'm not stupid. Just know that if an Asian Elephant Boy can rise to the top, there's hope for everyone. Also, if in doubt, I want you to know that every single tip, trick, or smartcut I have laid out is applicable to men *and* women, and whenever possible, I've tried to get a female perspective on the unique challenges faced by women in highly competitive (and political) industries like Wall Street. By no means are these ideas comprehensive, but my hope is they can help spur your imagination so you can crush it!

Beat C-3PO

There are many books on how to build a great career. This one is for the awoken among you who accept that working hard in the corporate world with all its warts is rarely enough. It's for those of you who practiced sleight-of-hand tricks as kids, delegated chores to younger siblings, and checked vending machines for loose change. It's for you who have realized that the most successful people see opportunity where others see obstacles. It's for those of you who want to learn skills that will prevent you from becoming obsolete—particularly in the not-so-distant future when you'll be competing for work against robots like C-3PO.

You won't learn what I am offering in any school. (I spent over a quarter million bucks at Harvard and Wharton, so I know what I'm talking about.) Our education system doesn't teach the softer elements needed to succeed in the world of high-pressured corporate finance. There are no tactical courses at Wharton or Harvard Business School on salesmanship, **emotional intelligence (EQ)**, or the human psyche, much less **cognitive dissonance** or biases. (You'll need to slum it at a liberal arts school to find them.) This book assumes you already have an out-of-the-park intelligence, so its primary aim is to help you take the next step and increase your emotional savvy. If you've never heard of EQ, that's a problem, because EQ allows you to identify and manage your emotions, as well as those of others. This book will teach you about EQ. If you have both IQ and EQ, in the business world you will be an awesome, unstoppable combination of Lex Luthor and Superman.

Succeeding on Wall Street or Whatever Street is all about doing the least amount of work for the most pay. Don't get me wrong. You still need to deliver and create great work or your career will be shorter than a reefer at Burning Man,[2] but pace yourself. Be the tortoise, not the hare. Be the smartest person in the room by lying in wait and making others think you aren't.

The secret sauce expressed in these pages includes interview tips (exaggerate), maneuvers for getting promoted (you don't need to outrun the bear, just the colleague next to you), ways to fit in (memorizing the top business movies so you can wax poetic about how little Hollywood actually knows about your industry), and ways to cover your ass (document everything—memories are short; emails are forever). I've also done a lot of work for you by summarizing key takeaways at the end of each chapter. Sometimes I'll read an entire book and want to scream, "Just tell me the elevator pitch! What's your point?!" My summaries are like CliffsNotes for grownups or those cheat sheets you bought off that brainiac in high school.

You can thank me now.

---

[2]Annual festival focused on community, art, self-expression, and self-reliance held in the western United States.

PART 1

Get in the Game

CHAPTER 1

Get Primed for Entry-Level Cattle Calls

Clean Your House

Y̶ou think you've been demeaned, disheartened, or even abused up to this point in your life? You ain't seen nothing yet. During the cattle call required to find an entry-level job, rejection can come faster than a blunt, "Better-Luck-Next-Time" four-word email. It's your first, startling indication that even getting your foot in the door will separate the plebes from the potentates.

The whole process of interviewing is ludicrous. If you do get hired, it's because you interview well, and not necessarily because you can do the work with any kind of competence. Interviews never made much sense to me because people perform differently in the field of play under the bright lights. Imagine signing a new quarterback through this process. He might give a great interview, but don't be surprised if on the first day of practice, the dude can't hit a moving target more than ten feet away. There's even a scientific explanation for it. It's called **interviewer illusion**, and it means the tendency for interviewers to overrate their own ability to interview and choose the best candidate. Who's the fool now?

But we're not here to break convention, at least not this one. This tried-and-true method probably dates all the way back to the Ice Age, when the first caveman asked his fellow hunter, "You do know how to kill a sabertooth, right?" Seconds before they were both mauled to death, he was probably thinking he should have done more due diligence.

So, obviously, the first rule in this playbook is to learn how to interview well. That's a talent all by itself.

But hang on, first you have to *get* the friggin' interview, so that's where we'll begin.

Scrub Those Leprotic Calluses

Landing an interview doesn't start with an email; it starts with a lot of prep work well before hitting the "Send" key with your cover note and resume. It begins with cleaning your social media house. Before going anywhere near a recruiter, a friend of the family who might help, or even your school's placement department, scrub your social media accounts like leprotic calluses on gangrenous feet. This is the arena where multitudes of warriors have fallen. Like the dormant chickenpox virus waiting to reemerge as the shingles, your youthful hijinks can hijack your career. Now is the time to search, destroy, delete. Then search again, destroy again, delete again.

At this starting point in the game, it's important to understand one very salient point. Corporate wonks have too many applications and resumes to cope with. Their mission is to find a reason NOT to hire you, and hundreds of others like you, so they can find the best three candidates worthy of an interview. If a quick Google search reveals a picture of you drunk on the roof of a house or having a penchant for racist memes, kudos for making their job really easy.

At the entry level, it's often the Human Resources department you're jousting with, so imagine them spraying luminol all over your life to uncover your darkest secrets. They're the bouncer at the nightclub; their ass is on the line if the firm hires a kleptomaniac, a slug, or a weaseler who got into Harvard pretending to be a champion coxswain.[1]

It's finally time to swab your Instagram, TikTok, Facebook, and any of the other dozens of apps where you deliriously posted about your bro trip to Mexico mingling with the local hotties or your NSFW weekend in Jamaica at your best friend's bridal shower, all in the never-ending quest to get followers. Purge anything that shows you in compromising positions—especially your most cherished posts. As a good rule of thumb, if your visceral reaction is "Dang, that's lit!" then hit delete. You never know who is judging you.

The TMZ Test

Practice the **TMZ Test**: Simply put, don't write anything or post any photos that you'd hate to see on the front page of a tabloid. That means if you've written anything you'd regret your priest seeing, it might be time to say *adieu* (French for *until we meet again*) to your favorite social media account until you're on *terra firma* (Latin for *solid earth*). Otherwise, you might be *f*cked* (French for *f*cked*).

At the same time, understand that since we know that nothing is ever truly deleted online, your efforts at evaporation might not completely succeed. So come up with a Plan B. If it's impossible to bury those pictures of you skinny dipping in the Red Sea or doing a keg stand on a diving board, then perhaps you may still be able to snatch victory from the jaws of defeat. Be prepared to smile earnestly and tell them you're an apostle of the "Work Hard, Play Hard" lifestyle. Even the most judgmental interviewers might envy you, or not, but at least you've given it a shot.

---

[1] You obviously did lie, because you have a dirty mind and don't even know that a coxswain is the person who steers the shell of a boat and is the on-the-water coach for a rowing crew.

Facebook and Instagram tend to be the top minefields, but buttoned-up LinkedIn can be equally treacherous. That's where most candidates put their resumes, but it's also where many feel the strange need to expose their inner selves or flaunt some higher purpose—like being on a mission to save all the pangolins in China. Remember, LinkedIn is not for making friends; it's your infomercial for getting paid.

On the positive side, job hunting is also a great time to take a good look at your LinkedIn account and be sure it's up-to-date and reflects your talents in the very best light. Dispense with the douchey descriptors like *Jack/Jackie of All Trades* (aka Master/Mistress of None) or *Strategic Visionary* (aka Good-for-Nothing). You'd be surprised how many bios I've seen that say at the top, *Self-Starter* or *Game Changer*. I recently saw a LinkedIn profile headlined, *Futurist*. Does that mean the person is a psychic? You might as well put as your headline, *Blithering Idiot*. If you're thinking, "Oh, dang, I thought I was actually being pretty clever," you're not. Instead, see how employees at your prospective employer describe themselves and do what every best-selling author does: copy and paste!

Also, check your references and make sure their contact information is current. While you're at it, have a clear idea of what each person will say about you, especially those who might have something negative, or even neutral, to volunteer. References are one way for an interviewer to fill in gaps about you, information that might not be reflected in your resume or transcript. The interviewer doesn't want any surprises, and you'll always know more about yourself than your interviewer knows about you. Make sure you control your own narrative and have several apostles lined up ready to praise your miracles.

Use **asymmetry of information** to your advantage. In contract theory and economics, this is the study of transactional decisions when one party has more or better information than the other. Don't be the ignoramus. Make certain you control your own particulars, rather than some A-hole ex-boss or professor who thought you were too big for your britches. This is another reason why you should scrub your LinkedIn. An ex-boyfriend might have linked to you in the past because at the time you were BFFs—although on Wall Street we prefer the term *Asshole Buddies* because nothing is forever. But now you're foes, and largely through your own laziness, that enemy is now available as a reference for any prospective employer to find. There's nothing like a backchannel reference to torpedo your chances faster than a German U-boat. So get ahead of it and know what they will say—or better yet, delink them from your network!

Key Takeaways

- Interviews are unreliable and risky due to *interviewer illusion*.
- Prospective employers try to find reasons NOT to hire you.
- Social media is where your youthful *hijinks* can *hijack* your career.
- Scrub *all* of your social media accounts like leprotic calluses on gangrenous feet.
- Practice the *TMZ Test*: Never post anything you wouldn't want on the front page.
- Due to *asymmetry of information*, interviewers try hard to fill the gaps.
- Delink bad backchannel references easily discoverable on social media.

CHAPTER 2

Don't Fight the Tape

Diligence Your Way to an Interview

In preparation for interviews, ask your close friends and colleagues what they thought of you at first contact. What were their brutally honest first impressions? Maybe your friend from kindergarten remembers you running around without pants. Or another remembers how you were sullen and listened to *Billie Eilish* on repeat. Regardless, ask only for the bad, or the things you need to improve. You probably already know what's great about yourself, but we're often oblivious to what makes us less than perfect.

Why is it so important to understand people's first impressions of you? It's not just that you want to put your best foot forward (and lock your worst foot in a safe room). People tend to hire those who are like themselves. It's all part of the field of **cognitive bias**, a discipline that uses psychology to explain why people make decisions, usually irrational ones. This field includes **affinity bias**—a concept that explains *why* employers tend to hire people who look like them and have similar beliefs and backgrounds.

On Wall Street, there is a phrase, "Don't fight the tape." It means not to trade against the market. If stocks are rising, don't sell. Obviously, this can be shite investment advice, but it's a useful maxim when you're first trying to get in the door on a job or a deal. So go with the flow, study the heck out of the companies, and try to determine their organizational biases. You may surprise yourself with what you can do to appeal to their affinity biases.

Diligence to Death

Let's start off with the obvious. Before trying to learn something about the people who will be interviewing you, it's essential to know the ins and outs of the companies where they work. Go deep in your due diligence. Learn everything you can about the company's history—its hierarchy, its distinct departments, and what each department does. Which one most interests you, what role would you like to play, and what makes you a perfect fit? Nothing makes you look like a complete fraud more than not really understanding the job you hope to land. Be prepared to answer these questions even if they're not asked. You'll want to be prepared with a deft pivot anyway, away from a question for which you don't have a brilliant answer.

Memorizing facts won't be enough. Look for any media, especially spin, about the firm. What do they claim about equal opportunity? Do they really just worship the dollar? Any disgruntled employees writing tell-all exposés? Any movie a thinly disguised parody of your employer of choice? Any alumni rotting behind bars?

On Wall Street, it's a given to work insane hours with bosses yelling down your neck for you to be at your desk the next morning at 6 a.m. to prepare for the unexpected. Your boss will be rolling in at 10 a.m., so that will give you plenty of time to prepare a 100-page report. Are you really ready for that? Do you think your interviewer will tell you, "Our company is awesome," while blinking "RUN!" in Morse code? In short, know what you're getting into (or out of, in case you don't get the job or if you're offered a much better one and can tell them to bugger off).

Be a Troll

At this point, just being knowledgeable about the staff lineup will help you wordsmith your cover letter. Find out who will be interviewing you and try to ferret out everything you can about the person. Troll them on the company's website, LinkedIn, Facebook, and anywhere you can get a sense of who these people are. What are their interests? Are they Dodgers fans, or do they prefer polo? Maybe you have mutual acquaintances. If so, don't hesitate to name-drop shamelessly.

Most important, try to determine the biases your interviewer might have that could prevent you from being hired. Conversely, think about possible biases that will help bolster your case to get you on the fast track. Biases cloud human judgment, so crack the code and use them to your advantage. I've been stereotyped all my life: Asian American males are super-good at math, have Confucian hierarchies etched into their psyches, and work crazy hard because, other than their mothers, women don't find them attractive so they don't waste time dating. So if somehow I slip it in during our interview that I'm a workhorse math wiz (even if I'm not), I'm 1000 percent dedicated to my career, and I'm a total Yes Man, then I won't have to do much selling. I'll simply be confirming a bias that probably already exists with my interviewer and she will see me as being worth my weight in gold.

Chris McGowan, former managing director at Madison Dearborn, former banker at Morgan Stanley, and now adjunct professor at the University of Chicago's Booth School of Business, tells his MBA students to take advantage of *affinity networks* in their job searches—to scour the web and social media sites to determine who went to the same undergraduate and graduate schools as they did. A common elementary school is even better to strike up nostalgic, bond-inducing conversation. "You had Ms. Chang in third grade, too? Remember those funny hats she wore?" Of course, just grin and bear it when they respond, "Oh, yeah, and I also remember you shat in your pants!"

"Don't stop with the obvious," Chris tells his students. "If you're making a career switch, see who took a similar path as you did. If you're into unicycling, find the other unicyclists."

Students need to understand how the game is played. On Wall Street, for example, some firms hire by organizing into school-based teams. If you're not from one of the top schools, you'll need to try harder, but at Morgan Stanley, for example, they had teams of employees made up of those with degrees from the top schools, so they had a Wharton team, a Harvard team, a Columbia team, etc. They're made up of alumni, responsible for reviewing the resumes and setting up interviews from their alma mater. It's just part of employers' leveraging affinity. They're also able to suss out the BS pronto, since they know which classes were *gut* classes and which were the *real* ones. They'll know which are better indicators of job performance. For instance, at Wharton, a C in Fixed Income Securities carries more weight than an A in Responsibility in Business.

Key Takeaways

- *Cognitive bias* explains why people sometimes make seemingly irrational decisions.
- *Affinity bias* is why employers tend to hire people like themselves.
- Research your target companies and try to infer their organizational biases.
- Exploit these biases by reinforcing those that will bolster your hiring case.
- Use *affinity bias* to your advantage by getting referrals from mutual acquaintances!

CHAPTER 3

Be the Holy Trinity of Deals

Your All-Important First Email

With your research at your fingertips, it's now time to reach out with that all-important first email. The first thing to realize is that the emails you send are treated like spam. So how do you grab the attention of the interviewer? The same way you started reading about the *Financial Crisis of 2008* and ended up scrolling pictures of *NBA Players Megan Thee Stallion Has Dated*: click-bait!

Give prospective employers a reason to click through and learn more about you by creating that perfect email that will get their attention. Be different, but be succinct. Err on the side of brevity. People are busy and their **return on time invested (ROTI)** is critical, so value your email recipient's time as if it were more important than your own, which it is.

Make Me Give a Damn

The first thing that will catch your reader's attention is a memorable subject line that summarizes the email's key message. This leverages another **cognitive bias**, **attentional bias**, the tendency to pay attention to some things while simultaneously ignoring others. It explains a person's focus on only one or two choices, despite there also being several other possible outcomes. It's another one of those brilliant scientific acumens that translates into solid, practical advice, in this case: Nail it in a sentence! This is all the more important in this era when the average Internet user has a shorter attention span than a goldfish.[1]

Be the pitch, like you would in a once-in-a-lifetime investment opportunity. Make it short and sweet because the first and last lines of your email are likely the only ones that will be remembered. Avoid the boring, like "Applying for Position" or "Seeking Advice." Instead, mimic the way a movie tries for a stunning logline or captivating sentence that sums up the whole shebang: "Jaws Meets Home Alone." "Clint Eastwood in Outer Space." "The Invisible Man Finds a Time Machine."

Usually if the logline sucks, so does the film, so make yours a good one. Here are some subject lines that weren't necessarily great, but did catch my attention:

- Looking for a Superstar Workaholic? Look No Further!
- Superpowers My Resume Doesn't Reveal
- Will Work for Free (or Almost Free)

My personal favorites which would get me to prowl deeper are those that make links to common acquaintances:

- Our Friend, Matt Lin, Thought We Should Connect
- Matt Lin's Friend Seeking Advice
- Have Dirt on Matt Lin

Using a mutual friend to make the connection has the power to encourage the reader to open the email and read it out of guilt or obligation—unless, of course, Matt Lin stole your wife. Or husband. But hey, snatch victory from the jaws of defeat. At least you and the recipient have the same lousy taste in friends. You can bond over that.

Watch the Trapdoors

The next step is to write the email. At this point, many job hunters experience the exact opposite of "You had me at hello!" Make the salutation respectful. If it's the initial email, I like "Dear Mr. or Ms." because it's so retro. Hardly anyone addresses people like this anymore. It goes without saying, don't send an email without a salutation like you would a text. We aren't *Gangnam Style* friends on WhatsApp. Also, be professional and don't begin with "Yo" or "Hey Buddy," or my personal

---

[1] According to a 2015 study by Microsoft, the average human being now has an attention span of eight seconds. You can imagine it's even worse now. https://time.com/3858309/attention-spans-goldfish/

anti-favorite, "Dear Mr. David A. Liu," which clearly indicates it came from a mass email merge. Show that your email is personalized, not personal. That will appeal to the person's ego and self-love by showing them they're important.

Here's a few more *Do's* and *Don'ts*:

- *Do* get to the point! Unless it's the latest *Dan Brown* novel, many of us hate to read, so don't waste our time or put us to sleep.
- *Don't* bury the lead. This comes from a bygone era when there were things called newspapers and journalists were taught not to hide the most important part of the story. *You're* the story here, so don't bury the most important thing about you somewhere in the middle.
- *Do* make it 100 percent clear right out of the gate why it's in the recipient's best interest to answer you. Here are some suggestions for opening sentences that will make your target read further:
  o I know you have a role to fill and I'm just the person who can fill it.
  o Here are the three reasons why I'm perfect for the job.
  o John Wong suggested I would be the best candidate for the role you're seeking. (Personally, I love this one because, assuming your target knows John Wong, it provides **social proof** that you might actually be the solution.)
- *Don't* repeat your resume unless it's something that really should be highlighted *and* is relevant. For instance, unless I'm the Green Bay Packers, I don't care that you won the Heisman Trophy, but I definitely want to know that you currently have an exploding offer from JP Morgan. (One caveat is we may want bragging rights for having Wall Street's Fittest Athlete. For many years, Wall Street had the Wall Street Decathlon, a 10-event competition which fuses challenges from the Olympic Decathlon and the NFL Combine. It was as stupid as it sounds and featured a bunch of washed-up, has-been college athletes looking to relive their glory days by impressing a bunch of nerds whose typical exercise is running to and from the kitchen in between stock trades to get bagels and lox. Thankfully, it has since morphed into D10, a more inclusive decathlon focused on charitable causes.)
- *Do* attach your resume, but make sure it's one page! No one is interested in a treatise on all your achievements dating back to your pre-K years. I'm not your Dad!

If you think you're a longshot for the job, you're going to have to take chances. You might want to consider some riskier catchphrases that might hook your reader, like "If you want me, I'm yours" or "I have other options" (i.e., shit or get off the pot).

The Rule of Three

Your goal is to provide a quick way of communicating why you're perfect for your potential employer. My favorite tactic is to use three bullet points. The **Rule of Three** is actually a writing tip that states a trio of points is more humorous, satisfying, or effective than other numbers. So give the impression that you're the love child of a Holy Trinity: the brains of Albert Einstein, the stamina of Optimus Prime, and the persistence of Wile E. Coyote.

Once you get past the opening sentence, let me reiterate a word of advice: Keep it short! People don't have time to read your version of *War and Peace*. They're too busy four-lettering their way through *work* so they can get on with *life* and *play*.

Ideally, your email will be readable on an iPhone screen in the bathroom. Yes, shocking, but you may not be someone's highest priority and the only time your target might have to scroll through your cover emails is the same place he has a chance to track his Amazon packages—when he's sitting on the can.

In your brief missive, it's also vital to link your skills with the firm's *specific* needs. This is where your research about the company and job openings will pay enormous dividends. You might even get lucky and what you really want to do is what the company really wants you to do. If you're a golf fanatic, have a degree from Harvard in communications, and don't get an interview for that social media position at Callaway Golf, you might as well pack it in. Even I can't help you.

Personally, I like bullet points, and again, three is usually the magic number. Maybe because I was raised at the altar of PowerPoint, I've found everything in life is generally explained in three short, quick phrases. If you have four really good ones, fine, but anything more than that tends to lose your audience, and anything less feels like you don't have anything to say. So think about the three key points you want to make. Every industry is different, but in banking, for example, here's what matters in order of priority: work experience, **grit** and hard work, and affinity. Let me explain further, as if I were receiving an email from you.

- *Work Experience.* Show me you've done this work before, ideally at an internship or previous job. Why? Because my time is valuable. I need to make sure

I have time for work, watching Netflix, and coitus (that last one takes less time as you age, but I still want the option). Time also means money. I want the highest **ROTI** on my hires. Remember that **ROTI, or return on time invested**, is the return on any time expended as valued in dollars. Translation: I want you to do all the work so I can make all the money. The fewer number of hours I need to train you in the basics (i.e., non-revenue generating work), the more time *you'll* have to make models, pitches, and other grunt work that will allow *me* to earn the moolah.

If you don't have the work experience, you're not exactly out of the running, but it does put you at a huge disadvantage. So be creative. Maybe there's something in your limited resume that can be reinforced in your cover letter. Underscore how you worked hard to get good grades in STEM while at the same time writing about Ponzi schemes for *Wharton Magazine*. Highlight something creative, even if it's a bit off-the-wall, like creating a PowerPoint presentation where *you* are the opportunity of a lifetime.

To get your juices flowing, I prepared a sample pitch (which you can get if you register on my website[2]) that highlights a mock candidate, "Mister Perfect," in the form of a hot IPO. Any resemblance to me is purely coincidental. Feel free to check it out and steal it if you wish.

Note that this is a high beta strategy because although there's a chance you appear unique, smart, and innovative, you're more likely to come across as a complete weirdo. But like good ol' Benny Franks said, "Nothing ventured, nothing gained," right?

One real-life unorthodox approach comes from Michael Henkin, former senior managing director of Guggenheim Securities. Someone who wanted to work for him agreed to work on a single company pitch as a trial run. This allowed Michael to assess him and ultimately "try before you buy." It worked. Michael eventually hired him. Talk about betting on yourself!

- *Grit and Hard Work.* Show me you'll put up with a lot of crap. A metric ton's worth. I'm talking about working all hours and not bitching. Expect to get last-minute changes from me on a presentation that you handed me a week ago. Or I'll give you my markup a few hours before the meeting and expect it to be flawless. Remember, crap flows downhill, from the CEO client pissed at me because there were errors in the presentation to you who handed it to me five minutes before the meeting. So it better be perfect!

One of the best bankers who worked for me was someone who had been a Mormon missionary. It dawned on me that nothing could take more determination than spending years selling God door-to-door in the farthest-most

---

[2] www.liucrative.com

regions of the Earth facing constant rejection by a bunch of heathens. I knew this person would walk through walls to get the job done. Plus, if he was any good at it, not only would he reserve his place in heaven (and maybe pull a few strings for me), but also chances were high that he was a natural salesman, which would bode well for his future rise in banking. I mean, if you can sell God to the damned, you can sell anything to anyone.

Personally, I earned my first grit-wings as a janitor at a Safeway supermarket. I was paid a minimum wage of $3.35 per hour to clean toilets, then got chewed out for failing to double-bag groceries. Nothing is more humiliating than feeling you aren't cut out to neatly stack shopping carts or clean all the piss out of a urinal. That experience put me knee-deep in grit. I worked in college out of pure desperation, but my three jobs while still graduating with honors with a dual degree helped me once I started looking for a job. It showed future employers that if I could put up with real crap, I could certainly stomach their metaphorical shit.

- *Affinity.* Show me that we have something in common. Maybe we're both Houston Rockets fans? Or both watch Pokimane on Twitch? OK, how about being left-handed!? Look for something fun or something you can mock together—school, hobbies, card games, odd habits, anything! But make sure it's not illegal, unethical, or just plain weird. Only your mom will tolerate that you munch on your toenails after cutting them.

Sreene Ranganathan, a member of Facebook's Corporate Development team and former Jefferies banker, shared how he first got into banking. When he was in school, by the time he decided he wanted to pursue an investment banking career, he had missed all the on-campus interviews. Undaunted, he did the research and found 107 alumni who worked at various banks and sent customized emails to each one of them. He highlighted recent school activities, figuring it might help him establish common ground with the recipients. It worked! Six answered back and helped him get interviews and, ultimately, a job. Sreene's persistence, coupled with using his noggin to establish some mutual affinity, got him a job.

One last point on affinity. Never, ever wade into the shark-infested waters of politics, religion, or race. You might as well bang your head against a landmine in Fallujah. Although it might not be obvious at first blush, you never know if you were dinged from the process because their God told them there were no open positions for Satanists. But if it does happen, look on the bright side. At least you can sue them for asking you an illegal question. Lemon from lemonade!

Go Out with a Bang

Now comes the finale—your signoff. People don't spend enough time on ending an email because they aren't aware of **recency bias**. It's the tendency of people to place a higher value on recent events than on ones that occurred in the past, which in this case means that the last few words of your email are more important than how you start. This is your last chance to make a final impression before you lose the recipient—potentially forever. So make it stick. Avoid the mundane and the boring. Sure, you can play it safe with something like *Sincerely*, the most vanilla in this category. No chance of totally screwing up with that one, but I always thought it a little weird—kind of like the written version of "To be honest. . . ." WTF? You've been dishonest and insincere this whole time and *now* you're finally going to tell me the truth?

Best or *Best Regards* has always been my personal go-to. If you're choosing between the two, I prefer *Best Regards*. It means I was willing to spend at least two words on you and I want only the best for you. Unfortunately, this makes *Warm Regards* and *Regards* the equivalent of a limp handshake. I'd avoid those.

Thanks is another one I like, as it can create a subliminal obligation for the recipient to reciprocate, which means you're taking advantage of the celebrated **reciprocity bias**, which is the scientific version of "You scratch my back and I'll scratch yours." If you still have no idea what I'm talking about, check out the Glossary and get a refresher. You know how much work it takes to write a book? Show some respect!

There are other, more personal signoffs that can work, but only if you have, or are on the verge of having, a personal relationship with the recipient. *Cheers, Your Friend, Adios Amigo,* and *Ciao* only work if you really know the person, or maybe even if you think you do. And please, no emojis! This isn't your group chat where you message your girlfriends about how your BFF just became your BF.

A few final tips for how to introduce yourself: Always add your email and cell phone and any other method of contacting you. It shows your availability 24-7, which bodes well for being a great employee in the grit department. But never, ever, ever include social media sites like Facebook or Instagram. You never know when one of your girlfriends will decide to tag you in a G.O.A.T. pic. Also, get a Gmail account. You millennials might not even know what I'm talking about here, but nothing screams tool or luddite more than *daveliu@AOL.com*. Those of you who do still use AOL, if you send me a check for $1,000, I can get you a Google account. I know people. . . .

One secret tip: No one ever uses P.S. (postscript) anymore, but frankly (I've been being frank the whole time, honest), I think it's a perfect vehicle to do something off the wall or get in a last comment or word. If you're one of the few people who reads this book aside from my Mom, use a P.S. and stand out. I sometimes use it to refer to something casual that was discussed during the interview and could help build affinity:

- P.S. Let's hope the Rockets recover from trading The Beard and have a better 2022, or I may have to become a Mavericks fan.
- P.S. If you're looking for a good bottle of wine, be sure to try the Rioja Gran Reserva. Spanish wines are so underrated!
- P.S. No one really uses P.S. anymore. I do. It shows you my respect for the past, present, and future.

One more super-secret tip: Remember **attentional bias**? Just checking. Well, think about ways to stand out but in a personal and meaningful way. I once got a thank-you note that was handwritten—in cursive! (I mean who the hell knows how to write in script anymore? I can barely write two sentences in block letters without it looking like I had a heart attack mid-sentence.) It means you've taken the time to gather your thoughts, write a personalized message, research my office address, place it in an envelope, lick it (OK, that's gross), spend some dough to put a stamp on it, get off your ass, and drop it in the mailbox. Now that's spam with heart, unlike the crap most of you Axiom passengers[3] will cut, paste, and send out ad infinitum.

And here's my last two bits of advice about emails: Proofread carefully for missing and extra words. And spell-check! Nothing can get you knocked out of contention faster than a few well-placed typos—especially in the anal-retentive world of Wall Street. Some of my personal favorites include:

- I'm very interested in working on Initial *Pubic* Offerings.
- I enjoy writing prospectuses. After all, the *penis* mightier than the sword.
- I have a strong attention *to to* detail.

You might be meeting with someone as anal as I am, so you'd better double-check and then do it one more time for me!

---

[3] Watch Pixar's *WALL-E* if you have no idea what I'm talking about. That's your future, couch potato.

Key Takeaways

- Assume you're SPAM, so create an email that gets their attention.
- *Return on time invested* is critical. Keep it brief and get to the point!
- Give the impression that you're the love child of a Holy Trinity: the brains of Albert Einstein, the stamina of Optimus Prime, and the persistence of Wile E. Coyote.
- Beware of *attentional bias*: Communicate key attributes most relevant to the job and validate them with mutual acquaintances.
- *Recency bias* dictates that endings matter. Think carefully about your closing salutation. Use a P.S. to build affinity (like your mutual misery over the Houston Rockets).
- Don't screw up prerequisites for the job. Proofread; then do it again. Otherwise, you might be saying you're interested in taking your penis public.

CHAPTER 4

Failure as Fertilizer

The Power of Persistence

You've sent the email, what's next? Do you just leave it at that and wait? No! Have you learned nothing so far? Although landing a job might be your #1 priority, chances are that your email (which you spent so much time agonizing over) has been either quickly forgotten or has landed in the Junk box, never to be seen again. So what do you do? Persevere. Persevere. Persevere.

Herald Chen, who co-ran Technology at Kohlberg Kravis Roberts (KKR) and is a former Goldman Sachs banker, recalls that when he was in college, he had his heart set on landing an internship at General Motors (GM). He sent a postcard to the HR department, explaining that he was an immigrant and that his father had always bought GM cars, but when they broke down, the Chens replaced them with Toyotas. The clincher was in the next line where he wrote, "I want to work at GM to make your cars better."

It worked. He got the job.

Here's another never-give-up story from Juan Alva, formerly of Goldman Sachs and now managing director of an alternative investment fund. Juan told me about a graduate of a midwestern university—which might as well have been University of Basket Weaving given Wall Street's preference to hire from the Ivies—who wanted to get into the investment banking division at Goldman. Now this was way before Google, so the persistent bugger called the main phone number at Goldman and continued to call every day, trying to speak with the head of the group. He got as far as the head banker's secretary, who put up a huge firewall, offering one excuse after another as to why her boss wasn't available. At some point, the pest started calling 15 minutes earlier each day, until finally he caught the head banker before his secretary had arrived. "You've been very persistent," he was told, and in the end, he got an interview and a job. That gnat became a top dog at Goldman and retired a very rich man.

The moral? "A lot of people don't appreciate that persistence really does pay off," Juan told me.

One last story. Eric Heglie, a partner at Industrial Growth Partners and an ex-banker at Jefferies, broke into the business the old-fashioned way: as a stalker. He graduated from UCLA with a liberal arts degree and wanted to work at Jefferies. The only problem was that at the time, Jefferies was largely hiring from elite business and finance schools. So when Eric wasn't invited to interview, he tracked down one of their bankers and approached him as he walked toward the parking lot. Eric regaled him with all the reasons why he'd make a great banker and wouldn't let him go until the banker finally agreed to bring him in for an interview. Without his persistence, Eric would not have become the powerhouse private equity investor he is today.

Bottom line: Be persistent. If you get a resounding "No," just remember that "No" is just a single letter away from "Now." Did you give up when you failed that sobriety test? When you didn't graduate high school because you flunked gym? When you proposed to your now-wife and she initially said, "No, no, a thousand times no?" Of course not. You learned from your screw-up, dusted yourself off, and got back into the driver's seat. Just like that, much of landing a job is having the willpower to persevere. Some call it **grit**, but I like to consider it being able to take a wallop to the gut. From day one of your job search, that's the posture you want to assume.

Be Unus

Sometimes when you're getting constantly rejected, the problem really is with you.

Rather than scream that everyone's stupid, learn from rejection and adjust. Iterate. Figure out what makes you unappealing. I can't help you burn off your warts or drain your cysts, but I do have some advice that applies to everything from getting a job, to a promotion, a deal, and even a spouse. Unlike the soulless, one-word advice Mr. McGuire says to Dustin Hoffman in the movie *The Graduate*, my advice isn't "Plastics." Mine is **"Unus."** That's Latin for "one" and "only" and is the root of the word *unique*.

Gina King, partner at Supernode Global and former Jefferies SVP, says, "Focus on making it clear how you are different from other candidates. In certain situations, I didn't have the relevant experience so I focused on bringing new perspectives and being additive to the team. I came across as unique."

Why **Unus**? Because the secret to getting in the door and ultimately getting what you want is projecting yourself as unique and taking advantage of scarcity. You're a durable good and you have to make others want to buy *you*, and only *you*. If you don't, then there is always some other chump who costs less, is more obedient, and is definitely better looking. So accentuate attributes that only a few can claim. Scarcity pays. Now hit that Send button!

Key Takeaways

What if you get rejected?
- Step 1: Contact hiring manager.
- Step 2: Get rejected.
- Step 3: Be *Unus*.
- Step 4: Try again; go back to Step 1.

CHAPTER 5

Strut Like a Peacock

Your First Impression Might Be Your Last

The interview process can take several rounds and will make you feel like you're a cast member in a reality game show, fighting for a coveted role while sizing up your competition. Your mantra has to be that you don't need to outrun a bear, just the other people it's chasing.

Rick Heitzmann, one of the founders of the venture capital firm FirstMark and former Houlihan Lokey banker, remembers as a kid working at a basketball camp run by Jay Wright, now the basketball coach of Villanova. Jay would say, "How bad do you want to be good?" and would tell the campers, "If you're tired, there are others who will gladly take your spot, so work as if you want it!"

I hope the campers remembered that advice, because for many jobs there will be thousands, if not tens of thousands, of wishful sycophants just like you competing for the same position. That means from the moment you walk in the door, you've got to stand out. You've got to show them the *wow* and do it quickly. From the first second you meet their gaze, you'll be sized up the way a tourist inspects Michelangelo's *David*. (Eyes up; get your mind out of the gutter.) In an instant, you'll be judged by what you're wearing, how you behave, how gracefully you shake a hand. Your interviewer will make a snap decision about who you are, your fitness for hard work, and your moral character.

Once again, I'm not making this stuff up. It's based on science and a very specific type of bias. Which one? **Initial impression bias!** Please don't tell me I need to spell this one out for you.

It won't be easy to break that first impression, so be sure it's a great one. Joanne Chen, general partner at Foundation Capital and former Jefferies banker, shared her experience: "There's no way I can be the stereotypical person people expect, so I don't even try. Instead, I focus on establishing credibility by being upfront and direct about my credentials and accomplishments."

So strut like a peacock. Come across as optimistic and enthusiastic, but also as a big thinker, self-directed, bottom line–oriented, a team member who builds confidence in others. You've got a great sense of humor; you're a motivator who accomplishes goals by working well with others; you bring fresh ideas to solving problems.

Wow, you sound great. Even *I'd* hire you.

Find the Greater Fool

Frank Baxter, former CEO at Jefferies and later the U.S. ambassador to Uruguay, advises young people just starting out to think of themselves as their own CEO, their own Internet brand. "You're not John Smith," he tells them. "You're *www.JohnSmith.com*."

Present yourself as if you're the investment opportunity of a lifetime. That's what your parents thought when they plowed all that dough into your education and extracurricular boondoggles. Prove them right by transforming yourself from a money-losing dotcom into a cash-gushing staple.

Show your value by leveraging one of the most fundamental tenets of investing: the **Greater Fool Theory**. It states that the price of an object is determined *not* by its intrinsic value, but rather by irrational beliefs and expectations. As a result, an investor might pay a price that seems *foolishly* high because one may rationally have the expectation that the item can be resold to a *greater fool* later. The entire market economy is based on this principle. Don't believe me? Tell that to Diana Duyser, who was lucky enough to sell a partially eaten 10-year-old grilled cheese sandwich with the Virgin Mary's likeness on eBay for almost $30,000. Believe me now?

In other words, be the fool*er*, not the fool*ee*. The only way you're going to stop living off the Bank of Mom and Dad and leach onto the payroll of a real company is to convince someone you're an excellent investment. The way to do that is to know what a prospective employer is *really* asking.

Here, I'll make it simple for you. The following table is loosely based on the pitch deck template of Sequoia Capital, the venture capital firm which backed Apple, Google, PayPal, Yahoo!, and YouTube, among others. You get the picture— they're rich as hell.

When You're Asked	What They *Want* You to Answer
What's your *purpose*?	To make you rich(er)
What *problem* do you solve?	A fresh body to replace the people who quit
What do you *uniquely* offer?	Three Bs: Brains, brawn, beauty
Why *now*?	One can only live on bread and water so long.
What *market* can you go after?	The sky's the limit.
Who *else* wants you?	Who wouldn't?
What's your *function*?	Your wish is my command.
How do you *make money*?	Giving you leverage on your time
Are you a *team player*?	There's no "I" in team (but there is a "me").
What's your *ROI*?[1]	Infinite! I'm not in it for the money.

Wear Some Damn Socks

Now that you have your self-worth in order, it's time to deal with the superficial—how you look. You should have already researched enough about the companies where you're interviewing to have a pretty good idea about how people dress. Dress to impress, and by that I mean, mimic. Remember, we're basing this on concepts like **initial impression** and **affinity bias** that explain why people tend to hire people who are like themselves. So if you're interviewing at Google and you wear a three-piece suit for the interview, they'll either think you're an insurance salesman or someone just died. Conversely, if you show up in jeans and the latest James Perse T-shirt at Goldman Sachs, they'll either direct you to the plants that need watering or someone will call security to have you escorted out.

Therefore, dress accordingly and appropriately.

But then again, inappropriate can work, too. At Jefferies, I interviewed more than a thousand candidates. In all that time, I remember one person who didn't wear any socks. Obviously weird, but he did stand out. We referred to him as "No Socks Guy." He had all the necessary qualifications and we were all set to make him an offer, until at the end of the day, we asked him, "Dude, why aren't you wearing socks?" He just said, "I forgot to pack them." That dropped him in our estimation. If you come in with a black eye, you don't tell people you walked into a door. You saved a child from a 7-foot-tall kidnapper. Sockless guy should have told us they were stolen, or a bear got into his sock drawer, or he gave his pair to a homeless person just before entering the building. *His* answer had us worried he wouldn't

---

[1]*Return on investment* is relevant because companies determine compensation by paying you the least amount possible to keep you from quitting.

pass the **Cleveland Airport Test**. "If I was stuck in some God-forsaken backwater hellhole like the Cleveland Burke Lakefront airport (not even Cleveland Hopkins International—they have a couple of good restaurants), would I want to have a frappé with this clown at the local McCafé?"

Here are a few more quick tips about your appearance:

- Be someone who the interviewer could visualize being part of the team.
- Dress like your interviewers, but not better. No senior bankers want to see you with the Business Class version of their Economy outfit.
- Bring an extra set of casual clothes (e.g., Banana Republic, J. Crew) for after-party or socializing activities. Nothing will make you look more like a tool than wearing a business suit to the hottest clubs.
- Always wear dark colors just in case you spill crap on yourself. Otherwise a nice coffee stain in the groin area of your light grey suit will be the highlight of the interview—not you.
- Wash your hands after using the bathroom.
- Bring a handkerchief in case your hands get clammy.

On many occasions, I've used that last bullet point to my advantage. I call it the **Clammy-Hand Test**. As an interviewer, I'm known for asking tough questions. When shaking hands at the end of an interrogation, I've noticed a definite correlation between the sweatiness of the interviewee's palms and their propensity to lie, or at least stretch the truth. The test has never failed me, so be sure to wipe your hands clean before you shake your interviewer's hand. Nothing leaves a nastier impression than the transfer of sweat goo from your paw to my unsullied digits.

Now that you've gotten your self-esteem and wardrobe down pat, it's time to get ready for *The Show*. Interviewing is just another form of dating. In the era before courtship went online, the skills honed at your local watering hole would have been invaluable in today's interview process. You would have found it second nature to stand out from the crowd and accentuate your most appealing features, diving fearlessly into the fray. Seamlessly slipping from idle chitchat into a deep soulful conversation that maximizes your appeal, you would have intuited the subtext behind every question or gesture. You also would have gotten good practice rebounding from your multitude of rejections.

Alas, in this swipe-happy generation, many of these skills have gone down the same drain as single-tasking, civil behavior, and doing things IRL (In Real Life, for you dinosaurs). Until you figure out how to swipe right for a job, you'll have to work on your magnetic personality.

Master Half-Truths

As we all know, life is rarely black and white; it is most often different shades of gray. Exaggeration is no different, so become an *artiste*. Think about how that menial summer job you had can be turned into a tour de force. Worked as a janitor? No! You were a Sanitation Engineer. Parked cars? Nope. Automotive Custodian. Got coffee? Hydration Manager. So master the power of exaggeration without lying. Half-truths are OK—politicians do it all the time—but outright lies will inevitably come back to bite you. And never, ever break the law. I don't have any tips for surviving jail.

Here are a few *exaggeration-without-lying* examples that may inspire you:

Half-Truth	In Reality
Demonstrated *leadership* in the face of adversity	Made sure the house didn't run out of alcohol at the Super Bowl block party
Exhibited superhuman *endurance*	Pulled three consecutive all-nighters crushing it on *Fortnite*
Displayed practical *ingenuity*	Created Facebook apps to siphon personal information for sale to advertisers
Showed impressive *teamwork*	Supervised my classmates in a group study to analyze the mating rituals of rats
Had *intuition* in the face of adversity	Prepared for this interview by reading this book multiple times

Exaggerating without lying is OK, but be forewarned. I know a firm that employs *intuitives* on their staff to smoke out the liars and cheats. These human beings are naturally gifted at reading people. So make sure whatever you say is the truth, and if it's a half-truth, make sure you can live with it. Otherwise, be prepared to get ejected out as an imposter.

COVID-19 changed the way we interact with people, but you can't let your guard down. (Just ask Jeffrey Toobin.[2]) Rick Heitzmann was recently conducting a Zoom interview for a senior-level job at his company. The dude was crowded in the corner of his bedroom (which, of course, is fine. . . . I don't want to judge!), when suddenly the door opened in the background and his wife walked in and started making his bed! Rick was appalled: "Didn't she realize her husband was interviewing for a job? I mean for God's sake, there should be some minimum level of professionalism." Needless to say, the candidate, who was also disheveled and seemingly unshowered, did not receive an offer.

---

[2]For the vast majority of you who don't read anymore, he was a journalist at the *New Yorker* and made a very serious faux pas on Zoom.

My own meetings during COVID-19 are online and it never ceases to amaze me how people nonchalantly deteriorate over time. At first, people are dressed as though they're going to church in their Sunday best, but soon the scene devolves into something from the movie *The Hangover*. Please have a little decorum and try to pretend you're still in the office. Remember, you're the same person who always laughed at old guys who forgot to zip up their pants after going to the bathroom. If you don't course-correct soon, one day you'll wake up and be that guy doing online meetings naked and not even know it.

Customize; Don't Compromise

It never hurts to go out of your way and make your mother proud with a dose of "Please" and "Thank You." Remember, it's all about making a connection with the person who's interviewing you and making yourself look good in the eyes of your inquisitor. So at the end of any interview, *immediately* send a thank-you email, and not a generic one. As Harry Nelis, former Goldman Sachs banker and now partner at the venture capital firm Accel, recommends, "Try to remember something specific from the interview so your email distinguishes you from all the others."

Please read over your thank-you note carefully before sending it. Some email programs allow you to build in a delay, which I would highly recommend for those of you who tend to write like you speak—with reckless abandon. Otherwise, you might get some of these classics I've received:

- "Thank you so much for meeting me today. I really enjoyed speaking with you and learning more about your firm. [CUSTOMIZE INTRO AS NEEDED]." Nothing like getting a generic email to make you feel special.

- "Mr. David Liu, I really enjoyed speaking with you about career opportunities at your firm for Latina women. You are clearly a beacon for us." And here I thought I was only a role model for Asian American men.

- "Mr. Dave Loo." My personal favorite, especially from British candidates who showed immense self-control. I know I wouldn't be able to keep it together if Johnny Shitter interviewed me.

- "Please excuse typos. Sent from my iPhone." You do realize that a typo is grounds for termination on Wall Street?

In general, I'm a big fan of **pre-mortems**, especially when it comes to interviewing. They're a tool I've used in which I imagine a best-laid plan failing and then work backward to figure out how it could have gone wrong. After I've prepared all I can, I replay in my mind all the ways I could screw up the interview and try to cover my mistakes with that last "thank-you" email before the interviewer either calls me back or sends me into the dumpster fire of dissed candidates. A good practice is to draft the email beforehand. Make sure to add something specific from your meeting which forces you to prepare to discuss something that has commonality with your interviewer; then be ready to press Send after the interview is over.

One final tip: Bribes work. The origin of *to bribe* is from the Old French, *bribeor* (beggar) and before that, the Romanic word, *brimber* (to beg). You should never be above groveling for a job; it greases the wheels of business, and in many cultures is even expected. So consider bribes as begging in polite company. But don't be gauche. Stick with the lowest level of **Maslow's Hierarchy of Needs**.[3] Food is always welcome, and generally donuts and coffee will suffice. No cash, nothing too expensive, and definitely not sex.

This works because of **reciprocity bias**, or the impulse to do what Jesus said: "Do unto others as you would have them do unto you"—but in a positive way. Wall Street is built on this. You do my deals, and I'll do yours. If you invest in my fund, I'll invest in yours. What started out as one caveman asking the other to scratch his hairy back, quickly devolved into co-investing in each other's funds to perpetuate a Ponzi scheme. Imagine, Wall Street might not have existed if a caveman had invented the back scratcher.

Know Oliver Stone from Oliver Twist

Hiring right is all about finding a great **cultural fit**. This is one of those insidious terms that no one can explain, but its absence is always grounds for not hiring someone. A simple way to think about it is as the sister of **affinity bias**, and one way to project this is through your media consumption, especially your movies. Now, everyone knows Hollywood doesn't know crap about Wall Street, so be sure to come across as the most astute cinephile this side of Orson Welles who can wax poetic about how off-the-mark these movies are when socializing with your

---

[3]Maslow's Hierarchy of Needs is a theory of motivation which states that five categories of human needs dictate an individual's behavior: physiological (food and clothing) needs, safety (job security) needs, love and belonging (friendship) needs, esteem needs, and self-actualization needs.

interviewers, future boss, or anyone at the office who will listen. To help prioritize your time, I've listed them below in order of viewing priority:

- *The Godfather* (1972). What does the Mafia have to do with Wall Street? Everything! Every senior person you meet will liken himself to Don Corleone, even the women. Watch and learn. Oh, and if you're ever referred to as "Fredo," watch your back!

- *The Godfather: Part II* (1974). Watch this to see what happens when you betray your firm. It doesn't end well. It also explains why your boss is such a jerk. They didn't start like that. Society made them that way.

- *Margin Call* (2011). All-time true-story fiction showing how Lehman Brothers really came within a gnat's hair of ending morning Starbucks macchiatos for everyone on both coasts.

- *The Big Short* (2015). Ever wonder how the Great Recession led to you moving to a trailer park? This is "Securitization for Dummies."

- *Trading Places* (1983). Confidence-booster that provides scientific evidence that any schmuck can make it on Wall Street.

- *The Wolf of Wall Street* (2013). Mostly fictional account of the glamorous life of fourth-tier stockbrokers who you'll never meet at a real investment bank. Oh, except the dwarf-tossing. That's authentic.

- *Glengarry Glen Ross* (1992). This is about real estate salesmen, but they coined one of the mantras of all salespeople all over the world: *ABC—Always Be Closing*. Don't think defining your job as sales is too lowbrow. It's all about the sale! And don't think you deserve anything if you aren't generating sales. Remember Alec Baldwin's warning: "Coffee's for Closers!"

- *Wall Street* (1987). 100 percent complete and utter crap; a classic example of a Wall Street movie written by a Hollywood outsider who created characters that are bastard composites of multiple jobs. Little to no redeeming qualities except for creating the one-liner every wannabe investment banker cites to simultaneously prove how knowledgeable and douchey he is: "Greed Is Good."

Key Takeaways

- Treat the interview like a performance; rehearse, rehearse, rehearse. Do *pre-mortems* to double-check yourself.
- Be aware of your *initial impression* as it will set the stage for everything.
- *Be* the pitch that satisfies what your prospective employer *really* wants and recognize that you're a walking example of the *Greater Fool Theory*.
- Pass the *Cleveland Airport Test*.
- Treat interviewing like dating.
- Exaggerate with half-truths, but never lie; otherwise, you might fail the *Clammy-Hand Test*.
- *Reciprocity bias* means bribes work.
- Know your target industry's media to project *cultural fit*.

CHAPTER 6

Ace the Personal Bake-Off

Interviewing as Performance Art

I've said it before, but it bears repeating: Connect. Connect. Connect. It's all about connections: who you know, what you have in common with the interviewer, and how you can help make crates of cash for the company. That's your mission. Got it? Now prepare for your personal bake-off like your life depends on it.

Show Time!

Before you get a formal interview, try for a pre-meet. An informal opportunity allows you to continue gathering intelligence and learn about your audience. Although this may not seem like a lot of time, fifteen minutes can feel like fifteen hours if you're a bore.

The first-round interview is the most straightforward, but riskiest, stage. Typically, it's done with a single interviewer, so if someone peed in your interviewer's Cheerios, you're screwed. On the flipside, if their favorite NFL team won the night before, or if they closed a deal they've been working on for months, chances are they'll be in a great mood! Regardless, don't forget to strut like a peacock and stand out.

Your first interview will likely occur at your school. As an alumnus working at Jefferies, I was part of the Wharton team of about a half-dozen interrogators. We'd travel to Philadelphia and interview approximately 300 hopefuls on campus. After a few days of interviewing, we'd eliminate most of them immediately.

Imagine yourself in the place of your interviewer: in a windowless room listening to a succession of naive undergraduates or MBA bores drone on about how challenged they were in some meaningless school project. You, too, would be watching the clock waiting for cocktail hour. Keep telling yourself to be memorable, because your competition is breathing down your neck. Since you're being interrogated to sniff out any BS on your resume, recite unique behavioral factoids that show why you'd be perfect for the job. Remember, *you* are the pitch. Tell stories that illustrate how you'll crank out whatever is needed—budgets, business plans, financial models, laundry lists—until your laptop explodes. Feel free to embellish to the ethical speed limit. It'll show you have the potential to be a senior executive one day.

Super Saturday

If we interviewed 300 applicants at Wharton, we'd probably invite 50 or so to headquarters for another cattle call. This one is much more intense, filled with one-on-one speed dating–style sessions, commingled with idle chitchat lunches with multiple executives and candidates.

This next round may start on Friday with a limo ride from the airport to your hotel. The next morning, dozens of impeccably dressed candidates show up at headquarters for what on Wall Street is called *sell day*, or *Super Saturday*. Each candidate is assigned to a particular room where your first interrogator is waiting. After ten minutes or so, you'll rotate to another interview, each time getting grilled to see what you know, but equally important, to see if *they* know *you*. Remember, it's mostly about a **cultural fit**. You may get a case study or two, but unless you made up those Medals of Freedom on your resume, it's all about sizing you up using—yup, you guessed it—the **Cleveland Airport Test**.

Each candidate might endure up to eight or nine separate interviews, often concluding with the person who interviewed you on campus playing the good cop: "Hey, Dave, good to see you again. How'd it go today? What're you thinking? Do you have any questions for *me*?" This is another opportunity to shine because you've come prepared with astute, brilliant questions they've never been asked before. There are lots of ideas you can glean from books, but most of them are terrible. Never, ever use these:

- "I spoke to I-Forgot-Her-Name-Because-I-Was-Too-Dumb-to-Ask-for-Her-Business-Card and she mentioned a Deal-I-Can't-Remember-Even-Though-We-Just-Spoke-about-It-Two-Hours-Ago. Can you tell me more?" There are multiple variations of this classic question, and they all drive me nuts. If you can't remember details like this, how am I going to explain to you the 50 finance scenarios I want you to run for the client in 24 hours?
- "This place is pretty laid back. What do you do for fun?" Work. Next question?

- "I don't have any questions." Seriously? Unless you wear the Infinity Gauntlet and zapped your unimaginative ass into the future, how could you possibly have no more questions after spending a total of 14 hours with us? That's one workday on Wall Street!

I've also discovered some that are insightful, specific, and memorable. A few examples:

- "I liked meeting Mr. Big Managing Director. He told me how he got his start after graduating from the University of Basket Weaving. How did you get your start?" If you haven't already asked this one, it's an oldie but goodie. It shows you were listening, and it gives the interviewer an opportunity to brag about how they walked through a hailstorm, barefoot, and stood in the arctic for hours to get a job. Nothing strokes an ego better than listening to them wax on about how awesome they were.
- "I'm very curious about this specific deal that the firm completed. It looked like you maxed the leverage and created a holdco structure to minimize the equity check. Can you tell me more about how you syndicated that deal?" Very nice! Shows you won't need much training from me and that I'll make that afternoon tee time if I hire you. Unless you spilled hot coffee on your groin, I'd hire you now, and even then, I've spilled hot coffee in my nether regions and if you've lived to tell about it, you're the perfect underling for me.
- "What will it take to get hired here?" I like it! Aggressive but consistent with the "Don't Ask, Don't Get" school of begging.

So come prepared with savvy questions. Sreene Ranganathan, a member of Facebook's Corporate Development team and former Jefferies banker, put it succinctly when he said, "I hate it when people don't do at least a minimum amount of homework. I mean how much friggin' work does it take to look me up online and find out one or two interesting things about me? It shows me that I'm not just one of thousands of bankers and firms you're meeting with." Nowadays, given how easy it is to stalk someone online, if you don't do it, it shows you're really not that interested.

Being the interviewer is really quite mindless because every candidate has the same answers to the same questions. So try to stand out, either because you're not wearing socks (this strategy is risky), your last name is Musk (or even Elon), or you've done your recon and can recite every deal the firm completed. I once had a candidate who read every interview I'd given in the *Wall Street Journal* and watched every presentation I'd delivered at industry confabs. That showed me a real interest in the industry, my firm, and, most important, me. In an ocean of candidates just looking for a safe port in the storm, nothing differentiates a candidate like a real, genuine interest in finding the right ship.

The Inquisition

So how exactly might you come off as unique? By providing one-of-a-kind answers (in a gregarious way[1]) to predictable questions. Here are some Q&As that should help get those gears turning:

- *What's your biggest weakness?*

  Good answers: Almost any answer that doesn't relate to the job is good. For example:
  - "I care about people too much."
  - "I love animals more than some people."
  - "I get very emotional about hunger and homelessness."

  Turn any weakness into a strength. Here are a few others:
  - "I'm obsessive." Generally not great with boyfriends or girlfriends (see the film *Fatal Attraction*), but it can be a superpower if harnessed, particularly if proofing numbers and fonts is your bag.

  - "I'm always pleasing people." Again, not perfect if you're in *Fifty Shades of Grey*, but senior managers and bankers secretly love this. We all want loyal employees who will go the extra mile, and there's nothing like someone who's motivated not just by money, but by an innate drive to satisfy *our* every desire!

  - "I love the weeds; I get lost in them." Perfect because someone needs to check the work. It sure won't be me. I paid my dues and I'm done reviewing numbers and fonts that no client will ever check because they'll assume that we did!

  Terrible answers:
  - Anything that could be translated in your interviewer's mind that you would not be a good employee and would be clearly bad for the job. Examples would be sloppiness, tardiness, and lack of enthusiasm. Tread carefully.
  - Anything that presumes you're too good for the job you're applying for. In other words, don't overstep your bounds, and don't make it seem like you think you should have your interviewer's job.

---

[1] Seriously, are you that hopeless? One good rule of thumb is to pretend the interviewer is the hottest guy or gal you've ever seen and no one else on the entire planet exists. You're Eve, they're Adam, and the future of the human race depends on you acing this interview.

For extra credit: What I look for most in a candidate is self-awareness. There's something called the **self-enhancing transmission bias**, whereby people share their successes more than their failures. This can lead to a false perception of reality and the inability to assess situations accurately. People with big blind spots are a recipe for future disaster. So if you take too long to answer when I ask you about your biggest weakness, that makes me think you're probably a narcissist, a sociopath, or both. So make sure you know your weaknesses (or at least have good answers), and don't hesitate before answering. If you don't have any weaknesses, *Mazel Tov*. Be sure to send me your name and address so I can refund the money you spent on this book and address it to your real name: Jesus Christ.

- *Why do you want this job?*

  Everyone knows the only honest answer to this question, but no one wants to hear it: "Moolah, dinero, buckeroos, Benjamins, cashola." Stay away from that answer because it sends the signal that you're just a mercenary jerk. Instead, do your homework and respond with something that specifically relates to the company, such as the following:

  o "Because of the culture." I know you're thinking that's a lame answer, but I will tell you that this is the most important thing in choosing a place to work. In most jobs, you'll be with your coworkers more than anyone in your life—that includes your drinking buddies who bum off your food. So even though you think you're an adult, you're still growing, and just like how peer groups affect teens more than anything else,[2] your coworkers will shape the professional you'll become. But just so you don't sound like a complete suck-up, make sure you have examples of how their culture differs.

  o Compensation, promotion, and client practices are all good fodder. And better yet, if the firm has been a great feeder into other careers like non-profits or politics, that works too.

  o "Because of the deals you've done this quarter." Make it obvious you've studied their deals, products, and projects. Better yet, make it clear that you would early-decision them in a heartbeat like you did your college admissions.

- *How many balloons can you fit in a truck?*

  This is a real question, and equally inane queries are the favorites of highly paid interviewers, maybe because they're bored out of their minds asking dead-end questions like "What are your goals?" and "What do you perceive as your strengths and weaknesses?" Or maybe because they really think they might learn something about the candidate by their reaction. There are a bazillion variations of this sucker. How many squirrels would be needed to blanket

[2] Judith Rich Harris, *The Nature Assumption*. https://www.latimes.com/archives/la-xpm-1998-sep-12-me-22017-story.html

the Moon? How many golf balls could you stuff in your colon? You get the idea. Each question is more absurd than the one that preceded it.

Lest you think I'm making this up, ask around. These are actual questions asked at top investment banking and management consulting firms like Goldman and McKinsey. Why, you ask? Because they want to see how you think "out of the box," as they say. I know; it's stupid, but make sure you walk through the methodology in a coherent manner. Obviously, no one has any idea what the real answers are; they're just interested in how you think under pressure. The only right answer is to play along, but at the same time show you can think out loud logically. Ask clarifying questions. Remember that a big problem is just a bunch of small ones, so break them down and solve them one by one.

Take a lesson from Spencer Wang, a former banker at Credit Suisse and Salomon Brothers, who retired as the chief investment officer of Seasons Capital. When hiring, Spencer always asked candidates his own version of the balloon question. "I'm going to flip a coin 10 times," he'd tell them, "but first I'm going to give you $1 million of my money to bet on a coin flip. What's your bet on the first flip? What will be your bet on the 11th flip? Now what if it's *your* $1 million, does that change your answers?"

Spencer knew these questions were atypical. Many would say it's a 50/50 proposition so it shouldn't matter what they bet. Spencer's take was that while these interviewees were book smart, there was nothing innovative in their answers. He generally rejected people who jumped at an answer without asking questions. One person Spencer did hire was a candidate who, once he learned he could ask questions, fired them off: "Is this a two-headed coin? Is it equally weight distributed? When could he stop and take his winnings?" Spencer hired him. Why? Because this person demonstrated intellectual curiosity, took charge of the situation, and turned it into one most in his favor. Spencer recently told me he still believes in this fellow, and that he invested in his fund, which has vastly outperformed the market during its lifetime.

I have some experience myself with these "moonball" questions. One of my interviews out of Wharton was at a top management consulting firm, where I was asked by a smug interviewer the "Squirrels on the Moon" question. I actually knew how many squirrels could blanket the moon and told him. As we were about to wrap up, he asked me if *I* had any questions. I was young and had already decided I didn't want to count crap in the ocean for a living. So I asked him, "How many tires can you fit in the Pacific Ocean?" He nervously laughed off my question and bid me farewell.

- *Pitch yourself.*

This is another common ask, and a favorite of mine, particularly for more senior positions because I'm trying to gauge how people sell themselves. Some just panic, while others pitch themselves like a hot Internet stock. Personally,

I go aggressive and pitch myself as the second coming of Amazon at IPO. Sometimes this strategy can backfire if you sell too hard, but at least it will get a few chuckles.

A variation, albeit less aggressive, is "Tell me about yourself." This is a favorite of Bret Pearlman, co-founder of Elevation Partners and former senior managing director at Blackstone. He says it gives him insight into what a person thinks is important to know about themselves and gives him an opportunity to gauge potential fit. Of course, many a fool has answered this question by going on too long, repeating their resume, being a bore, or unveiling something about themselves that should have been kept secret. If you do get this one, remember that form is more important than substance. You've already made it this far because you have the quals. Now it's time to show them you have the energy and gusto. That's how you'll win the audition.

Lauren Wu, former equity analyst and CFO of venture capital at J&W Seligman and Merrill Lynch banker, says it's important to be proud of your accomplishments and make it clear you deserve the job. She adds that women tend to say "We" when talking about accomplishments, while men tend to say "I." She suggests that women candidates say "I" more often.

Alexandra Lebenthal, senior advisor at Houlihan Lokey and former CEO of Lebenthal Holdings, adds that women can be their own worst enemy. "I think in many cases, we can have a tendency to feel like we aren't qualified. People joke that if there are four qualifications for a new job, a woman will think she needs six while a man will feel like he is in good shape with two. We cannot be afraid to take on new challenges; women shouldn't back down from pursuing their passions."

- *Tell me something no one knows about you.*

OK, this can be really dangerous, so be prepared for variations of this question, like "Tell me something that isn't on your resume" or "If I Googled you, what would be on the back pages?" Here are some suggested answers that should keep you in the game:

  o Volunteer something you think your interviewer and you may have in common, perhaps a hobby not on your resume or an interest that seems geeky but makes you appear multidimensional. For me, it was always about being a cartoonist—the Chinese Stan Lee!

  o Another good option is to talk about an aspect of yourself that isn't on your resume or cover letter but will make you even better suited for the job. For me, it was my skills in COBOL, an archaic programming language designed in the 1950s. Jefferies was actually using a COBOL mainframe system for doing securitizations and I fit the bill of being a perfect grunt to take it over.

One important reminder concerning these commonly asked questions:

DON'T BE BORING! Put yourself in the shoes of your interviewer, who has spent all day listening to people just like you drone on and on about their achievements, why they want the job, what makes them great, blah, blah, blah. After a half-dozen of these, any sane person thinks about jumping out the nearest window. So be entertaining. Use what you've learned from the zeitgeist and from collecting dirt on your interviewer's interests. Take the conversation wherever they want but be prepared to gossip about other topics. Try to be a Renaissance person, equally adept at discoursing about FDR, the FDIC, or Jay-Z.

Over the years, I've forgotten the details of almost every interview. However, one I remember vividly had nothing to do with the job for which we were hiring. We were both from Texas, and once this candidate found out I was a Houston Rockets fan, we spent half the interview talking about how bringing Clyde "The Glide" Drexler to Houston mid-season in 1995 was the greatest trade in NBA history. Finding a Rockets fan in L.A. surrounded by Laker bandwagoners was like finding a hundred-dollar bill stuck to the bottom of my shoe. It made my day.

Finally, when interviewing, beware of the **hot-cold empathy gap**, which states that we act differently when in different psychological states. *Hot cognition*, initially proposed in the 1960s by Yale University psychologist Robert P. Abelson, is the theory that a person's thinking is influenced by their emotional state. It contrasts with *cold cognition*, in which the processing of information is motivated by facts and intellectual judgment, independent of emotional involvement. Since hot cognition is led by emotion and often leads to rapid, automatic decision-making, it may cause biased and low-quality conclusions. (It's why you should never, ever make financial decisions while getting busy with your significant other. You're liable to break the bank.) So during the interview process, make sure you're cool, calm, and collected when an assignment is suddenly sprung on you.

Overall, interview questions can be perplexing. Living in Silicon Valley has exposed me to a whole different array of crazy questions from wacko tech people trying to outdo each other:

- On a scale of 1 to 10, how weird are you?
- What do you know is true but no one else agrees?
- What is your superpower or animal spirit?

Some questions may be more reasonable, like the one Rick Heitzmann, founder of the venture capital firm FirstMark and former Houlihan Lokey banker, uses to evaluate candidates: "What are three things you love in either your business or personal life, and three things you hate?" He feels that the answers give him a good idea of the candidate's strengths and weaknesses.

My favorite interview question comes from Harry Nelis, former Goldman Sachs banker and now partner at the venture capital firm Accel. He asks all his prospective hires, "Do you consider yourself to be an intuitive person?" Then Harry follows with his trump card: "You say you're intuitive, so what do I think about you?"

Saturday night is the big switcheroo—the reverse selling, as you're treated to an expensive meal and some form of entertainment. This is all for show. It'll be years before you're treated like this again, so starting Sunday, get used to raiding the office fridge weekdays at midnight for eight-week-old yogurt.

But there is a meaning behind this madness. The firm wants to see how you interact with its brass—specifically, if you're fun to hang out with. Don't have too much fun. Do I even have to say this? Don't get drunk. Many a great candidate has lost an offer by acing the day's interviews and then, at night, vomiting on a senior banker's shoes.

Key Takeaways

- Play the broken *affinity bias* record: It's all about connections.
- Get ready for multiple rounds of interviews where *cultural fit* is key.
- Practice and rehearse your interview, especially the gotcha questions.
- Beware the *hot-cold empathy gap*, where we act differently when in different psychological states.

CHAPTER 7

Grownups Ask for Directions

Map the Salt Mine

Now that you've been hired, you need to know how to excel at doing the required work. But before I get into the ins and outs of elbowing your way up the **corporate ladder**, you have to start with perfecting the basic rules of the game. I get that you want to hear more tricks of the trade and how to stop some jerk from getting the job you're pining for, but first you must map the salt mine you're about to enter.

The importance of getting oriented prior to planning, then executing, your attack is, of course, not original. Over 2000 years ago, Sun Tzu wrote about it in *The Art of War*, where he underscored cunning strategies to win battles and manage conflicts. He cautioned his readers to know your enemy as you know yourself. In the case of corporate combat, this consists of all the forces working against you as you try to get ahead in your career, beginning with the person in the next cubbie and moving on to the managing director in the corner office who you can't stand. Sun Tzu admonishes, "Those who do not know the lay of the land cannot maneuver their forces." So before you act, scope the battlefield. To me, that meant being the first person to know where both the bathroom and boardroom were the moment I walked into the office.

Map Your Way to Greatness

Many people enter employment without having a clue as to how job progression *really* works within their company. They start work barely knowing what their own job really entails. Remember **asymmetry of information**? It goes both ways! While you're snickering about how your new employer didn't do their full due diligence to find out you were busted (but never charged) for shoplifting when you were 12, they didn't tell you that your job would entail using your fancy college degree to bind presentation books at 3 a.m.

Not only do most people not do homework on their own job, but they also only have a vague inkling as to their immediate boss's job. Seriously? Would you begin a journey without knowing the destination? Why would you start a job to build a career without knowing where it could lead? Well, maybe you would if it didn't make any difference to you if the pot at the end of that rainbow was gold versus one not worth pissing in. But given that this book is all about employment and moving up the chain of command, it behooves you to know the job. Know how the movie ends before you decide if the ticket is worth buying.

Lauren Wu, former equity analyst and CFO of venture capital at J&W Seligman and Merrill Lynch banker, recommends doing your due diligence to figure out early on how to identify the key players in the hierarchy and how they relate to your career goals. "A good place to start," she suggests, "is with a deep dive into understanding your company's different departments and its rungs up the **corporate ladder**."

So on the off chance you didn't do this for your interview, get off your bloody arse and do it now! Get the org chart from the corporate website and ask to have coffee with people who appear to have roles you'd like to have in the future.

Dave Wargo, board member of Discovery, Liberty Broadband, and Liberty Global, and former Putnam and State Street Research investor, would look around his office, and later the entire industry, and try to identify those people who were clearly the best and pledge his allegiance to them. In his words, "I figured that eagles only wanted to spend time with other eagles. Eagles soar together and I wanted to be one of them."

Don't stop there. Every organization has a *shadow org chart*. Yes! Is your mind blown? It's why some people seem to have a lot more influence than their corporate title suggests. Like that banker with a corner office with blackout shades that appears to be two pay grades above their station. So how do you map out the shadow org? Most of the time, it comes from tenure and keen observation, but if you're looking for a **smartcut**, find the grand pooh-bahs at the top of the heap and befriend them. On Wall Street, and many corporations, this role might be held by someone with a "Vice Chairperson" title. They don't have any direct reports but may sit on the Board or executive committee and hang with your CEO. They appear most often when the proverbial crapola hits the fan and your CEO is looking for trusted advice. Think Tom Hagen in *The Godfather*.[1] They're even more influential and powerful than the Godfather's sons. Spend time befriending these shadow lords; it will bear huge dividends in the long run. But beware of the imposters. At Jefferies, we had a few vice chairmen, and it was well known that not all of them were equal. Some seemed to hold enormous sway getting their deals approved while others seemed to be on a one-way train to the glue factory.

---

[1] Did you not watch *The Godfather* like I told you in Chapter 5? Tom is the Godfather's consigliere or *jūn shī* (军师), Chinese for wartime counselor. These guys didn't have any soldiers directly reporting to them but wielded enormous power by guiding the commander's overall strategy.

Gina King, partner at Supernode Global and former Jefferies SVP, realized that her direct boss wasn't always the person in charge of the purse strings. "Revenue generators exist all across the firm and they weren't always directly in line of sight on the org chart," she says. "So I spent time getting to know who these people were so that they could give testimonials on my behalf when the time came for comp or promotion."

Like other industries, investment banks are filled with multiple departments, like Corporate Finance, Capital Markets, Research, and Sales & Trading. What each department does isn't really important (or that interesting), but know that once you enter the corporate world, you're essentially a cog in a machine, in a factory, on an island. Learning how you fit on the island is important, but note that **initial impressions** are often wrong and everything is not necessarily as it appears. People, departments, and relevance to the organization vary widely, and it usually takes experience, with the help of strong mentors and managers, to ultimately figure out the real path to success. How do I know all this? I started to learn it at a young age, so before we go any further, let's take a detour down memory lane.

Swallow the Red Pill

In the movie *The Matrix*, the main protagonist is offered the choice between a red pill and a blue pill by the rebel leader. The red pill reveals the truth, unpleasant as it may be, and the blue pill allows him to remain happily ignorant. Luckily, I swallowed the red pill at the beginning of my career.

As you know by now, I wanted to be a cartoonist, but I went into investment banking. (In my defense, there are some similarities. Both professions use words and pictures to sell fantasies for a living.) Truth be told, I did it primarily because it seemed like a great way to make a lot of money quickly—and boy, did I need money. It was 1993, and I graduated from Penn with over $100,000 in debt (in 2021 dollars). For you English majors, that buys a lot of ramen noodles: about 100,000 packages, to be exact, or enough to feed me for fifty-five years, assuming I eat five packages a day. I needed a job, one that paid well, and I needed it fast. My family couldn't help me. In 1993, my mother was selling costume jewelry from our one-bedroom apartment in Houston, my father was estranged somewhere in Canada, my younger brother was still rotting in high school, and my other brother was just wrapping up his last year in college and had his own mountain of debt.

I knew what I had to do; I'd been preparing for it for years. I had Management & Technology (M&T) degrees from the School of Engineering at Wharton, which was crawling with graduates choosing between either investment banking or management consulting. In 1993, many were flocking to those careers because of the compensation, the prestige, and the access to C-level executives. An undergraduate at the time could expect to make $40,000 to $80,000 a year in investment banking or management consulting versus settling for a typical corporate job that might pay $20,000 to $30,000.

Wharton prided itself on being a Wall Street factory. Portraits of financiers and magnates like Donald Trump adorned the walls. Classes like Finance, Real Estate, Insurance, and Fixed Income Securities were all geared toward creating über bankers.

During my junior year, I had gotten a taste of investment banking by working at Goldman Sachs as a summer analyst. I had entered through a program in information technology for analysts. It gave me the chance to work in a technical support role for a revenue-generating department. In my case, I ended up working in the Fixed Income Technology Group at 85 Broad Street, Goldman's corporate headquarters. The work was supremely dull and boring, but the money was not, particularly for someone who had never earned more than $8 an hour. It was also my first real introduction to the corporate world.

My bosses were a curious bunch. There was Sam, a Chinese American who took me under his wing and was always generous with his time. He seemed to know a lot more than anyone else, but he never took credit for his work, so he never received it. That was an early lesson. Sam was the smartest person on the team, but also the most invisible. There were times when others were clearly in the wrong, or just plain stupid, but he remained quiet. I took note. Just like the squeaky wheel gets the grease, sometimes the loudest voice gets the attention.

Which brings me to Sam's boss, John. He was a VP and a hard-nosed, funny fellow who took a liking to me as well. He would yell expletives from his cubicle like some hobo on a street corner, but always seemed to know the right angles to get things done. The three of us would have ritual lunches together at Yips—a Chinese restaurant across the street that we used to call "Yucky Yip's." Even though I barely had enough money for lunch, I knew it was important to socialize with Sam and John and pick their brains, so I forked over the six bucks rather than squirrelling it away by having ramen noodles at my desk.

Finally, there was Francis. I could never quite figure out what he did, except he was at the same level as Sam, but clearly a dolt. He didn't actually know anything, and he worked the least of anyone I met in the department. He would arrive late and bolt out the door like Fred Flintstone an hour before everyone else. I later found out that he lived in some palatial estate in Connecticut that required a three-hour train ride to and from Manhattan. He had been a veteran of Goldman for many years and was clearly inferior to Sam, but rumor had it that he was a winner of the genetic lottery and may have even been related to some of the partners. I always assumed he had dirty pictures of someone important. It was my first inkling that perhaps there were smarter ways to get ahead than appeared on the surface.

My job that summer was humdrum and mundane, a far cry from the work I had prepared for as an M&T student. It became obvious to Sam and the team that I wasn't being challenged, but there was always a subtext of "Well, at least you're getting paid." In the short time I was at Goldman, I saw how the Francis of Wall Street, of which there were many, worked: Do the minimum possible so that you were still adding value, but at the same time you weren't showing up either your superiors or your peers. I learned the latter point the hard way. Being the precocious smart-ass that I was at 19, I was in a meeting and felt compelled to correct Francis on a point that he had gotten wrong. Little did I know that his boss was in the meeting. Francis glared at me like I had killed his first-born. He never invited me to another meeting for the rest of the summer, which taught me a very important lesson: No one likes a know-it-all.

Working at Goldman was an eye opener into the power and money of Wall Street. The headquarters had extensive artwork on every floor worth more than I could possibly imagine. (I'd be lying if it didn't cross my mind that I could just lift one painting off the wall and disappear forever.)

Every day I would ride the Goldman Sachs elevator. Contrary to what you read on @GSElevator, I never heard anyone say anything of interest. The cafeteria was a different story. It was as though truth serum had been injected into the cappuccino station. I would overhear the most inane *First World 0.1% Problems*. Here are some memorable ones:

- Complaints about mistresses wanting alimony to support their illegitimate love children
- Debates over whether the latest Lambo or Ferrari would make them a better "chick magnet"
- Kudos about making exorbitant fees picking off the dying carcasses of bankrupt companies
- Bitching about how the lobster tail in the Goldman Sachs cafeteria sucked

Nothing like hearing the unvarnished truth to show you how the world really works. It certainly made a searing imprint on my young, impressionable mind.

Once I was indoctrinated into Wall Street that summer, it was clear to me that if I wanted a career at Goldman, or at any other Wall Street firm, I could make it happen. I fit the ideal profile of what they all want at the entry level—a gearhead. On top of that, I was Asian! It quickly became obvious to me that the ideal job candidates were people, typically Asian males, with zero dating prospects, a magnetic affinity for numbers, and a singular focus on making money. The shoe fit perfectly!

I still remember the recruiting season at Wharton. Every investment bank had interview sessions. It wasn't just the Goldman Sachses and Morgan Stanleys of the world who were viewed as the crème de la crème of Wall Street, but also the boutique, smaller firms. I was in a good position to work at Goldman, Bear Stearns, Lehman Brothers, and a boatload of others. Then I got a random call from Jefferies, a small firm in Los Angeles. When I first got the call, I was skeptical. I had never heard of Jefferies and wasn't even sure if they were a real bank. I even thought they had spelled their name wrong by adding an extra "e" in the middle. But two of the bankers who interviewed me were Wharton graduates. I liked them immediately because they didn't fit the traditional banker mold and we had the shared affinity with Penn. They were down-to-earth, no-BS guys, who swore every third word and seemed to really enjoy what they were doing. Most important, unlike most people outside of Philly, they could tell the difference between a real cheesesteak and a steaming cowpie. I decided to give it my all and was invited to fly to Los Angeles to attend a Super Saturday interview session with the team.

The trip from Philly to the West Coast was the clincher. I was picked up in a limousine and booked in a palatial suite at the J.W. Marriott in Century City. I felt like a rock star. I ordered room service and made sure to raid all the goodies from the minibar. That would feed me for at least a week back at school. I almost took a velour bathrobe, but nothing screams hillbilly faster than walking around in a stolen robe with a hotel logo emblazoned on your breast.

The next day I went to their offices at the corner of Santa Monica Boulevard and the 405 freeway. It wasn't as opulent as Goldman's, but I admired that. Less money on the walls meant more money in my pocket! At the end of the day, I was offered a job and I took it. I thought I was going to be the Man!

I was so wrong.

Banking for Dumbos

So now that you know my origin story, let's get back to our regular programming.

Entering investment banking at the junior level is like joining the military or being a digger in a salt mine. There is a strict hierarchy and everyone does a "tour of duty." There are no shortcuts unless you're super-smart and well-connected. Implicitly, everyone is expected to give their life to the job. No outside hobbies, no significant others—no social life, at least not one that would come ahead of your work. Work is your spouse and everyone else is your mistress or mister. The learning curve is incredibly steep, and for that reason alone, I don't think there's much more you can do as a 20-year-old that is more challenging.

Like most new recruits, I started with a two-year tour of duty in the Analyst program, where you're the lowest person on the totem pole but exposed to sophisticated finance tools. You quickly learn that the world revolves around money and the ability to raise it. The skills you learn as a newbie help you throughout your career.

I think the biggest surprise was learning that the tools needed to raise $1 million are the same as those required to raise $1 billion. Both require salesmanship—something that really isn't taught in schools because it's considered "low brow." But once you enter the real world of investment banking, you'll see that your selling techniques are more infomercial than high-finance persuasion. In banking, the tools for selling, whether it be a concept or a security, are basically the same:

- *Business Plan or Selling Document.* Primarily used to cover the client's ass so no one can ever say they didn't disclose something. "Yes, we did! It's in six-point font in footnote 144!"

- *Financial Model.* Usually an Excel spreadsheet, which is the most important document, but no one really double-checks it except for the junior bankers. It's the foundation for why a deal makes sense, and once the juniors check it (and swear on their mothers' lives that it's correct), everyone from the senior bankers to the clients to the clients' shareholders all assume someone else checked the numbers. By the way, this is how nuclear reactors melt down.

- *Financial Presentation.* Usually a PowerPoint and the only real document that matters because no one of importance ever reads the first two; they're typically delegated to the junior people to "check." This is the pièce de résistance because it's essentially the lazy man's way of getting the gist of the whole shebang.

Rising in the ranks of the investment banking world is no easy task. The firms typically have multiple departments, but the one that the general public is most familiar with because of Hollywood is the Corporate Finance Department. This is the group that identifies companies to buy, invest in, or sell and that raises capital for them with the goal of generating a healthy return for stakeholders.

I climbed the ladder in the corporate finance function at Jefferies and spent my career helping companies find liquidity. I started in the proverbial "janitorial suite" as an analyst, where I was routinely asked to do financial analyses, assist in presentations, order late-night takeout, and carry the deal books to meetings. Typically, this is a two- to three-year stint where you give your life, after which you're asked either to stay on and be promoted to associate or told to leave and either go to business school or enter another profession. I stayed for four and a half years, went to business school, then returned as a vice president. After a few more years as VP and a short stint as SVP, I was promoted to managing director and ultimately became co-head of an industry group. In totality, I stayed with the firm for almost a quarter century until I retired, but not before doing a lot of deals and making a lot of money.

If you're still confused about the hierarchy in banking, like most jobs in the corporate world, it's structured like a pyramid. While the specific titles may vary, here is the general pecking order of power:

Formal Title[2]	Real Title	Description
Analyst	Janitor	You're the lowest of the low. Crap flows downhill, and you're the drain that leads to the ocean.
Associate	Head Janitor	You're responsible for the analysts, but don't get a big head. The only thing separating you from them is your fancy MBA. Everyone knows you really don't know crap.
Vice President (VP)	Lieutenant	Welcome to management! You're the sole reason the SVP and MD no longer have to read or review anything, so you better not have faked your way here.

[2] Title on your business card or what you tell Mom.

Formal Title[2]	Real Title	Description
Senior Vice President (SVP)	The Man-Lite	This is the most dangerous job, like being trapped on a boat crossing the River Styx. Make sure you get to MD ASAP or you're going to be unemployed in the next RIF.[3]
Managing Director (MD)	The Man[4]	You have arrived. You now have the career longevity of a pro athlete and are expected to deliver revenue and pay for all the stooges below you.

There are also bastardized titles, like "Senior Analyst" and "Senior Associate," but they're like Dwight Schrute's[5] role as "Assistant to the Regional Manager." It doesn't make you "Assistant Regional Manager."

Many companies, Wall Street firms included, are like the Borg from *Star Trek*, where you either assimilate or face rejection, so once you've been hired, you'd better know what the work actually entails so you can be the best at doing it. In fact, it still surprises me how many people don't actually know how their company really makes money. They can't identify the highest value-added their companies provide to their clients. It's critical to know this because almost always, the seats of power are right at these epicenters of money making. You need to know the source of your company's money machine because all career paths lead back here.

So lay your map on the dining room table and chart the must-knows. In investment banking, here are the kindergarten basics:

- *Mergers & Acquisitions.* This could also be known as Marriages & Alliances. Just like a human Tinder, you find companies for others to acquire by examining the cultural, financial, and strategic fit. By combining all those "fits," you could be creating either the *Brady Bunch* or *Game of Thrones*. And, most important, is it worth your while? In other words, is there synergy (the most potent and dangerous word in the English language)? Synergy is what happens when you take two lemons and make lemonade. It's Wall Street's version of the **free lunch**. Every merger has synergies on paper. It always works well on PowerPoint, but in real life, it rarely exists. In fact, most M&As fail.[6] Oh yes, there's one other question that trumps all others: Will the firm make a fat fee?

---

[3] RIF is an abbreviation for Reduction in Force, a euphemism for getting canned. Wall Street is a cyclical business, so expect these RIFs every few years. You better be generating a high ROI when this comes or you're screwed.

[4] Because Wall Street is a dudefest, there really isn't a female equivalent of this. In reality, the women who make it to this level should be called the Queen Bees.

[5] Character from the TV show *The Office*, one of the few British imports that is actually pretty awesome.

[6] A 2012 KPMG study found that 83 percent of deals hadn't boosted shareholder returns, while a separate survey by A.T. Kearney concluded that total returns on M&A were negative. https://www.cbsnews.com/news/why-mergers-fail/

- *Debt Financing.* I'm talking about raising the Benjamins. Debt should be well known to all you recent graduates. After all, you owe more than *one trillion* dollars of it. Companies can borrow money in a host of exotic ways, but the key is that the more you borrow, the more financially distressed you become. But something magical happens when you borrow a shit ton. John P. Getty, who for a time was the richest man in the world,[7] once said, "If you owe the bank one hundred dollars, that's *your* problem. If you owe the bank one hundred million dollars, it's the *bank*'s problem."

- During the last several decades, debt innovation used to raise money has rivaled the explosion of Internet pornography. The variety of acronym-infused products is astounding. The number of mortgage-backed securities (MBS), asset-backed securities (ABS), agency-backed securities (ABS), and commercial-backed securities (CBS) issued by Wall Street will blow your mind. Notice what they all have in common? They're full of BS. They're primarily designed to serve a simple function: to get money from investors willing to accept different levels of risk–reward tradeoffs and to exploit varying degrees of their **risk aversion**. Some like it hot and spicy, others cold and bland. There are many different ways of doing this, but all track back to *securitization* where you can sell securities to investors who have neither the knowledge nor the ability to judge what they're really buying.

- *Equity Financing.* The other way to raise money is by selling stock in a company. This can be done via venture capital funding when the company is still private or going public through a process called an *initial public offering* (IPO). These deals garner the most press because they mean someone other than you just became fabulously wealthy and successful. Generally speaking, however, people have only a faint understanding about investment banking, mostly garnered from the headlines they read and the many fictional and real-life villains, like Gordon Gecko, Bernie Madoff, and Dick Fuld, to name just a few, who have been in jail or should have been.

So there you have it. Now you know enough about Wall Street to recognize yourself in these stories regardless of your desired or current job. I've spent time with thousands of companies in all sectors of the U.S. economy, so I know there are enough similarities between Wall Street and Main Street that many of my lessons can be applied to any workplace. The only difference is Wall Streeters get paid better.

Key Takeaways

- Don't rush into battle; understand the lay of the land.
- Study the org chart or, better yet, the *shadow org chart.*
- Know your company's money machine because all career paths lead back there.
- Wall Street is the same as Main Street, just better paid.

[7] J. Paul Getty was the richest man in the world in 1966, worth an estimated $1.2 billion.

PART 2

Play to Win

CHAPTER 8

Your Career Isn't Just a Job; It's an Adventure

Stay to Win

Now that you're in the door, it's time to dance the dance and go the distance so that you'll be showered with financial rewards and prestige when you reach the top. Contrary to what your frontal lobe may be telling you, the name of the game is not speed, but longevity, and that means making the best possible decisions early in your career to ensure your rise.

The best way to approach any intense, competitive workplace is to think of it as a *game*—a game that's played by rules that include a few explicit ones, but a lot that are unwritten and lurk in the shadows. These may include why some coworkers seem to do so little and yet get the plumb promotions and why some office assistants seem to wield more power than VPs.

Every workplace is different, but the fastest (and easiest) way to discern these rules is to find that seasoned veteran who seems to have an outgoing exterior masking an undercurrent of cynicism. We all know them. They're that mid- to senior-level person who appeared to be on the fast track, but now seems to be stuck in Dante's Purgatory. They've clearly been there long enough to know the unwritten rules of the office, and if you play your cards right and demonstrate fealty to them, they may just take you under their wing and spill the beans. But what's in it for them? Therapy of course! We all need someone to commiserate with and explain our station in life, and who better than a young apprentice who will lend a soft ear and nod compassionately no matter how idiotic the explanation? In fact, on my first day at Jefferies, an MD, who became a valuable mentor to me and my office sherpa, quoted me his own rule of survival that had served him well: "To have a long-term career as a banker, you need the adaptability of a cockroach."

OK, I know what you're thinking right now. Easier said than done. Well, you're right. Most of us know we should exercise and yet we are overweight.[1] We know what we need to get done today but we procrastinate. Hell, I've been staring at this same paragraph for an hour as I do more important things like tweeze my ear hairs. Change is scary, and we're resistant because with change comes risk, and we all know we have a tendency toward **risk aversion**. This means we generally prefer situations with less variability or less change, even if the situations with greater variability can lead to a better outcome! Meditate on that for a minute. We have a tendency *not* to choose an outcome that we know has a chance of leading to a *better* outcome. Talk about being scared of your shadow. And it can get worse. It can even extend into **cognitive dissonance**,[2] that uncomfortable feeling you get when you hold two or more contradictory beliefs, ideas, or values. No, not when you're listening to someone speak and imagining them naked. It's when your own belief, or gut, is turned into knots because of some new evidence. To reduce the psychological pain, you either have to change your mind or your behavior so that the contradiction is resolved. Or you fool yourself. It's how I justify to myself that tweezing my ear hairs is more important than finishing this paragraph.

Later we'll talk more about how to change yourself, but the first step is awareness and knowing you have a problem. To paraphrase the amazing work of top academics like Dan Ariely and Angela Duckworth, it's all about developing *habits*, stupid! This is the key to adapting your behavior and having a long-term, successful career. As a young man, I remember visiting Frank Baxter, former CEO of Jefferies. On his office desk, prominently displayed was a cartoon of a dinosaur with a caption that is the secret to a successful career anywhere: "Adapt or Die."

Be Water

What this means for you human buggers is that you've got to figure out how to be flexible and contort yourself into whatever is required at the moment. Using the immortal words of the great Chinese American warrior-philosopher, Bruce Lee, "Be like water making its way through cracks. Do not be assertive, but adjust to the object, and you shall find a way around or through it." To say it more plainly, the talents that gain you entry at the bottom (e.g., detail orientation, hard work, financial acumen) are not the same ones that elevate you up the **corporate ladder** (e.g., salesmanship and being a political animal). In fact, much like the quirks of your

---

[1] Over two-thirds of Americans are overweight or obese, and I'm pretty sure they don't wake up in the morning thinking it's in their best interest to stuff yet another muffin in their pie holes. If they're oblivious to their predicament, they have the other third of skinny Americans to nag them to get off their asses.

[2] This phenomenon, first described by Leon Festinger in 1957, helps explain why so many people will vigorously defend, excuse, justify, and keep their sacred beliefs, even when confronted with irrefutable proof they're wrong.

significant other that initially seemed so gosh-darn adorable, your best skills can quickly become the claws-on-a-blackboard irritants that cap your career, or even get you fired.

So take the time to survey the land and be patient. Harry Nelis, who you should remember is a partner at Accel, suggests that the newly hired "not come out of the gate too fast." Rather, he says, it's best to "lay low and figure out the lay of the land, then gradually show your true colors and opinions only after you've deciphered how the place works."

Harry and I both have seen plenty of people injure their career within their first two weeks to such a degree that it takes a long time, if ever, to repair the damage.

Who Moved My Caviar?

When we first walk through the doorway of any company after the mollycoddling we received as an undergraduate or in business school, we're all naive and, frankly, idiots. Part of the problem is that there's a good chance our naiveté comes from being victimized by the bait and switch. You may not see it coming, but it won't take long to recognize. Maybe you've already had the experience, like I did, of being lured during recruitment into thinking your new job will vault you into a glamorous life of expensive cars and beautiful people. I bet you thought you were going to be the God or Goddess of the universe. I sure did. How could I not, when my only experience at the firm was during Super Saturday, being shuffled around town in a limousine, partying with the rich and famous at Beverly Hills nightclubs, and having wine and dinner at overpriced LA restaurants? (At one restaurant, I saw Tom Cruise eating at a nearby table and thought he and I were certain to become BFFs frequenting the same day spas and latte watering holes for the hoi polloi. Instead, the closest I've come to seeing Tom again is as a billboard cutout offering me a free personality test on Sunset Boulevard.)

But don't beat yourself up too much. Again, we're inclined to believe what others tell us even though our Spidey Sense may tell us the other person is full of it. We believe communication is honest—which frankly makes us all easy pickings.

Slaving and Hazing and Crazing

So what's the reality? Well, Thomas Edison once said, "Genius is 1 percent inspiration, 99 percent perspiration," probably right after he screwed Nikola Tesla out of a patent. Succeeding as a Wall Street warrior might be 1 percent street smarts rather than inspiration, but that same 99 percent perspiration applies. For more than

20 years, I worked 80 to 120 hours per week.[3] I couldn't plan for birthdays or holidays or be relied upon by my family when they needed me. I even hid my grief when I was told in the middle of an important negotiation that my uncle had died and I couldn't make his funeral because a client demanded my presence at a meeting. I was stressed out of my mind. I sought release anywhere I could, like 11 p.m. exercises at 24 Hour Fitness and drinking a half-dozen cups of coffee in the morning and another half-dozen Diet Cokes in the afternoon. That's almost 1000 mg of caffeine a day, or just 200 mg shy of what the FDA says can cause seizures. Compound that over 20 years and you have over 7 kg, or a bowling ball's worth, of caffeine that's coursed through my body. It's amazing I'm not anxious or high strung!

Wall Street is an extreme, level-ten rollercoaster. Some days we lived like rock stars, but most days we lived like rocks. In my junior years, I shared a single office with three dudes. Our office was split into four cubicles, with a banker jammed in each one. We practically lived in that office, cranking out presentations and having little to no social life. There was a newly minted associate who sat across from me who had a particular penchant for BS and always talked up his banker life to his bros. One day, he was chatting with a buddy on the phone and he said out loud for all of us to hear: "You know me! I'm doing deals, getting laid, and going to parties on the weekend!"

What a crock! He was spending his Saturday nights in the office checking for typos like the rest of us.

But I digress. In the early years, nothing should deter you from doing what's needed for the job—in particular, anything personal. You're setting initial impressions, and even though companies want you to have a balanced personal life, it's only because they think it will make you a better worker bee. Otherwise, we'd all work for companies who let us screw around doing our personal stuff, right? So it's important to prioritize wisely. If your adopted step-sister from China is getting married to the love of her life during an important IPO roadshow, you should go to the wedding. Or ask her if there is any way she can change the date. However, if it's a cousin who only invited you because he thinks you're a rich investment banker and will buy overpriced crap on his Williams-Sonoma registry, send a card—a paperless one. If you think you're having a heart attack, for God's sakes, go to the hospital. If you're dead, you can't do a financial model. But if you tear your ACL the night before a big pitch, get a knee brace and some good painkillers. This is a marathon, made up of dozens of sprints, and if at any time you burn out, you can't play the game.

You've also got to learn to put up with the crazies. Early in my career, one associate treated the entire office like his personal frat house. If a phone rang more than once, he'd scream until someone answered it. He'd remind me that it was my job to answer the main line and if I wasn't smart enough to do that, how the hell could I be trusted to build a balanced financial model? If we ordered takeout and either screwed up his order or didn't have enough for him, the entire city block would know it. Of course, he had a simple solution. He'd eat mine.

---

[3] For you skeptical math savants, this is humanly possible. There are 168 total hours in a week. If you sleep approximately 7 hours per day, you can work just under 120 hours per week. Of course, by the time you reach my age, you're unlikely to be able to string more than two sentences together without having an editor correcting your work.

One VP would insist I order takeout for him regardless of which city he happened to be in—even if I was in a different continent! Zappos, an online shoe company, became legendary for their customer service, which could include ordering pizza for their shoe customers. I'm not impressed. I was a walking Zappos call center long before they came around and stole my business model.

When I was 20 years into my career, I was scheduled to jointly pitch a client with another MD. He was a perennial tardy bastard and finally arrived over 30 minutes late. Instead of apologizing to the client, he blamed me for the scheduling mix-up and smacked me in the back of the head so hard my teeth rattled! I could have decked him right there and then, but I chose the high ground and kept my cool. I live by the mantra of sometimes "losing the battle and winning the war"— especially when it comes to crazies. A few years later, we fired his ass.

Sometimes there's a fine line between slaving and hazing, which is simply another way of developing affinity among the slugs, of indoctrinating them into the group by making them conform to the norms. This is why in my experience, people from war-torn countries or low-income backgrounds make the best junior-level employees, especially Asians. We're hungry, and if we don't perform and lose our jobs, there might literally be an extended family, or even an entire village, that won't eat. So you put up with the hazing, the grueling hours, the asshole boss changing the deal in the final hour. Until you don't.

The pressure is enormous and can break you, like it did with a colleague of mine who, like the rest of us, was working around the clock. He was forever grumpy and stressed. One night a group of us were toiling deep in the salt mines when this analyst got a call at 2 a.m. from his MD, a particularly disorganized muckety-muck who had just looked at the pitchbook for the first time, even though it had been delivered to him days before. When he finally got off his ass to look at it, this MD had wholesale changes, which radically altered the final recommendation and required a rework of the entire presentation. Essentially, this analyst's all-nighters had all been for naught. So he hung up the phone, stared at his computer screen, and, after mumbling unintelligibly to himself, got up and walked out the door.

Walking by his cubicle early the next morning, I did a double-take when I saw confetti all over his desk. Upon closer inspection, I realized he had shredded his business cards into tiny pieces. Given we were running a respectable joint and not some bucket shop,[4] our cards were made of fancy cardstock that you couldn't tear easily. So unless he was the Hulk, it must have taken this dude a hell of a lot of time and energy to rip each of them one-by-one into shreds.

A few hours later, the analyst walked back into the office with a Joker-like smile, acting as if nothing out of the ordinary had occurred. He started cranking out his work again as the rest of us tiptoed around him like he was a suicide bomber. A few weeks later, he left the firm, and the investment banking industry, and never returned.

---

[4] A term of endearment given to firms that sell crappy securities to unsuspecting rubes. Yes, like the one you bought that bitcoin fund from last week.

In a similar circumstance, a colleague and I would always bitch and moan among ourselves about being exhausted and overworked, promising that one day we'd quit together in solidarity. Every day was quitting day, but we'd always return to the grind as soon as we had let off some steam. One morning, however, I saw him walk into the MD's office and through the glass, his smiles turned to scowls and I could hear him yelling at the top of his lungs. The MD just nodded, barely saying anything. When my colleague finally finished his rant, he walked out the door, waving and muttering as he went. That was the last time I saw him until almost 25 years later. He's now his own boss, running a billion-dollar hedge fund.

Always Be Learning (ABL) so You Can Always Be Closing (ABC)

How many times have you heard this? "You're a real asset to this company." Translation? You're an expensive, souped-up laptop, programmed to make money. So as your career progresses, always be mindful of your **return on investment (ROI)** to your employer. You may start off as a negative ROI project early in your career when you barely know how to spell your name, but if you don't generate positive ROI soon, guess what happens to you? That's right—you're headed to the same resting place as those Tickle Me Elmo dolls—the local trash dump.

As you become more senior in your career and beg for greater compensation, you'll need to generate a higher and higher return if you want to keep your job. As your seniority grows, so does your cost to the organization, so it's critical to learn new skills as you progress up the ranks. In fact, a variation of *Always Be Closing* (ABC, from the motion picture *Glengarry Glen Ross*[5]) is the equally important *ABL—Always Be Learning*.

Once reality sets in as to what you've gotten yourself into, it's time for you to get with the program. You'll quickly have to accept the fact you'll be living, like I did, within the four walls of your cubicle (i.e., jail cell), working around the clock for the next several years. During my first tour of duty, before leaving for business school, I fulfilled my role as master apprentice by following my boss around like a puppy and never letting go. I became a living, breathing positive ROI project because I was constantly trying to improve my skills. I was *ABLing* my way up the ladder.

My MD even leant me his Porsche 911 Targa. Why? Because I had ingratiated myself to him. Remember **reciprocity bias**? I was an unapologetic workhorse and was doing everything possible to lead the charge. A wise old banker once told me

---

[5] *Glengarry Glen Ross* is mandatory viewing for anyone intent on climbing the corporate ladder. Among other pearls, it tells the story of how the more senior you become, the closer you can smell the Holy Grail of revenue and sales. This is not something you should forget. Consider tattooing "ABC" on your forehead, so every day when you look in the mirror to clean out your blackheads, you're thinking about how to close business.

that a career in banking "isn't just a job; it's an adventure." Of course, he stole this saying from the Navy, where I'm sure they coined it to motivate young cadets to risk their lives for country. (The worst thing that can happen to you on Wall Street is getting a hernia from carrying too many pitchbooks.) Part of what makes careers on Wall Street more than just a job is the daily learning and interactions that come with the work. It's a project-oriented career where you get to work with a wide variety of companies, industries, and personalities. That's what makes it an adventure—the constant sailing to and from different destinations. I also think this mantra is a good North Star. When work no longer seems like an adventure, it's time to find a new career.

Chris McGowan, former managing director at Madison Dearborn, former banker at Morgan Stanley, and now adjunct professor at the University of Chicago's Booth School of Business, agrees with the work-as-an-adventure comparison. "Slow and steady always wins the race," he tells his MBA students. "The tortoise beats the hare because the hare gets distracted surfing his phone at work, chitchatting with the receptionist, developing a drinking problem, and maybe even getting hooked on drugs."

Key Takeaways

- *Grit* and *longevity* are the keys to winning. Speed kills.
- Treat work like a *game*—one with both *written* and *unwritten* rules.
- Be water and adapt to the circumstances.
- Fight *risk aversion* and even *cognitive dissonance* by being adaptable.
- To rise through the ranks, you must change. Use *habits* to begin this process.
- Work is a marathon, so don't burn out or you can't play the game.
- *ABL* so you can have positive *ROI* and *ABC*.

CHAPTER 9

People Are Irrational

Science Your Way Up

I've worked with C-level executives and many successful people my entire career and to be blunt, it's not their science, technology, engineering, and math (STEM) knowledge that distinguishes them. Certainly, having at least a basic knowledge of STEM is a prerequisite in today's competitive world, but that's not what makes an individual stand out. If you want to succeed, you'll need to get people to do what you want and will have to study *people* and not just books or spreadsheets. You'll need to have knowledge of the theories that underlie human behavior. Think of it like being a great magician. You first need to understand the basic rules and techniques, like sleight of hand or misdirection, and then adapt them to suit your needs.

No idea what I'm talking about? BINGO! That's your problem, and chances are, you're selling yourself short. Moreover, if you've ever been told the following, you're in serious trouble:

- "You're not a team player."
- "We're trying to mix up the complexion of the group."
- "Have you considered changing your attitude?"
- "It's not you; it's us."
- "You're too aggressive."
- "You're not aggressive enough."

Chances are, many of you have been participating in the raging Bull Market for STEM and the Bear Market for the social sciences. You can rectify that problem by gaining knowledge about **cognitive bias** and **behavioral economics**. If you understand this body of research and apply it to your work situation, you'll find an easier way to the top of the totem pole. I will admit that it wasn't always obvious to me, but now in my aging years, I realize a lot of my success has been because I stumbled in the dark applying some of these theories. They've helped me become more strategic in my actions, empathetic with colleagues and clients, and proactive in plotting my career trajectory. So for the impatient among you, the following should help.

Get with the Program

Cognitive bias and **behavioral economics** theories are based on the premise that human beings not only are *imperfect*, but also are fundamentally *irrational*. Among many other examples, that's what ad agencies depend on when developing misleading commercials and what movie companies depend on when creating trailers that pique an audience's interest.

The black belt masters of applying these theories to commerce are the Internet companies. Ever wonder why Netflix, Amazon, Google, and their Silicon Valley ilk are swimming in dough? It's because they know the value of these magical theories. In fact, the godfather of the field, Professor Daniel Kahneman, held court at a 20-person, invitation-only con-fab in the wine-drenched hills of Napa Valley.[1] Now this wasn't some *Eyes Wide Shut*, mask-wearing bacchanal, but it was an orgy—an orgy of social psychology and cognitive science. Dr. Kahneman gave tech titans like Jeff Bezos, Larry Page, and Sergey Brin a personal primer on theories like **risk aversion**, **planning fallacy**, and **utility theory** over a two-day period. To what end, you ask? To share his latest research on how people *really* think so that they could use it in their businesses. I believe it's a big reason why these tech giants have been able to sell you shows you'll never watch, tchotchkes to clutter your house, and smart devices you swear you need in that closet.

Still skeptical as to the importance of this field? Well, McKinsey, the powerhouse management consulting firm, thought it was so critical that they established thought leadership in the space.[2] They identified that reducing decision biases should be the top priority of boards and senior executives for improving performance. Of course, enterprising capitalists that they are, they used this as an opportunity to charge millions in fees to their clients to diagnose, design, and implement ways to root out **cognitive biases** in organizations. And here you thought this book was overpriced!

[1] Edge Master Class by Daniel Kahneman: "A Short Course in Thinking about Thinking." Since you aren't a billionaire techie, the likelihood of you getting invited is the same as an ELE (Extinction-Level Event). But you're in luck! You can get the CliffsNotes version without wasting time mindlessly chit-chatting about the model of your private jets or the furnishings in your fourth vacation home: https://www.edge.org/events/the-edge-master-class-2007-a-short-course-in-thinking-about-thinking#album
[2] McKinsey, "The Business Logic in Debiasing," May 23, 2017. https://www.mckinsey.com/business-functions/risk/our-insights/the-business-logic-in-debiasing#

Professors Daniel Kahneman and his pioneering partner, the late Amos Tversky, wrote *Thinking, Fast and Slow*, where they highlight that, in a nutshell, human beings make irrational decisions, economic and otherwise. Remember that time you bought that Indestructible, Perfect-Fit-Belt from an *As Seen on TV* infomercial? Forget that it doesn't even fit your expanded waistline; you couldn't resist buying something that promised to be perfect! You justify it by telling yourself that you'll shrink into it.

Being a Smart Dummy

Understanding irrational behavior and motivations has been under scientific study for many years. In the early 1900s, Professor Lewis Terman developed an IQ test as a way to measure general intelligence and predict future success. Here are just a few of his findings that are still relevant:

- Intelligence does not equal rationality. Don't assume people act logically. It explains why Sir Francis Bacon, a brilliant philosopher, died of pneumonia from spending too much time in the cold stuffing a chicken with snow.

- Motivations are the key to understanding human behavior. Wonder why Warren Buffett is still working? *Hint:* It's not about the money.

- The most overconfident are often the most ignorant because they have blind spots. They're know-it-alls who think everyone's a friend. Just ask Julius Caesar about his amigo Brutus.

- Wisdom can trump intelligence. Look at Benjamin Franklin, who dropped out of school at the age of ten but had arguably the greatest career in American history. Although he was a scientist, statesman, counselor to presidents, and Founding Father of the Constitution at the ripe old age of 81, he will forever be known as the source of the Wall Street career phrase: "It's all about the Benjamins!"

- **Overconfidence** in intuition can end with **dysrationalia**[3] but it can also be helpful in decision-making. Henry Ford trusted his gut and doubled his employees' wages in the midst of rapidly declining sales and employee turnover, despite all data showing it would be suicidal. It worked, and turnover and the business recovered. (By the way, using your gut is also super-helpful if you're lazy and just want people to follow your advice. It's the work equivalent of "Because I said so!")

---

[3] The inability to think or behave rationally despite having adequate intelligence.

- Organizations can either benefit from the **wisdom of the crowd** or sabotage themselves with **groupthink**.[4] The former led to the crowdsourcing of some of LEGO's greatest designs, whereas the latter is responsible for every major investment bubble, from tulips, to dotcom stocks, to NFTs.

You might think this is all great, but how do you use this to advance your career? You should know by now that a great way to better understand other people's motivations (as well as your own) is to master **cognitive bias** and human psychology. Harry Nelis, former Goldman Sachs banker and now partner at the venture capital firm Accel, underscores this notion. "You have to realize that people aren't instinctively against you," he told me. "Being against someone is a lot of work. Most people's motivation is a preoccupation with themselves."

Harry's point is that you might have thought you were competing with the go-getter in the next cubicle, but you're really competing against yourself. Others are so focused on getting what they want, they likely don't have the energy or inclination to purposely sabotage you. Of course, you may encounter the occasional disciple of Machiavellianism who enjoys winning at the expense of others. The key to rooting them out is to become knowledgeable in these social sciences in order to understand what truly drives a person's behavior.

There's not a lot of literature out there that tackles the practical application of **cognitive bias** in the workplace. (That's why you should read this book cover to cover!) But rest assured, I'm by no means alone in my obsession. Hank Paulson, ex-CEO of Goldman Sachs and former U.S. Secretary of the Treasury, says just coming up with a bright idea is not enough. "Everybody can learn the computational skills, analytical skills, and so on, . . . but it's the people skills that matter most," he said when interviewed at the Stanford Graduate School of Business.[5] "Almost as important as *what* you do, is who you do it *with*. Getting anything done requires working with others. It's all about interpersonal relationships."

One great way to learn how to deal with people is in sales. Lloyd Blankfein, ex-CEO of Goldman Sachs, started as a hot-dog salesman. Frank Baxter, who went on to become CEO of Jefferies, began selling newspapers at the age of eight and the following year even hired someone to help him. Another Goldman CEO, Sidney Weinberg, entered the workforce selling newspapers, shucking oysters, and carrying feathers. He later started at Goldman as a janitor's assistant, where he cleaned partners' hats and shoes. I guess back in the day, you really could be a janitor and rise through the ranks at an investment bank.

I hope I've given you food for thought and opened your mind to another set of tactics you can use as you ascend in your career. Remember, the key is to first see the world through this new lens, inferring people's motivations and, ultimately, their behavior. If you're able to do that, you're well on your way to gaming the system. It has certainly served me well.

---

[4] The practice of thinking or making decisions as a group in a way that discourages creativity or individual responsibility.
[5] https://www.youtube.com/watch?v=gTGybnPatQk

Key Takeaways

- Studying STEM got you this far, but to go further, study people.
- Humans are not only *imperfect*. They are also fundamentally *irrational*.
- *Cognitive biases* explain why individuals make irrational decisions—sometimes even against their own interests.
- Mastering *cognitive biases* will give you insight into motivations, which are the most important way to understand human behavior and game the system.

CHAPTER 10

Office Politics

Only Friends and Very Good Friends

O ffice politics is an epidemic in all companies. Show me a company that does-n't have any and I'll show you a company devoid of people. It exists because people are complicated, are consumed with their own goals, and need others to get stuff done or simply get out of the way. Whether they realize it or not, they're using every tool at their disposal to achieve their individual goals and engage in activities that shift balances of power to their gain. I've found that the degree of the politicization is directly correlated to the number of people in the organization—the more, the less merry. Gossip, innuendo, and backstabbing all seem to increase exponentially the more mouths there are to feed and the more hands in the cookie jar. So stand ready, hone your peripheral vision, and cover your back lest a dagger gets stuck in it.

Start Kissing Babies

The best way to deal with office politics is to stay above the fray. Take the high road and avoid getting caught in the muck with the pigs. Develop a solid reputation for being a team player, but also for being someone who isn't out to get everyone. Personal brand preservation is critical, and someone who isn't viewed as a threat is someone who will most likely survive—or at the very least bide their time until the moment is ripe for action.

The tools you've learned so far, like your newfound understanding of **affinity bias**, really come in handy when dealing with office politics because they further your ability to play the game well. So just as you did during the interview process, this is the time to pull out your dossier about company colleagues—their origin story, their fashion choices, their anonymous browsing history, their office fantasies, their drug of choice, and so on.

If your boss attends Zoom meetings in a Non-Iron Twill Button-Down Collar Shirt but just wears underwear and white socks off camera, don't be afraid to do the same. But don't be creepy and wear *exactly* what your boss wears. Instead, wear the Non-Iron *Pinpoint Spread* Collar Shirt, and sneak a peek at the label on their jacket—preferably when they're not wearing it. Get the same jacket but perhaps in a slightly lighter color. Don't go darker because that might look a little more suave and you never, ever want to show up your boss. If you follow this advice, I guarantee they'll be thinking, "This kid has good taste. Reminds me of me." If your boss is a different gender, you can at least shop at the same store or purchase the same brand of clothing. When you go on pitches together, you'll look like a "sib from another crib" or "sister from another mister."

But like everything, don't go overboard. What you wear says a lot about you. At a session where we were drafting a bond offering, I remember a banker from Credit Suisse who always wore a Harvard tie and matching cufflinks. Regardless of what you might think about the Ivies, nothing says "I think I'm smarter than you" more than wearing Harvard gear outside of Harvard Square. Obviously, my MD and I didn't let him get away with it unscathed. At group meetings, we would go full-on Statler and Waldorf[1] and make wisecracks like, "I didn't go to Harvard, but I think this should be a semi-colon." Then when it was time to order lunch, we'd tell him, "I didn't go to Harvard, but I think the turkey sandwich is better than roast beef." Nothing makes you look more like an elitist douchebag than wearing Harvard gear to a business meeting. Keep that crap for reunions.

Years later, I did attend Harvard, but I still wouldn't be caught dead wearing the school apparel at work. The Credit Suisse banker wore it to fit in and show how smart he was; his mistake was that he was working with people who were the opposite of impressed. Moral: Let your actions speak louder than your cufflinks. Prove to people you belong by your performance, not by the logo on your chest. Superman may wear his family crest there, but even if it looks stupid, who's seriously going to screw with Superman? You, on the other hand . . .

Do your snooping so that you know the particular interests of your direct bosses and the firm's partners. It might be time to pick up their hobbies. Golf. Bridge. Gourmet cooking. The list is endless, but the goal is singular: Build rapport and commonality.

While blending in and being part of the crowd may go against millennial dogma, you have to fit in right away; otherwise, you'll never have a chance. Just as when you were a teenager, like in *Clueless,* there are in-crowds and there are out-crowds. There are cool kids and there are pariahs. Assess the various groups and quickly insert yourself into the one that wields the most power. If you're unsure, follow the money; it's the yellow brick road to power. See who has the largest office or the corner one with no glass walls for lookie-loos. Or find the banker who seems to have gathered the best and brightest as their deal team. Winners want to work with winners, so leverage the work others have done and sound out the Pied Piper and follow their tune.

---

[1] Statler and Waldorf are a pair of *Muppets* known for their curmudgeonly opinions and joy from heckling from a theater balcony. No one knows what they do for a living other than make jokes at others' expense that only they find funny. I'm sure they're retired investment bankers.

Another way to offset office politics is with your ability to purview the lay of the land, as we discussed in an earlier chapter. Find the seats of power and understand that power abhors a vacuum and politics is ultimately the way one gathers strength in an organization. So know from where power emanates and who is trying to make sure they get more than their fair share. In other words, beware and be aware!

Be a Street Dog

Although you may think of the corporate world as dog-eat-dog where you have to sacrifice everything and knife someone in the back to succeed, I'm here to dispel that notion. You never know when your friends and allies might come to your rescue. For example, one year Lauren Wu, former equity analyst and CFO of venture capital at J&W Seligman and Merrill Lynch banker, was paid well and she later found out that it was due in part to her colleagues in the legal department who said she did a great job and deserved to be compensated well. Talk about manna from heaven!

If you treat work rules as guidelines and coworkers and higher-ups as resources, I'm confident you'll do well because everyone you meet will be a steppingstone to your financial freedom. Today's cubicle buddy could be tomorrow's CEO client, so treat everyone in your journey with respect.

People are inclined to do business and work well with those they like and who are like themselves. I mean, who doesn't love themselves? This is the crux of the **affinity bias**. The corollary to our unconscious tendency to get along with others who are like us is that it's easy to socialize and spend time with others who are *not* different from us.

So what do you do with these pearls of wisdom? How do you leverage this bias to your advantage?

Another of my mentors was the late Bob Lessin, who at different points in his career was vice chairman of Jefferies, vice chairman of Smith Barney, and advisor to the current CEO of J.P. Morgan, Jamie Dimon. In his heyday, Bob was a legend on Wall Street and was known as a banker extraordinaire. By accompanying him on pitches and observing his presentation style, through osmosis I learned a lot of tools that carried me throughout my career. Immediately after pitches, he'd give me sharp critiques of my own presentation style, and one day he told me something I'll never forget: "In this business, you only have friends, and very good friends."

The first time he said that to me, I wasn't exactly sure what he meant, but Bob was the most networked banker I'd ever met, and watching him work was like seeing Oprah disarm a talk show guest. When I accompanied Bob to pitch titans of the private equity world at firms like KKR, Carlyle, and TPG, Bob would be greeted by these masters of the universe as though they were asshole buddies. They would wax poetic about the Ivy their kids were attending, their recent multi-billion-dollar deal conquests, and the likely destination for their next ski chalet vacation. Bob would offer up a ton of pro bono work to curry favor with these titans. After the meeting, I'd comment to Bob about how much that executive liked him and how we'd soon be drowning in fees given the buckets of business we'd get given their relationship. Bob would comment without a tinge of irony, "He's a prick. He'll screw us." He reminded me that in the service business, there is no upside in making people aware of your true feelings unless you're looking for some fleeting sense of superiority, or even *schadenfreude*. There was only downside. Being enemies has zero upside, but being genuinely friendly can bear enormous dividends. Bob had no enemies—just good friends and better friends, and that meant he never disqualified himself from a deal.

Carl Icahn, a billionaire corporate raider, was rumored to have said, "If you want a friend, buy a dog." His point, paraphrased or not, is that Wall Street, like Corporate America, is a place for business and making money—not friends. I beg to differ. I've found that it can be both and, in fact, there is synergy! Having friends can only help accelerate your career by establishing alliances when jousting for internal power, marshalling advocates for your work at review time, or even generating business from clients who'd rather hire friends, all other things being equal. And frankly, work is just more enjoyable when you're surrounded by people who like you. So take the opposite view of Carl Icahn: Treat everyone like a dog, assuming you love dogs.

Besides, the opposite of a friend is an enemy, and having enemies can be exhausting. They usually lurk in the shadows, and trying to suss them out can be time-consuming and will distract you from your primary goal of getting ahead. Michael Corleone of *The Godfather* says, "Keep your friends close, but your enemies closer." True, but I prefer to live by the words of Abe Lincoln: "Do I not destroy my enemies when I make them my friends?" How? Do them favors; convince them you're no threat. Try to ascertain their goals and help them on their journey. Come across as the oblivious rube with no insight into their goals and motivations. Or if all else fails, become allies in helping them achieve their goals. Rather than trash their crappy deal at committee, support them so they will back you up the next time you bring some rancid opportunity to the firm. Work closely to win business for the firm and defer the knife-fight over credit until year-end.

Making allies out of enemies can work, but beware of what I call the **Sinister Six Syndrome**. I derived this from my youth of reading and drawing Spider-Man comics. Spidey would always kick the ass of individual villains until one day the morons realized they could beat him if they worked together. Their mutual hatred of Spidey created an alignment of interests. So Doc Octopus, Kraven, Mysterio, Vulture, Sandman, and Electro partnered up and beat the living daylights out of Spidey. Of course, you know how it ends. Marvel isn't going to derail their gravy train. But how does Spidey beat them? Well, it's almost always because once these baddies think they've vanquished him and their mutual goal is achieved, they turn on each other in the quest to be the alpha dog. Then Spidey reemerges at the denouement for mop-up duty. So take heed: Making alliances with enemies lasts only as long as you're mutually aligned. Once that goal has been achieved, or is perceived to have been achieved, then it's back to backstabbing as usual.

Sometimes you have to accept that enemies won't change and will never become friends no matter how hard you try. But don't despair. They can still be helpful in advancing your personal growth, particularly as it relates to identifying your weaknesses. When your adversary is vying against you for that one last partner slot, you need to ask yourself, what do they have that you don't? It could be that they're more adept at playing the game. Maybe they're better at sucking down stogies after hours with colleagues, flattering your bosses with praise and adoration, or simply killing deer on hunting treks with the senior partners. Whatever it is, use your enemies to identify where you might be deficient and try to rectify it. And lest you think you're perfect, take note of the science. Americans, in particular, have been found to suffer from **illusory superiority** where they overestimate their own qualities and abilities. It's also known as the **Lake Wobegon Effect**, named after the fictional town where all the children are above average. That's impossible, of course.

To What End?

One of my bosses used to say to me, "Know your station in life!" That set off all kinds of negative reactions in me, beginning with "WTF!" But after screaming into my pillow a few times, I thought maybe he had something else in mind. Well-run organizations do rely on a pecking-order mentality. You can't have inexperienced juniors running around trying to be senior executives; the whole place would fall into anarchy. So I learned to develop a thick skin, not only with my bosses, but with my peers. It helped that at all times, I kept the mantra "To what end?" close at hand. I highly recommend you do the same. To me, that meant not to seek revenge or retribution against someone, but at the same time not to be passive. Lie in wait, pick your battles, and heed the words of Pyhrrus of Epirus, "Win the battle; lose the war." Remember, your boss was in your role not long ago. Just be patient and soak up their knowledge. In other words, grin and bear it and wait your turn.

Just to show you that I'm not perfect (I know, shocker), when I was younger, I was a hypocrite and didn't follow my own advice. When I was rising up the ranks, another banker and I were vying for a single promotion slot. I got the job in large part because he was pretty ineffective, but he attributed his loss to my gamesmanship rather than talent. When he was pushed out, I didn't do anything to disavow him of this notion, believing that it would fall on deaf ears anyway. I didn't think much of it until years later when he was the CFO of a supernova Internet company and we were pitching for a role on his IPO. Even though we were the best bank to take them public, he didn't think twice about rejecting us. I later learned through one of the company's VCs that he still harbored resentment toward me and blamed me for his execution. I should have addressed his termination at the time and made it clear I wasn't doing anything untoward. Even though it might not have made a difference, in the highly competitive world of banking, you never know what might have tipped the balance in our favor.

Have a Shtick

Regardless of your color, gender, political persuasion, or food preferences, don't be a doorknob when attending office social events. Be interesting! Remember to ask yourself, "Would you want to hang with yourself?" If your answer is a feeble "Yes," become *more* interesting. Adopt some hobbies, watch movies, or read a book. Or be bold and get yourself a relationship coach to teach you how to get out there and rock and roll!

Edward Fu, president of Happy Masks and former banker from Jefferies, shared with me that he likens building friendships to dating. In fact, he studied pickup artists' techniques on YouTube and voraciously consumed the book *The Game: Penetrating the Secret Society of Pickup Artists* by Neil Strauss, a Bible among single men that highlighted some of the tricks to picking up women in the Los Angeles dating scene. Edward found these same tactics to be very successful in establishing rapport with strangers as he built his Rolodex[2] and career.

Gina King, partner at Supernode Global and former Jefferies SVP, adds that when she first started her career, she learned the importance of developing relationships outside of work. By attending a few happy hours and office functions, she was able to develop a camaraderie with her coworkers and get to know them and their families personally. This would bear dividends later when the time came to call upon her allies for help in everything from compensation to advocating for her promotion.

Sallie Krawcheck, CEO of Ellevest and former president at Bank of America, says that research has shown that for women in particular, having a strong network and a go-to squad of women colleagues who can help is one of the drivers for women getting ahead in their careers.

Many of you are going to have to develop a new mindset. Treat work like an improv stage. Develop a few amusing routines. Try them out with friends and iterate to see what works. Jerry Seinfeld, one of the most famous comedians of all time, tries out jokes in low-stakes clubs like the Gotham Comedy Club before using them at larger venues. If it works for him, it can work for you. After a while you'll have a few stories that can be conversation starters and you might even stumble upon a barn burner. But always be mindful of your audience and use EQ. This isn't *Mad Men*, so sexual and racial topics are verboten in this era. Spencer Wang, a former banker at Credit Suisse and Salomon Brothers, says that "EQ is a huge element of success, but so is situational awareness—like knowing when to crack the funny joke."

My own go-to stories were usually about my family, particularly with the older folks. Age comes with many disadvantages, like arthritis, incontinence, and memory loss, but when it comes to schmoozing, it can be an advantage because you have more in common with your firm's decision makers and prospective clients.

---

[2]A metaphor used by old businesspeople to describe their contacts. It's the business equivalent of saying something is "the bomb" or "rad." Nothing screams lame ass more than this.

You've lived longer and racked up a lot of experience, while younger people have been toiling away in the office talking only to their fellow associates or analysts. You can lament about the decline in the cultural scene in your hometown 20 years ago, compare the workmanship on your knee replacement scars, or simply commiserate about what your good-for-nothing kids are doing with their arts majors.

I try to engage younger people about their careers, but also with anything we might have in common. Sometimes it's about asking what my younger cousins are interested in doing or asking about the latest TikTok dance sensation. Picking the right topics can also overcome cultural barriers. With Americans, sports are usually a safe bet as long as you don't rub it in if your team has had an overabundance of riches; with the Chinese, travel and cuisine usually work. Chinese are always trying to find that restaurant in town that serves the best *xiǎo lóng bāo* (小笼包) or *dàn tǎ* (蛋挞) because most taste like microwaved leftovers. So when you do find one, mentioning it to your brethren is like sharing the location of the Fountain of Youth. It will earn you props to get at least another meeting or even a bosom buddy for life.

As you inch your way into the inner circle, here's a final piece of advice: don't stretch yourself too thin. There's a scientific theory, **Dunbar's Number**, which states that the number of people with whom you can maintain a stable social relationship is 150.[3] So choose wisely; this will be your tribe!

As the Roman philosopher Seneca once wrote, "Luck is what happens when preparation meets opportunity." This cliché has a nugget of advice. Consider every business meeting, every casual coffee or tea, and even every random encounter, as a chance to open another vein of opportunity. But the only way to truly exploit that opportunity is to prepare and use the tools you've learned so far to your advantage. Use them to make friends, not enemies, and fortune will eventually shine on you. Good luck!

Key Takeaways

- Politics are a fact of office life.
- Stay above the fray, but study your colleagues intently.
- Find the seats of power and latch on.
- Only have friends and very good friends.
- Enemies can become allies, but beware of the *Sinister Six Syndrome*.
- Lake Wobegon doesn't exist. You're likely average or below.
- Always ask yourself "To what end?" before acting.
- Study pick-up artists to learn relationship-building tactics.
- Have audience-tested stories ready as conversation starters.

---

[3] In the 1990s, British anthropologist Robin Dunbar discovered a correlation between the brain size of primates and the size of their average social group. Using the size of the human brain, he extrapolated a cognitive limit of 150 as the number of people with whom a person can maintain a stable social relationship. In his book, *Grooming, Gossip, and the Evolution of Language*, Dunbar explained it as "the number of people you would not feel embarrassed about joining uninvited for a drink if you happened to bump into them in a bar." Recent research out of Stockholm University (*Biology Letters*, 5 May 2021) disputes the validity of Dunbar's findings, but that's another story.

CHAPTER 11

Be a Stork, Not a Pigeon

Bring Value, Not Diversion

As I approach my 30th year of corporate life, I estimate that I have spent more than 30,000 hours in meetings[1]—many of which, in hindsight, were worthless. But they don't have to be. Use them wisely and make them a venue to showcase your talents.

The bottom line (and oh, how we all love bottom lines) is don't be that person everyone looks at and wonders why the hell you're sitting at the table. That makes you the dodo bird. But even worse, don't be a pigeon—someone who flies in, craps on everything, then bails.

Instead, be the person who arrives without pomp and circumstance, is on time with the delivery, drops the baby off with some real value-add, and then expects nothing in return.

In other words, be the stork.

Mind Your P's and Q's

Whenever you go to *any* meeting, *add* value. Remember how I said that when you make a job inquiry, the recipient might have the attention span of a goldfish? I told you, "Nail it in a sentence!" Well, the same applies when you actually land a job, with slight adjustments. Be brief!

---

[1] I estimate I've spent more than 25 hours per week in some *fakakta* meetings for almost 30 years.

When you have something to say, make it relevant. Don't waste everyone's time with inane comments or questions. That's a surefire way to earn membership in *Densa*, the low-IQ society—like when someone asks a question masquerading as an opportunity for them to sound smart and the speaker retorts, "So what's your question?" Everyone in the audience thinks, "Dumbass." Another is when the question exposes someone for being an inattentive jerk and the speaker states, "We covered that five slides ago . . . dumbass."

If you're lucky, or powerful, enough to determine the purpose for a meeting, follow a few key tips to make sure you're adding value for everyone invited. Before the meeting, send a concise agenda with any background materials and a clear delineation of the meeting's purpose and attendees. Focus on getting stuff done. Meetings for education purposes are a complete waste of everyone's time, particularly given that we all read and process information at different rates. Don't ever use a meeting to walk through the materials you sent in advance. Use it for Q&A. Make sure there is a timekeeper to keep everyone on track. This will reduce the airtime used by that suck-up to wax on about how awesome he is just so he can appear smart. How dare he! That should be your airtime! And finally, make sure there are clear deliverables. I was in many a meeting where I left thinking, "Damnit, I'm never going to get that hour of my life back." Make people feel that something is actually going to get done from that meeting.

Lauren Wu, former equity analyst and CFO of venture capital at J&W Seligman and Merrill Lynch banker, suggests coming with solutions, but to be specific. "Don't be vague. It will only diminish your credibility. Come with a well thought out, specific solution. Otherwise, why bother? You'll only hurt yourself."

If the meeting is meant for decision-making, come prepared with recommendations and earn kudos from your boss and colleagues. Why? People don't like to make decisions. They represent pain points because by making a decision, you close off other avenues. It's why you didn't completely dump that nice but boring guy you were dating. If your current beau turns out to be a Toad-in-Prince's clothing, at least you can always go back to Mr. Reliable. Deciding anything is exactly like that: It creates what's known as the **Paradox of Choice**, whereby we think we want more choices but in reality we don't. Rather than agonize over the choices, we either punt on the decision or, ideally, have someone else decide for us—and take the blame. A great way to add value is to educate your boss on the options, the pros and the cons, and then make a recommendation.

If I was ever in doubt as to how to act, I'd remind myself of **Prospect Theory**,[2] a Nobel Prize–winning theory that describes the way people behave when given choices concerning probability. Experts found that for most people, *losses* loom larger than *gains* and people give greater weight to *certainty* over *probability*. In other words, small *certain* gains will trump *probable* big gains. In layman's terms, human beings are twice more risk-averse than risk-loving.[3]

[2]Kahneman and Tversky, "Prospect Theory: An Analysis of Decision under Risk" *Econometrica* (1979).
[3]Richard H. Thaler, *Misbehaving* (2015).

I recognized that this is the reason why bosses are less willing to take bets on new people unless they provide sufficient downside protection and strong upside certainty. When I first joined Jefferies, I made sure I was a safe pair of hands for building balanced financial models, proofing presentations, and performing punctual work. I became known for the *Liu Triple Check* because everyone knew I made sure my work was impeccable before submitting it to my bosses. Once I had the table stakes covered, I'd show them I had more than half a brain and could make succinct client recommendations, manage the newbies, and identify new prospects. By punching above my weight class, I showed I had the upside potential to progress to the next level. In short, I became the living embodiment of **Prospect Theory**.

Too Smart for Your Own Good

In many corporations, as the low person on the totem pole you'll be asked to prepare summaries for your higher ups so they can swoop in and get credit for whatever you've worked on. This will be your perfect opportunity to shine. Be that distillery that takes the highlights of any report, any meeting, any topic, and condenses it to its essence. Find the lead and deliver it to your boss.

None of us have enough time. You're probably reading this wondering how much longer until I get to the punchline.

When you prepare your work, it's good to remember the **curse of knowledge**. It occurs when a person assumes that other people they're communicating with have the same knowledge (and background) as they do. Another way to put it is that people who are smart or well-informed might not understand that other *regular* people might not think like they do. Take the TV show *The Big Bang Theory*, where scientist Sheldon Cooper has no clue what his waitress-neighbor, Penny, is thinking. He's a pedantic know-it-all with genius-level IQ and nonexistent EQ. She's . . . well . . . normal. The result is often a complete miscommunication that leads to a hilarious outcome—usually at the expense of one of them. Understanding the **curse of knowledge** can help you better communicate with, and educate, others.

But there's also another danger here. For many people, knowing too much can cause analysis paralysis, so watch for this in your bosses. You can add value by being the one to help them separate the signal from the noise. Providing a high **signal-to-noise ratio** is easier said than done because there's so much misinformation out there. I know someone who constantly uses his grandfather, who smoked three packs a day and lived to 100, as evidence that smoking is not unhealthy. It's an argument that ignores the possibility that his grandfather was an outlier.

This danger is intensified in this age of short attention spans, which, combined with laziness and the lack of bandwidth,[4] results in people preferring not to delve into the details. That's where you come in. I've found a formula for success is to be a human Google—or **Hoogle**[5]—by ingesting everything you can on a subject, then morphing into a walking CliffsNotes so you can help others easily understand a topic by providing a well-thought-out, succinct summary. I have found this to be the single best way for a junior professional to turn from a pigeon into a stork.

In fact, when I became a VP and had an eye toward becoming a big, bad MD, I started to think about ways I could generate business. Fortunately, the dawn of the Internet had begun and there were more than enough companies to cover and prospect. Unfortunately, there were almost too many. So I started to think about how the Internet would continue to grow like a trash dump for human thought. In 1999, there were already over 3 million websites,[6] much of it complete crap like MySpace.com, TheGlobe.com, and Boo.com, and I wondered how we were going to make sense of it all. My time was precious, so I started to employ the **signal-to-noise ratio** to my own identification of prospects. If the site helped people find what they wanted, if it identified the signal from the noise, then I knew it was adding some value to Internet users. From that point onward, as I focused on the Internet and ultimately became co-head of the group, I always used this filter to determine if the company was worth spending time on. It worked. Don't believe me? Think about all the sites you frequent and decide for yourself if they adhere to this principle.

Early in my career, senior bankers would ask us to create **Public Information Books,** or **PIBs.** These tomes were gigantic documents that contained every publicly available piece of information about a company, including annual reports, Wall Street analyst writeups, public 10-K and 10-Q filings, press clippings, etc. Senior bankers would then take their time perusing this material to *appear* as though they knew everything about a company in a one- or two-hour client meeting. Edgar Nye coined a phrase originally used to describe a river but has since been adopted to describe every senior banker on Wall Street: "A mile wide and an inch deep."

Recognizing their use, I quickly developed my own version of the PIB and it came to be known as the *LIUMEMO.* It was essentially a one-page summary of all the key points in the PIB that I thought were relevant for any upcoming meetings. I found this added tremendous value to my bosses because it provided the breadcrumbs needed to figure out how we were going to impress our client and not waste their time in some mindless pitch meeting that made them wish they had a time machine.

---

[4] "I don't have the bandwidth" is the millennial's version of "Do it yourself."
[5] Don't try to Google this. It's a word I made up and have trademarked for future royalties.
[6] In 2020, there were over 200 million *active* websites. That of course doesn't include your blog, which is part of the 1.5 billion *inactive* sites.

But be advised: The information you disclose to your superiors, subordinates, and colleagues is critical because what you say or show can have a direct impact on their decisions. You need to start slow and offer up distilled versions only if you're confident that you aren't missing anything critical. Summarizing the company's key facts but failing to mention that they hired Morgan Stanley last week and now there's no fee opportunity for your firm is grounds for being nominated for the *Darwin Awards*.[7] You only have the power to drive a situation in your favor if you carefully craft the information-sharing.

Eric Heglie, a partner at Industrial Growth Partners and an ex-banker at Jefferies, has some great advice for those who are confident in themselves: "At some point in your career, you have to take a risk by developing a point of view and making it known." He says it takes a little bravery at first, but once you overcome your fear, the rewards can compound over time. If you make a bet on yourself and it pays off, it gives you the courage to do it again and continue to make a solid impression down the road. Of course, the converse is also true. Don't screw up!

People's most precious asset is time, so use yours and your boss's wisely. One trick is to start your summaries with the end in mind. Personally, I like to do a cheat sheet of the key takeaways to be sure I've included all I need. Think of everything you write as a selling document, and if you find something that doesn't make sense or is extraneous, delete it. Once I ascended to a senior banker role and got the mic, at every client presentation I would start, somewhat tongue in cheek, with the Executive Summary and state to the audience, "Please give me your undivided attention for the next ten minutes as I rattle through these key points. After that, you're free to check your phone, go to the bathroom, or zone out because the next 100 pages are simply back-up." It's amazing how often this would elicit not only smiles and approving nods of "Thank You, Allah!" but also rapt attention for the next ten minutes. It was as though I was performing to an audience who had PTSD[8] from a lifetime of meetings and had finally met a therapist. But be ready to clarify or double-click on ideas, particularly if they're questioned. Otherwise, your audience will think you just read some how-to book on gaming the system called *The Way of the Wall Street Warrior* and are just summarizing stuff without synthesizing it.

Chris McGowan, former managing director at Madison Dearborn, former banker at Morgan Stanley, and now adjunct professor at the University of Chicago's Booth School of Business, used to tell his junior bankers that anybody can do a spreadsheet, export it into a PDF, then leave it on someone's chair. The challenge

---

[7] The Darwin Awards recognize people who contribute to human evolution by selecting themselves out of the gene pool by dying or doing something so stupid it warrants death. It's a real thing—look it up! You may qualify.

[8] Post-Traumatic Stress Disorder. A disorder in which a person has difficulty recovering after experiencing or witnessing a terrifying event. It's most commonly associated with the brave people who fight for our country, as well as the laid-off investment bankers who now have no idea what to do with their free 100 hours per week.

is whether at 3 a.m., while still in the office, you can write two or three cogent lines explaining your conclusions so your boss doesn't have to wade through the red meat.

"Lots of good people can do the 85 percent, but the great people do that extra 15 percent," says Chris. He suggests leaving a note with the summary—a summary of the summary, if you will. "When you get a stack of information, be the first to read and boil it down to the basics; then send your key takeaways to your bosses."

One more tip for you geniuses out there. You're likely younger than your boss and probably know a hundred times more than they do about technology. Use that to your advantage. While your boss is still using a flip phone and having their secretary print out emails to read on flights, you should impress them with your mastery of the hundreds of tech resources that are replacing the role of investment bankers and other skilled workers. Use LinkedIn to stalk potential CEO clients, WeChat messages to reel in valuable Asian prospects, FactSet to create models at the push of a button, and DealBook to figure out how many months of cash your client has left. You have all these tools at your fingertips, so maestro your way to greatness and wow your boss. Remember Arthur C. Clarke's words: "Any sufficiently advanced technology is indistinguishable from magic."

Mute That Crap

Unless you've been living under a rock, you were likely trapped on Zoom for most of 2020 and beyond. Meetings took on a whole new dimension online, but it's important to understand that the same tips and tricks applied, but with a few adjustments. First, there is a high likelihood that unless you get straight to the point, the recipients are checking their latest fantasy football stats rather than listening to you drone on about the latest state of the business or product. Treat every online meeting as a performance. You're one of many actors in a sideshow carnival and you're trying to get passersby to stop and gawk at you. Use the smaller real estate of the screen to your advantage. No one is going to care about that coffee stain on your pants because they'll be focused on your wonderful visage.

Zoom doesn't give you the opportunity to strut around a room and gesticulate wildly to get your point across, but it does have one big advantage. Much like being able to practice in front of a mirror, Zoom gives you the opportunity to perfect your own performance because you can watch yourself. You can see if your facial expressions are animated enough to express your enthusiasm or too overdone such that your audience thinks you're nuts. That digital mirror will help you hone your skills and become a better presenter, so stay focused, peer into the camera, and perform like an actor. No need to wear pants, but please comb your hair and check your teeth.

Oh, and one last very important tip. If you're on a conference call and aren't saying anything, mute for God's sakes! One fine Sunday morning, my team and I were conferenced on a bridge line with our client. We didn't have cameras on because this was pre-pandemic. We had a *Chinese Fire Drill*[9] so we all dialed in from wherever we were. Normally I would've expected the team to be dialed in from the office, but I'm pretty chill so I didn't care as long as they were working on a Sunday! I started going through some boring but important legalese with the client on their upcoming offering and all my juniors were on mute, taking detailed notes and learning by osmosis. I asked one of them to follow-up on a specific task and he forgot to mute his line after yelling an affirmative. Suddenly, in the middle of my performance, I heard the nastiest bowel movement. Then a few groans of relief followed by a pregnant pause. Then a vile encore that ripped through the call like a horn trumpeting the Apocalypse. Finally, a flush and a zip. So what did I do? Nothing. I continued with my advice to the client without missing a beat. No point in bringing attention to something none of us could do anything about. I later found out one of my juniors had some food poisoning and had a serious case of the runs. Despite his poor state of affairs, the trooper still managed to get out of bed and get on the call. The silver lining was this was pre-Zoom. So what's the lesson learned? Keep your conference line on mute, damnit! No one wants to hear you in the can.

Welcome to 7-Eleven

While you spend your time researching and writing succinct reports, always try to get your inbox to zero by the end of the day or ideally every hour. In this day of always-on, constantly connected, instant-messaging, if you don't instantly answer your boss or client, everyone assumes you're either on a plane and too cheap to spring for Wi-Fi or undergoing open-heart surgery. And if you're a junior banker or lower-level staff person, you shouldn't be flying around with your ass in business class anyway. You should be planted squarely at your desk, ready to take orders from your boss. Be a 7-Eleven—open 24 hours a day, 7 days a week to take on projects, then more and more projects.

---

[9]This Wall Street term is used so often, many have forgotten its racist origins. It was coined in the early 1900s when a ship run by British officers and a Chinese crew practiced a fire drill for a fire in the engine room. Nowadays it's typically used when there is a state of confusion and everyone is running around as though their hair is on fire. It's used by the same morons who use *Oriental* to describe their Asian colleagues.

So why are you checking your email only every five minutes?

Show you're constantly on the ball and instantly responsive. If the email is asking for Heaven, the Moon, and the Stars, just reply that you'll get back to them. At the very least, you've probably bought yourself a few hours to figure out how the hell you're going to fit it in with all your other work. A tip is to ask your boss to prioritize for you. This is so your boss takes ownership of all the projects that have been assigned to you. Of course, this falls apart if you have more than one master, which is usually the case on Wall Street, as in life. In that case, do what every great businessperson does when they can't make a decision: Pass the buck! Inform your multiple masters about your conflict and have them duke it out over whose project gets your love. The worst thing to do is let these requests fester. Many junior people spiral into nervous breakdown by not responding immediately. Not good. If you have time, Google "I Love Lucy, chocolate factory." Go ahead. I'll wait. . .

You see what can happen? The chocolates are all the things you need to do, but less tasty. So be responsive! Don't procrastinate; speed wins.

I used to get emails from my boss that had "911" in the headline. Once I was in Hong Kong and I got a "911: PLEASE CALL ME NOW" in the middle of the night. No other message aside from that. I saw it for the first time when I woke up at 5 a.m. Hong Kong time and called him back. My boss greeted me with, "Why the hell didn't you call me right away?"

"Because it was 3 a.m. in Hong Kong and I was asleep."

He didn't think that was a good answer. Apparently, I shouldn't have put my phone on silent.

One final piece of advice on how to be a stork, not a pigeon. Forward your office phone to your cell, and say something in your voicemail to make the caller feel important, something like, "Hi. I'm so sorry to have missed your call. I'll get back to you as soon as I'm able. In the meantime, leave me a detailed message so when I do call you back, I will have addressed your issue."

I always tell my subordinates, "Bring me a plan that I can say *Yes* to." Don't come to the party with only problems and no solutions. Work that requires me to hunt for the answer or, heaven forbid, finish on your behalf, is called half-assed! If I have to do that, then what the heck am I paying you for? Nothing pisses off your boss more than making them do your job. So don't ever come to your boss with unfinished or unsolved work. Bring ideas to solve issues, solutions to problems. Be a *stork*.

Key Takeaways

- Meetings suck. Keep them to a minimum and use them for taking action.
- Get to the point and bring recommendations. Be brief, damnit.
- Don't be that person who everyone wonders why they're in the meeting.
- Remember *Prospect Theory*: Be a safe pair of hands with strong upside.
- Don't have the *curse of knowledge*. Think like your audience.
- Be *Hoogle* and provide a high *signal-to-noise ratio* for your boss and clients.
- Zero-out your inbox or you'll be living in an *I Love Lucy* chocolate factory.
- *Always* deliver a plan your boss can say *Yes* to.

CHAPTER 12

Quack Like a Duck

Learn the Lingua Franca

"If it looks like a duck, swims like a duck, and quacks like a duck, then it probably is a duck."

Wh en first starting out, you're raring to go, ready to conquer the business world and make your mark. But before you open your trap, know that the corporate game plays by a different set of rules, and there are forces that propel you up and down the ladder like gravity—you can't fight them, so use them to your advantage. Do everything possible to learn the rules, the backdoor entrances, the human hacks, and play like a pro.

If you have followed my sage advice, you know your boss's interests and hobbies and you've shifted your drink of choice from Miller Lite to Pappy Van Winkle. It's a good thing because if everyone's a duck, you need to look and sound like a duck. So let's get quacking.

Speak the Lingo

All companies are made up of tribes, some more territorial than others. The key to being accepted into the tribe is not only to look the part, but also to speak the unique language that develops in every workplace, particularly on Wall Street.

Nothing demonstrates that you're part of the group more than if you learn to speak the tribe's *lingua franca*. Otherwise, it's like stumbling upon a pack of cannibals. If you have no way to tell them that you have syphilis, they will eat you alive!

Let me tell you how I learned to quack like a duck and became a mallard of Wall Street. Even though I was born in America, I grew up in Asia, so all I knew about American culture was what I learned on TV. Naturally, I thought all Americans were conniving (*Dynasty, Dallas*) rednecks (*The Dukes of Hazzard*) who lived in a sci-fi world (*Star Trek*) where their cars talked back to them (*Knight Rider*).

Thank Yahweh, I went to the University of Pennsylvania, which is over a quarter Jewish. I was lucky enough to have an amazing roommate my freshman year, an Orthodox Jew from Israel. He made it his mission to teach me key Yiddish words so I wouldn't be a *schmuck*. As freshmen, we would joke that I knew *bupkis* and how by *schlepping* to class and *schmoozing* with our professors, we'd learn the *shtick* and the *spiel* necessary to win them over. Of course, we had the *chutzpah* to fake it till we made it, so although I was a *goy*, at the end of our freshman year, I was truly his *mensch*.

This experience served me well on Wall Street, as I had a lot of Jewish coworkers and clients and I would often overhear them setting up meetings at their synagogues to talk shop. To fit in, I leveraged my basic knowledge of Yiddish and would make sure to drop a word here and there. Subliminally, it worked, and soon they were asking me, "You sure you're not Jewish?" *Mazel Tov* to me! That's when I knew I had them or at least could pass as a trusted friend to the tribe.

Whatever the lingo is in your industry, learn it and become a master of it. It takes practice, but make the effort to understand the hidden meaning of key phrases. I've done the heavy lifting for you with this list of Wall Street language, which I'm willing to bet translates well into almost any corporate environment:

When Your Boss Says	What Your Boss Really Means
"Do you have extra bandwidth?"	Prepare to get pounded with an all-nighter's worth of work.
"I did the math."	Your report has an error even a lazy ass like me can spot.
"Good enough for government work."	Good enough for *my* boss or the client; they'll never check it anyway.
"In all fairness . . ."	Prepare to get hosed.

When Your Boss Says	What Your Boss Really Means
"To be honest . . ."	I've lied to you all along and everything previously said on this topic is null and void.
"I have a small project for you."	I have a boil-the-ocean project for you.
"Money isn't everything."	I'm about to screw you on compensation.
"Can we talk?"	I hate talking because it takes away from money-making opportunities so be ready for really bad news.
"Strap it on!"	I'm heading home while you stay here all night checking numbers.
"It's been a tough year."	Prepare to get screwed on compensation.
"You're not a team player."	Your enemies have won, and I'm about to eject you from the Game.
"I'm sorry. . . ."	Not really. Prepare to get screwed.
"There can't be any daylight between us."	I'm right and you're wrong.
"That's below the bar."	This has nothing to do with my drinking problem. That business is beneath me, but we'll do it because I need to pay for you.
"You da Man or Woman!"	Don't feel special. I say the same thing to my cocker spaniel.

Tap the Same Wavelength

Confirmation bias prevents us from looking at the entire picture because we tend to filter out information and focus on facts that confirm or validate preexisting perceptions. We subconsciously ignore or dismiss anything that threatens our worldview, since we surround ourselves with people and information that confirm what we already believe. Think Fox News and MSNBC.

The best way to use this bias to your advantage is to realize that if someone (i.e., boss, clients, colleagues) *likes* you or *thinks* you're *similar to them*, they will have blind spots to your faults and your flaws in logic. This explains why

Emperor Palpatine was defeated by Darth Vader (sorry, spoiler alert; too late!). Palpy underestimated Darth, thinking he would kill Luke, his own son, because that's what he would have done. Snoke made the same mistake with Kylo Ren because he clearly forgot to watch *Episode VI: Return of the Jedi* (sorry, another spoiler!).

This is another reason why at the beginning of your career, the third rails of *politics* and *religion* should be avoided at all costs. These can easily make a boss think you aren't anything like them, particularly if you bleed *red* and they bleed *blue*, or if they're a God-fearing Christian and you're a Satanist. My tip is to leave the pentagonal earrings at home and be a chameleon—or a duck. Take a page from Lloyd Blankfein. He self-identifies as a registered Democrat and a Rockefeller Republican; conservative on fiscal issues and more liberal on social issues. It worked for him. He became CEO of Goldman Frickin' Sachs!

Master the Unspoken

I hope you now realize the power of corporate jargon and business-speak in the workplace. It helps you fit in and understand the nuances of the work. It's a way to show you're now a card-carrying member of the club. But body language and intonations can sometimes be as powerful as the spoken word. Keen observation will help you pick up the signs. When I started my career, it was important to get certified with a Series 7 license, which entitles you to sell most types of securities. At Jefferies, they withheld your business cards until you passed the test. Understand that as an analyst, I was already working 120-hour weeks. There was no way I had time to study and take the damn test, so for more than a year I didn't have business cards, which at some point became a running joke. At meetings, the MD on the deal would go out of his way to make a show of exchanging business cards, like we were in Yokohama. When clients asked for my card, he'd interject with "Sorry, the SEC hasn't yet allowed him to talk to anyone" or "This is a special treat. We don't usually let him out of his cage" or "The dog ate all his cards."

Each time he'd make a joke at my expense, he'd give me a look that's usually reserved for a frustrated parent: the hairy eyeball. I used to get this when I would make a stupid joke or do something that would elicit disdain. With that one glance, he was saying, "Dude, seriously, take the test and get the damn cards, you're embarrassing *me*!" Needless to say, once I couldn't put up with his crap any longer, I finally took the Series 7 and got my damn business cards!

Key Takeaways

- Learn the *lingua franca*. It will keep you out of trouble and help you fit in.
- Beware of *confirmation bias*, which will focus you only on facts that confirm or validate your preexisting perceptions.
- Learn the body language of work. It can be more powerful than spoken language.

CHAPTER 13

Read the Room, Not the Prospectus

Profile Your Audience

A s a junior banker, I prepared thousands of reports for the higher ups, and as I zoomed up the flagpole there were plenty of occasions when I was asked to summarize or present my findings. Early on, I learned that when delivering a sales pitch, a business plan, or even a prospectus, reading the room was infinitely more valuable than reading any document. In other words, to hack your career, scrutinizing the people around you and understanding their goals and motivations is way more important than the written word. If I could go to school all over again, I'd not only get a degree in psychology, but I'd also take courses in FBI profiling.

When I first started my career, I didn't know my ass from my elbow. I had spent my time buried in engineering and business books. I could decipher a quadratic equation, but ask me what someone meant by some passive-aggressive comment? Fuggetaboutit! Early on, I learned the full extent of my stupidity.

I was a newly minted analyst and was rearranging my desk in my cubicle so that everything would be perfect for me to conquer Wall Street. Senior bankers sat along the edges in glass-walled offices overlooking junior banker cubicles in an area known as the "bullpen." I thought, so appropriate! Like jocks of finance, we were pro baseball pitchers staying warm, ready to be called up at a moment's notice to play in the big game. What a fool. A few months later, I realized the term more likely stemmed from its original meaning in the 1800s. Bullpens were holding cells for inmates where they were watched over by police officers, or "bulls." Sometimes ignorance really is bliss.

My bullpen was stationed right outside one of the most senior MD's offices. I didn't speak to him and he never acknowledged my existence. He was an old-school banker who had cut his teeth at the venerable firm of Drexel Burnham Lambert, the original crack house for the junk bond industry. One day I was called into his office. Without missing a beat, I sprinted into his office and took a seat in front of his massive desk. After staring out the window at the 405 freeway contemplating life, he turned to look straight at me. He said nothing, but gave me a sardonic look. I simply looked back through my aviator glasses, waiting for him to speak. After what seemed like an eternity, he said in a matter-of-fact voice, "What the hell are you doing?"

I replied, "Sorry, sir. I was told to come into your office."

After sufficient time for his blood to stop boiling, he said, "If I ask for you, it's not to compare notes, shoot the shit, or do whatever the hell kids in your generation do. It's because I want you to do something for me."

I responded, "Sorry, sir, I understand—"

He stopped me mid-sentence by raising his index finger in the air and saying, "Forgetting something?"

"Sorry, I don't think so," I replied in all honesty.

"Get a damn pen and paper because I'm only going to tell you this once!"

That was my first lesson in reading the room, and from that day onward, I always brought something to write on whenever I was summoned by my boss. I hated not knowing how the other person was going to react and made it my mission to understand people's true intentions. That, and I hate waiters who don't write down my order. Get a damn pen!

Read Like an Open Book

After almost 30 years in business, one of the key skills that has kept me out of trouble and made me successful is one I share with FBI profilers: the ability to sniff out BS artists. It has helped me figure out who is an ally and who is an enemy, if my bonus can be increased, when I can expect that promotion, and if I'm going to win the deal. People are like open books if you know how to read them. You just need to learn a few tricks and, like all things in life, practice!

Early in my career I learned that there is a big difference between *hearing* versus *listening*. *Hearing* is scribbling down every single spoken word without looking up, whereas *listening* is studying body language while writing down notes in shorthand. *Hearing* is accepting verbatim what comes out of someone's lips, whereas *listening* is discerning the truth behind the lies. Once I became a senior banker and had juniors working for me, I'd instruct them to take detailed notes, allowing me to focus 100 percent of my attention on my prey.

If I had to master only one thing about reading people, it would be to figure out when they're lying. That's more than enough in helping you on your path. It takes skill and practice, but the first order of business is to determine the natural state for your audience. Establish a baseline. How do they normally act when they say something you know is true? How do they change their body language when they lie? This comes with familiarity, but over time you conclude the same thing as your Friday night poker buddies. We all have *tells*, like they won't look you in the eye, or they look down if they're feeling a little guilty. Dilated pupils are another dead give-away because lying taxes our brain, and heart, more than truth telling. If someone tries *not* to break eye contact for more than seven seconds when you ask about your promotion or gives you chapter and verse on why the bonus pool is smaller this year, then that's a sign of fibbing. Master the amateur hour giveaways like evading questions or inconsistent answers, then perhaps one day you'll be able to discern Bernie Madoff from Bernie Sanders.

I learned the hard way to pick up these cues. Seasons of broken bonus promises were my tour of duty, but my real training came when I started to pitch and win business. I'd quickly discern when a prospect really intended to hire me versus when they were just humoring me for the sake of their VCs. On many a bakeoff that I would eventually lose, I'd see incessant blinking or vague references to their decision-making process, which made the NFL Rulebook seem simple. One CEO took fidgeting, a liar's tell, to a whole new level by excavating boogers from his nose as if they were buried in China, and another just kept smiling as though his face were petrified in plastic.

When you're a junior, take the time to learn these tricks and tells. Study FBI tips on YouTube. These skills will become even more critical as you rise up the **corporate ladder** because you'll become more client-facing and be exposed to more senior executives in your own firm. Unfortunately, chances will also increase that you'll run into psychopaths, the profile of many CEOs and senior bankers.[1] Being able to sniff them out more quickly will save you a lot of time and heartache.

Use What God Gave You

Now that you've learned how to read all the liars, it's time to learn how to turn bystanders into allies and enemies into supporters. The key is to develop relationships with both. Like when your book publisher says, "Make it funnier," it's easy to say but hard to do. But it's the secret to success in work and in life. I've *never* met a successful person who *wasn't* good at developing relationships. Is there a pill you can take to make it happen? Nope. It's not that easy or we'd all be backslapping and high-fiving one another to kingdom come. But I believe it can be learned, because that's how I did it.

---

[1]Kevin Dutton is a psychologist who specializes in the study of psychopaths, or people with persistent antisocial behavior; impaired empathy and remorse; and bold, disinhibited, and egotistical traits. In 2011, he published the "Great British Psychopath Survey." The role with the highest proportion of psychopaths was the CEO. In 2011, *CFA Magazine* published "The Financial Psychopath Next Door" by Sherree DeCovny, in which she estimated that 10 percent of people in the financial services industry are psychopaths. And that's a conservative estimate, according to Christopher Bayer, a Wall Street psychotherapist cited by DeCovny.

For most of my childhood and early adult life, I was trapped inside an obese introvert's body. I had few friends and was teased a lot. Not in the "Hey, fat ass, did you bring me a pair of *baos* or are those just your man boobs?" kind of way, but more in the unflinching stares of horror, curiosity, and pity. It was tough to make friends and for the longest time I don't even remember lifting my gaze from the ground except to greet my mom. Or a glazed donut.

But once I entered the corporate world, I basically told myself, "Screw this. If you're going to amount to anything in life, you'd better hold your head high because book smarts and good grades will get you only so far. You'd better learn how to develop relationships or welcome to a life of building models in some office dungeon." It wasn't easy, but much like potty training, the learning curve gradually flattened and I started to get the hang of it.

Here are some of my tips to cultivate relationships:

- *Listen.* The proverb "God gave us two ears and one mouth" is made up of sage words. In simpleton terms, you should spend twice as much time listening as speaking. As an introvert, I learned to be pretty good at this. Whether someone quoted the world's greatest soliloquy or espoused some verbal diarrhea didn't matter to me—I was equally attentive. People just want to be heard, so I fulfilled that desire. It's the table stakes in building a relationship. Without it, you might as well just talk to yourself all the way to the funny farm. Oh, and note my own addition to the proverb: "God gave us two ears, one mouth, and one ass." Only talk out of one.

- *Be Interesting.* It isn't as hard as it seems. Even the most mundane story can be made interesting if you learn *how* to tell it. Arguably the best movie of all time, *Citizen Kane*, is the story of a reporter trying to figure out why some rich dude said "Rosebud" as his final words. And that's the best movie ever! If you're still thinking you're boring, practice. Find a few stories and try them out on friends and family.

  Eric Heglie, a partner at Industrial Growth Partners and an ex-banker at Jefferies, says that to build relationships "you need to somehow connect with people. You need to develop common points of view and to have the ability to develop a dialogue." He says it requires sales skills, but that you also need to be likeable. "You need to be someone who others would want to sit next to on an airplane for four hours." Remember the **Cleveland Airport Test**?

- *Be Interested.* This is the hardest one to master, but the most important. You have to show genuine interest—or at least *appear* to be genuinely interested— because it's easy to spot the fakers. You know why? Because we all have a benchmark—our parents. As far back as you can remember, your parents were interested in your amazing work. Or, let's face it, crap. But they were your parents and no matter what, they really loved that incoherent speech you gave or your drawings that looked like bear poop. So we all know what genuine interest looks and feels like. Showing interest in people, no matter how inane their stories or travails, helps us get closer to them. Find common ground, something that ties you together. Mutual love or mutual hatred? All good.

Jon Seiffer, senior partner at Leonard Green & Partners and ex-DLJ banker, says they have a running joke in their office—"Oh, my gosh, we're just like you!" It's how they build relationships. He says they do this by eliciting information from the other side and finding commonalities. "The easiest way to form relationships is to ask them about their life."

Check Out That Body

How do you know if any of this is working? Sometimes it's obvious because of verbal cues like "I agree with you" or "Great question!" But often people aren't as overt. You need to become a master in reading body language so you can adjust accordingly.

In many ways, the signs that someone is an advocate, or becoming one, are the same as when you know someone is sexually attracted to you. Here are some elementary tells that work for me:

- *Mirroring.* When someone does what you're doing, like following your gesticulation or, ideally, finishing your sentences, that's a good sign you're on your way to cha-ching! They like what they see and hear.
- *Laughter.* Laughter is the gateway to a person's heart. If they laugh at your stupid jokes (which you practiced and mastered with your friends), then you're in the HOV lane of relationships.
- *Handshakes.* If they have clammy hands, you're in good stead. (Just checking to see if you were paying attention!) Not even close. If this happens, run; don't walk! But if they give you a firm handshake clasped with *both* hands, that's a winner!
- *Liar Mode.* Liars are curt or evasive, they shy away like you have a bad rash, they simply avoid eye contact, or they act like there's a restraining order on you.

I'm sure some of you are wondering, does this crap really work? Can body language really tell you all this? Take it from the geniuses at the MIT Media Lab. Those brainiacs could predict the upshot of negotiations, sales calls, and business plan pitches with almost 90 percent accuracy simply by studying body language—all without a single spoken word.

I hope by now you realize the power of reading the room. In every meeting, there is a hierarchy, and understanding who has the seat of power is critical to getting what you want. Oftentimes, it's not the person who sits at the head of the table or the person who shouts the loudest or talks the most. Sometimes the alpha dog lies in wait until everyone else has said their piece.

When I was starting my career, one of the reasons I went to Jefferies was to learn at the feet of senior bankers who I wouldn't normally interact with at larger firms. At Goldman, we had working group lists that summarized everyone working on a deal. It struck me that the analysts would be listed at the bottom under mountains of associates, VPs, SVPs, and MDs. As an intern, I didn't even make the list because they needed to save space for the client's logo. So going to Jefferies gave me the promise of exposure to grizzled veterans. Early on, I was a 21-year-old punk sitting in Underwriting Assistance Committee meetings where the firm's leaders would decide what deals to approve. Committee members would give the deal team a proctology exam and if they failed to answer correctly, the deal would be torpedoed. At every meeting, I'd sit to the left of Frank Baxter, Jefferies' CEO, and I noticed he'd scribbled all over the memos, clearly showing he had read them. He wouldn't say much during the presentation, but he would always end the discussion with an incisive question that got to the heart of the matter. Usually his question came from listening to the discussion and not what was on the page. By observing him, I learned that powerful people don't always say much, but when they do, you better frickin' listen!

Practice Makes Perfect

The best way to learn these tells is practice. When traveling on business, I scheduled additional meetings with prospects with a low probability of hiring us or ones that I frankly didn't care about. I'd meet with these companies as a young VP and practice my spiel on them. Initially, it was a disaster. I'd trot out a 100-page presentation and bore the audience to death. I wouldn't pick up the obvious cues and trip all over myself. One time, I pitched a company an IPO thinking the meeting was going great. As I kept tap dancing, I didn't notice that the CEO was getting increasingly agitated as the meeting stretched from an initially scheduled 30 minutes to over an hour. Finally, he cut me off and said, "Look, we're going with Bank of America on a bond deal so there is no business for you here."

Thankfully, I improved. Eventually, I learned to not even open a pitchbook, but instead, just to have a conversation. I learned how to pick up people's cues, and that's how I ultimately built my own book of business and started on the path toward the big dance.

The next time you're on a business trip, book an extra day and stay overnight. Schedule practice meetings with low-chance candidates. If you botch the meeting, no big deal, and if you manage to get some business out of it, fabulous! Perfect your powers of observation one step at a time. Start with your dog, office assistant, coworkers, and then work your way up to your boss. Focusing on one target will help you establish a baseline and give you the confidence that you're picking up the right cues.

If none of this works for you, then maybe it's time to take a couple years off and go to Quantico or join the World Series of Poker. If that fails, then maybe you should stop reading now and go back to that mind-numbing work in your office cubicle.

One final warning: What's good for the goose is good for the gander, so unless you want to be the stooge, make sure your own tells aren't obvious. There is zero upside to anyone knowing what you're really thinking, so make sure you aren't flashing a sign above your head with your innermost secrets. How? Practice in front of a friendly audience. Pantomime in front of the mirror. Hire an ex-FBI agent. Do whatever it takes! Then when you're ready, head to Vegas. If you come home fleeced, you have work to do.

Key Takeaways

> - Reading the room is infinitely more valuable than reading the prospectus.
> - Master the *tells* that show someone is a liar, is an ally, or is just disinterested.
> - Learn early because the psychopaths only become more common the higher you go.
> - Build relationships with your ears.
> - Study body language for nonverbal cues.

CHAPTER 14

Don't Walk Around Blind Without a Cane

Wake Up!

You've strutted like a peacock; delivered like a stork, not a pigeon; and quacked like a duck. Sounds like you could be the star in the Aviary Exhibit at the San Diego Zoo.

Not so fast. Chances are, with all your birdbrain activity, you haven't discovered your Achilles' heel, your Kryptonite . . . your *blind spots*. Anyone who drives a car knows what I'm talking about. You're cruising down the street, looking for the nearest gas station before your bowels explode. Some slowpoke ahead of you is sticking to the speed limit, and you solve that problem by starting to turn into the left lane. Then, out of nowhere, a blast of a cacophonous horn, accompanied by a distant, "Learn how to drive, dipstick!" shoos you back to your lane.

That's the infamous automobile blind spot, but it's no different than when you swerve into the oncoming traffic of a big meeting that you aren't prepared for or when you think you're in the fast lane to promotion only to learn you were really on the offramp. Sometimes the blind spot is so powerful that it sabotages your career or chases away the love of your life. Usually they're difficult to locate; otherwise, they'd be called *obvious spots*.

The **self-serving bias**, the **blind spot bias**, and the **self-enhancement bias** all speak directly to this flaw. They can cause us to create fake news about ourselves, like we're better than we actually are, or smarter, more creative, and more just about anything. Ask anyone, "Are you a good driver?" and see the response you get. Or ask 100 Americans if they have above-average intelligence. More than 65 percent will tell you they do.[1] Using my simple math skills, that means there are some serious dullards out there!

---

[1] According to two national surveys completed by Heck, Simons, and Chabris in 2018.

These biases are particularly problematic because they also affect the way we judge our own decisions, which we view as rational, accurate, and free of bias. They make us think we're better decision-makers than anyone else and explain why we *always* think our bosses are morons when we disagree with them.

But I'm an Ostrich

Some of you skeptics may be thinking, who cares? It doesn't affect me, and even if it does, I'll just shove my head in the sand. I'll keep my head down, work hard, and everything will take care of itself. Well, I'll tell you why.

I've had hundreds of bankers report up to me during my career and, unfortunately, I've had to give a lot of them negative feedback. Typical messages ranged from "Sorry, not this year" to "You might be a better fit at a smaller firm" to "Have you considered a different line of work?" I've had to put people on PIPs, or "Performance Improvement Plans," an HR euphemism for we're going to give you one last false hope before we toss you onto the street. Almost without exception, the recipient of the message was surprised—in certain situations, borderline suicidal. In their tender 20s or 30s, it was as though I was the first person to tell them they're less than perfect. Now I will admit that some were playing possum and feigning shock to test the limits of my magnanimity, and some I'd clearly failed as a manager by not having forewarned them along the way, but I believe that the vast majority suffered from major blind spots to their own capabilities and career trajectory.

As I said earlier, Wall Street has a hierarchy where each of the roles commands a different skill set. It's very hard to know until you're on the field of play actually doing the job whether you can be good at it. And that's where I saw tremendous career blindness. Candidates would see themselves as doing great in a certain role and assume it would carry them to the next level. They'd also be blind to much of what I've described so far in this book. I couldn't blame them. If they were top performers in school and early in their career, they could do no wrong. There was no need to master the human elements that factor into getting noticed and promoted. They assumed blindly that just by keeping their head down they would succeed.

These blind spots are especially acute when you're a different gender or race from the majority who decide your fate. I had an exceptional foreign-born analyst who thought he was a superstar and saw his path to greatness as an associate without the typical MBA. However, when it came time to discuss his potential promotion, I told him he had abysmal marks from not only the people who managed him, but also the junior analysts he was assigned to train and mentor. His reviews had choice descriptors like "lacks social skills," "uncommunicative," "arrogant," and "unmanageable." He had no clue that his abrasive personality was demoralizing others, inhibiting his management capability, and derailing his chances of promotion. He started to tear up as I gave him this feedback and told him it might be best for him to go to business school.

On a more senior level, I once had a VP who was clearly never going to make MD. He was an amazing field general managing the troops, but he demonstrated no ability to develop deep relationships with prospects and seemed to miss the buffet line when they were doling out EQ points. I got feedback from clients that he was socially awkward and lacked a certain *savoir faire*. We would go to client dinners and this VP would drink too much and ask about the nearest watering hole for single women—not exactly appropriate conversation with a religious CEO who'd been happily married for 30 years. When I finally had to break the news to him that he lacked the salesmanship necessary to make MD, he proceeded to berate me about how blind I was to his innate talents.

You can certainly be an ostrich and stick your head in the ground, but note that having blind spots is part of life. Just try to identify the big ones—the fatal ones that can derail your career.

Find Buried Treasure

Not much is accurate about the film *Wall Street* besides a single line, when Gordon Gekko tells his disciple, "You're walking around blind without a cane, pal." He's telling him not to close his eyes to reality. But how *do* you figure out your flaws lurking just below the surface? It can't be that easy, right? Right! It takes diligence and open-mindedness to unearth that buried treasure. You need to *want* to find them and, even then, they will change and differ over time. Accept that to ace your career and your life, you'll need to play *Whack-a-Mole* with your blind spots forever.

When I was first starting in my career, I thought everyone was trustworthy, hardworking, open-minded, and magnanimous. What a naive fool I was. I thought the world was colorblind and I'd sail on the jetfoil of money, fame, and power. But then I started to wise up, using a few tips I learned along the way.

- *Own It.* Just like you learned at your Alcoholics Anonymous meeting (or will one day), the first step in solving any problem is recognizing there is one. You can't solve a problem by pretending it doesn't exist, and you can't find a resolution by making excuses. Only after admitting there's a problem can you explore the causes. Acknowledge the issue, not just the symptoms. Make an honest and painful dig into the roots to analyze the cause and effect. Don't think you're biased? In a sample of more than 600 residents of the United States, more than 85 percent believed they were *less* biased than the average American.[2] My money is on you being in that 85 percent.

---

[2]Irene Scopelliti, Carey K. Morewedge, Erin McCormick, H. Lauren Min, Sophie Lebrecht, and Karim S. Kassam, "Bias Blind Spot: Structure, Measurement, and Consequences" (2015).

- *Ask Friends.* Start by asking your closest friends to tell you about your faults. Remember we talked about that way back in Chapter 2 in the context of preparing for a job interview? Do it again once you've arrived in your comfy cubicle or have settled into your office with a view (even if your line of sight is of the dumpsters). Ask people whose advice you won't reject out of hand. You know who I'm talking about—the person who initially makes you think, "They don't know what they're talking about," and then you slowly acknowledge that they probably know you better than you know yourself. Note that your current spouse or partner might not be the best person to ask; they may not want to damage your fragile ego.

- *Ask Enemies.* This is a good time to do some sleuthing and figure out why your enemies hate you. Maybe there are clues from your childhood, your sorority sisters, or colleagues at your previous job. Like your ass in that chair, go wide, go deep. The more you know, the better you can offset these negatives to become the star you are. But be forewarned: Always consider the source! Sometimes people orgasm at the moment of *schadenfreude.* You know it must be common when the Germans have a word for it.

- *Ask for Feedback.* In the workplace, it's imperative to obtain 360-degree feedback to know your real faults. During my reviews, I would tell my boss that I didn't want to hear any of my positives. I'd always say, "Let's use this time to discuss how I shat the bed this year and can do better." This helped me a lot in my career because I knew I would get honest, constructive feedback. Everyone likes to criticize, especially if given permission. But it takes a *real* person to want negative feedback. I'd say 99 percent of people who asked this of me got all defensive and went into such an emotional tizzy that they failed to hear the message. They would nod appreciatively as their face turned red and their eyes said, "Screw you jackass! You don't know me. I should go to your house, eat all your Hot Pockets, and steal your dog." The other 1 percent went on to have great careers.

- *Check the Score.* It always amazed me how Wall Street attracted some of the brightest analytical minds who could map the future performance of a company onto a fancy Excel spreadsheet, but who rarely took a similar analytical approach to their career. I always knew that looking at data is one of the best ways to determine if the results are happening for the right reasons.

  Early in my career, we were a small firm and pitching everything under the sun. I started to track my own productivity. I realized we were winning less than 10 percent of every deal we pitched when I first joined, and there was almost no correlation with the quality of work that I, the junior schlub, produced for the team. Instead, it almost always came down to the quality and capability of the individual MD. Some were Babe Ruth while others were Babe the Pig. So over time, I learned where to focus my energies and pledge my loyalty.

When I became a senior banker, I had the benefit of our CRM, or Customer Relationship Management system. This software helps management track client meetings and interactions. It was an easy way for my bosses to make sure I wasn't just lounging at home watching *Star Wars*. Using this system, I'd analyze my entire customer funnel, from cold call to closed deal. By looking at my productivity and success rate, I could see my overall effectiveness as a senior banker. The data didn't lie and I'd see patterns of incompetence in my own performance. This helped me figure out where I was failing and could do better.

- *Take the Test.* Business school and early career years are full of psychological tests—Myers-Briggs Type Indicator, the Caliper Profile, the Hogan Personality Inventory—you get the drift. They're all designed to put you in a box and determine if those boxes lead to career success. In general, I've found them completely useless for identifying successful career traits, but I have found them to be very useful in identifying areas that I *lacked*. You do enough of these silly tests, and patterns form. You come to realize not exactly the location of hidden treasure, but at least the ZIP code. Of course, if these tests reveal you have an insatiable appetite for killing small animals, keep that to yourself.

- *Conduct a* **Post-Mortem**. After every project, deal, or assignment, take stock of how you did and ask yourself what you did right. What did you do wrong? Did the project succeed in spite of you? After every pitch, I'd always ask my team what I could have done better. Of course, when a junior banker told me I should have worn a darker suit, I owed it to myself to tell him he's a doofus. At my compensation review, I'd ask how to get paid the highest. I'd welcome criticism and not get defensive even if I thought the feedback was wrong.

- *Hire a Coach.* If you're really in a rut, pay someone to find your weaknesses. Just like white-hat software engineers who get paid to hack a company, hire a career coach to hack your system and find your weaknesses. It's the difference between someone beating you up and you *paying* someone to beat you up. See the difference?

- *Meditate.* No, I'm not talking about dressing down to a loin cloth and hiding in some Himalayan mountain. I'm referring to *really* reflecting on the answers. Introspection is key! If you get the same messages over and over again, you've hit the nail on the head. If you learn something new, bless you! Don't get defensive. You're on the road to recovery.

- *Do Unto Others.* As you rise up the ranks and have minions of your own, be sure to learn from your own management. Sometimes one of the best ways to recognize your own blind spots is by observing them in others. When I was a young associate and had my harem of analysts, I would give them feedback and identify shortcomings that were clearly my own as well. Of course, I didn't admit it to them, but rather I'd scurry back to my cubicle, quickly forgive myself for being a hypocrite, and then try to fix my own house. At first, I'd be cold and dispassionate when delivering the bad news to my underlings, but over time I learned one of the key tricks of the trade—the **Shit Sandwich**. I learned of this tasty morsel as a method of delivering bad news, typically around compensation season. It's used to ensure that the person hearing the bad news, advice, or rejection actually listens to what is being said so they can eat and digest. Mine would take the form of "We think you're awesome and a rock star, but we're going to pay you like a has-been." So if you ever deliver sobering feedback to a subordinate, be sure to wrap that feces in a nice focaccia.

• *Read This Book.* Use it to open your mind. This isn't a recipe; it's not even a treatise. I'm not a psychologist, but I am a businessman. This is a way for you to recognize that the world around us isn't always what it appears to be. And it's not just because people think and do stupid things; it's because we're also stupid. So wake up! Finish this book. Share the Key Takeaways with a friend and your faux Faceblab friends. Tell them to buy it and share the Key Takeaways with you. Rinse and repeat. By the way, if I happen to get on a bestseller list as a result, consider it a happy coincidence.

What Could Possibly Go Wrong?

Related to blind spots is the problem of **overconfidence**, which leads you to take greater risks than you should. You might have a brilliant product idea but your team might lack the ability to execute it. You run out of time on a project because you thought you could do two days' worth of work in one. I would always underpromise and overdeliver by using the tried-and-true method of sandbagging. I'd also do a **pre-mortem** to make sure I wasn't sculpting a statue I couldn't finish (although, if you create the Venus de Milo, that ain't so bad).

I've encouraged you to use your intuition as well as your smarts, but don't get too overconfident early in your career about your intuitive prowess. Your inexperience in this realm could lead you directly into your blind spots, especially if you're new at it. People often see what they want to see, which is a blind spot in itself and which gets in the way of evaluating something intuitively. This is particularly true when you find yourself in a tough situation, so if you're feeling stressed, don't make rash decisions. Take a chill pill, regroup, and stick to the plan.

A clue that you're succumbing to **overconfidence** is if you hear yourself thinking to yourself, or worse, saying aloud, any of these dangerous words, which could be your last:

• "What could possibly go wrong?"
• "I can't see us losing."
• "I'm definitely getting this promotion."
• "It's in the bag, baby!"

My Boss, the Bat

Now that you've self-diagnosed yourself and are on the path to greatness, I'm sure you're bothered by one last observation. You've probably looked at your boss, and hell, maybe even the CEO of your company, and thought to yourself, "They've got major blind spots and look where they are! They're blind as a bat!" It's true. Some people were just hit on the head with the lucky stick. You aren't one of them, so keep reading.

We can't fix everything. If we had to do it for you, we'd be here for millennia. So prioritize. Figure out your blind spots and determine what could be fatal. When I'm not an investment banking maestro, I'm doling out dating advice to many of my female friends. Their dating patterns were eerily similar. They'd meet Prince Charming one night and see a future where they'd marry, have kids, and get old together. All in a fortnight. Then a few weeks later, Prince Charming would be Prince Charmin Toilet Paper and he'd be on the outs. My question to these friends is the same one I give to you. When you find Prince Charming, ask, *"What's the catch?"* We all have blind spots, especially in the heat of romance, and the best way to figure out if we can see a long-term life with someone is to figure out all their ticks and tacks. So figure yours out quickly and see if it's something your career can live with.

As for me, I was very naive and frequently taken advantage of. Then I woke the hell up. As I progressed up the **corporate ladder**, I started to identify my blind spots one by one and tried to mitigate them. But new ones popped up. I was quick to judge people based on *initial impressions*. I was a young man in a rush and had a massive case of **attentional bias**. I had immediate disdain for people who didn't work as hard as I did. I was a micromanager and couldn't get leverage on my subordinates because I had massive **risk aversion** and didn't accept failure as an option. I lacked empathy and compassion, and I would tell others to get the hell out of the way if I thought they were incompetent. In other words, I became a massive *jerk*.

I still am. But at least I know my blind spots!

Key Takeaways

- *Blind spots* are hard to find. Otherwise, they'd be called *obvious spots*.
- Don't be an ostrich; even you are likely to be average, biased, blind, and in serious need of help.
- Discover your blind spots through friends, enemies, and feedback.
- *Pre-mortem* everything and don't suffer from *overconfidence*.
- Answer *"What's the catch?"* as soon as possible and make sure it's not fatal.

CHAPTER 15

Turn Liabilities into Assets

Harness Your Superpower

Unless you're Buddha, Mohammed, or Jesus, you have weaknesses, defects, or things that make you less than perfect. Some defects are overt and some aren't. So just because you don't fit in, know that you're not alone. You have plenty of company and the key is to remember that there is no such thing as a handicap, just features that make you who you are and are destined to make you stronger. When the time is ripe, you can turn your liabilities into assets by heeding Sun Tzu, who said, "Appear weak when you are strong and strong when you are weak."

When I was a young man, I took a sociology course at the University of Pennsylvania taught by Professor Michael Useem. He explained a controversial theory, but one that has stuck with me throughout my career. The higher up you go in an organization, the more uncertain the outcome, and the more reassurance and confidence you want from your team. A CEO's decisions on any given day have a greater impact on the future of the company than its janitor's decisions, and the far-reaching ramifications of the CEO's decisions are not known for weeks, months, or years. In the face of this massive uncertainty, senior people are even more inclined to surround themselves with like minded people, which results in less diversity at the top.

To my caveman brain, this made sense on an instinctive level. If our tribe of *Homo sapiens* were going to hunt wild boar, I'd rather have another of my kind covering my flank than a Neanderthal who may be more interested in eating me than the boar. However, it's now a given that cultural diversity benefits companies. It allows for new perspectives and greater insight into the mind of the customer—particularly when the target customer is more likely to be a 20-something Latinx woman from the inner city rather than a middle-aged Caucasian guy from Celebration, Florida.

Houston, Do We Really Have a Problem?

Things are getting better. We have the #MeToo movement, #BlackLivesMatter, #StopAsianHate, and other initiatives to improve **cultural inclusion**. But in my almost 30 years working on Wall Street, in Silicon Valley, and a little bit in Hollywood, I see almost no *real* emphasis on management diversity. It's as though the focus is on getting a veritable melting pot at the base camp of Mount Everest, but not at the summit. That's why, if you're part of a marginalized group, you need to assume that aside from my trusty book as your sherpa, you're on your own! No one is coming to save you.

Wall Street is a white man's frat house. The only diversity you really see is at the junior scrub level or in the firm's food takeout orders. C-suites, boards, and leadership positions are not diverse. The CEOs of America's biggest banks are white dudes, as are most leaders of asset managers, private equity firms, and hedge funds that make up the rest of Wall Street's hit parade. U.S. government reports and hearings show that the executive level at the largest banks is a sausage fest with over 70 percent bros.[1] At Morgan Stanley and Goldman Sachs, almost 80 percent of their senior executive level are white bros and across all major banks, white people made up 81 percent of the executive suite. That's less diverse than a snowman convention!

Why? **Affinity bias** again: Recruiting favors the majority in power and people tend to hire those who mirror themselves. Bosses prefer to promote dudes who laugh at the same penis jokes and have the same ridiculous hobbies. Clients, who are mostly white, rightly or wrongly prefer to have their deals and dough handled by people who look like them. The cycle goes on like *Groundhog Day*.

The same government reports and hearings show how women are screwed from the get-go. *Working Mother*'s Gender Gap research shows women are a third less likely to recognize **relationship capital** and the importance of monetizing it. Women and people of color aren't told that leveraging **relationship capital** is absolutely critical in their early careers. (They must be the unfortunate few who skipped my book.) They start out behind the eight ball and it snowballs from there. For you enterprising women, to get ahead you need to accept you got a raw deal and quickly build that capital. Build relationships by truly understanding the mind of your male colleagues. If your poison is Wall Street, the male mindset is really quite simple. Just think five-year-old boy. Hell, I'm almost 50 and I still enjoy a good fart joke.

---

[1]"Diversity and Inclusion: Holding America's Large Banks Accountable" by the U.S. House Committee on Financial Services, February 2020.

Lauren Wu, former equity analyst and CFO of venture capital at J&W Seligman and Merrill Lynch banker, suggests seeking out female mentors either at your employer or in the industry. "As a woman, particularly of color, it is so important to find women who are just like you, ideally with the same ethnic background. They can best empathize with your situation and guide you how to navigate the male jungle of corporate America."

Ruth Porat, CFO of Google and former CFO of Morgan Stanley, emphasizes the importance of securing a sponsor. "A sponsor is someone who will take a risk on you and has the power or authority to put you in a position that is the door opener," she says.

It is possible, however, to turn the table. A minority female managing partner at a large hedge fund and ex-investment banker says that "being a woman and minority is both an asset and liability." She says that when she was rising up the **corporate ladder** there was really little awareness of gender and race issues. For example, one of the things that irks her to this day is golf. She would never be invited because of her gender and that hurt her prospects. "Forget that I couldn't play; I was never invited. So that's less time for me to bond with others." But she didn't let that hinder her. She channeled her energy. "I just worked harder." Now plenty of dudes work for her fetching her golf balls.

If you're in one of these disadvantaged groups, there is a silver lining. Things are improving—even on Wall Street. You're more likely to attend an online course on sexual harassment than a strip joint with your boss. Gender, race, and sexual orientation are now all the third rail in investment banking. So guys, keep your dirty thoughts to yourself. Remember, you're now in a fishbowl. Cheerleaders on the trading floor, nudie magazines—all gone. Even dwarf-tossing. In 2003, investment banks, including SG Cowen, Lazard, and Jefferies, threw a $160,000 bachelor party for a former Fidelity star trader. It was alleged to have included an appearance by Madonna, female escorts, Ecstasy pills, and a dwarf named Danny Black, who self-described himself as the Heidi Fleiss of dwarf talent. Although Black was originally hired as a waiter, he allowed himself to be tossed by guests. This would be unlikely to happen today!

All firms now have an all-points bulletin out for minorities and women. The time is now. Getting in the door has never been easier. Staying in the game and rising to one of the head honchos, however, is a whole different matter.

Appearances Are Deceiving

So why do I think I have the moral high ground to talk about this? Well, because I came from one of the disadvantaged groups. I was a non-white male born with a hole in my face. Not some small pockmark from picking a zit, but a big honkin' hole right in the center of my visage. My lips and palate weren't fused together at birth, and so when I popped into this world, I was a sight to behold. About 1 in every 700 babies is born with a cleft lip, a cleft palate, or both,[2] making it one of the most common birth defects in the world. Babies with this defect need special care from a team of health professionals from birth to young adulthood. The cleft repair team usually includes nurses, social workers, nutritionists, audiologists, speech-language pathologists, geneticists, pediatricians, dentists, orthodontists, and pediatric surgeons. It's a freaking village! Unfortunately, many kids go untreated or, if they do, get only the first initial repair but lack the resources for ongoing treatment. Many just learn to live with the ongoing physical and psychological impact.

I was lucky enough to be born in the 1970s in Houston where one of the top specialists in the world worked. I say lucky, because I have one of the most severe cases of the disability. I had almost a dozen surgeries from birth to adolescence, which left deep facial scars and made my voice more Bob Dylan than Fran Drescher, but, thankfully, without a severe speech impediment which plagues most kids with this disability. Still, if you asked my high school classmates what was I most likely going to become in a decade, half would say mad scientist, the other half Unabomber, but all would agree I'd be a 300-pound contestant on *The Biggest Loser*.

At Jefferies, I was quiet, but intensely focused on building a successful career and making a ton of money. I was progressing up the ranks at an accelerating clip and was one of the fastest to be promoted to associate and VP in the firm's history. But by the time I hit 30, I could see the cliff ahead. All the quiet diligent types, of which my ethnic brethren were the majority, got blown out before getting a taste of senior status. I knew that if I ever wanted to progress beyond VP and not become yet another casualty of middle management, I needed a radical makeover. To satisfy the prerequisite of being a senior banker, I started to actively call on clients, develop industry expertise, and invest in long-term relationships.

To rise, I also knew I needed to change my appearance. I ditched the TJ Maxx clearance racks and massively upgraded to Armani and Hugo Boss. The glasses were replaced by contacts and, eventually, Lasik. A stylish satchel replaced a goofy backpack. I changed my facial appearance. As one of the few Asian men who could grow facial hair, I grew a meaty moustache and a sharp goatee. For a while I even grew my hair long and looked like an extra in a Japanese gangster film.

Post my revamp, the way people looked at me radically changed. I went from Walter White to full Heisenberg.[3] My wife said my RBF, or Resting Bitch Face, became that of someone who would kill if given the wrong glance. I'm doubtful that it had any real effect on my capabilities, but I became even more recognizable as that big Chinese dude with a badass 'tache. I found my groove and started to win over clients. In a sea of uniform Brooks Brothers bankers, I was your Yakuza Hit Man. Seriously, who would you rather negotiate your deal?

----

[2]According to the American Academy of Pediatrics.

[3]*Breaking Bad*, one of the greatest shows on television, follows the transformation of high school chemistry teacher Walter White into a drug kingpin, Heisenberg. If I didn't become a banker, I could easily have been a crystal meth dealer . . . on TV.

When you're growing up with such a disability, you search for role models—someone you can point to and say, "Well, if he has it but is still successful, then I can be too." Unfortunately, I couldn't find any others. It was the Mojave Desert. My mom liked to point out that the actor Stacey Keach had a cleft lip and partial palate, but I couldn't relate to him. When he got busted for cocaine possession and served time, that was the kisser. So in searching for a role model, I've tried to become one. Eventually I became one of the firm's youngest MDs and one of its first and only persons of color to reach that level. I'm not quite perfect (and I'm modest, too), but for those of you who have a disability of any kind, take comfort in knowing that if I can do it, anyone can.

Unleash Your Superhero

I believe we all have superpowers—if we know how to use them. That power could be your gender, ethnicity, or simply one defining positive attribute. That's all you need because when others take that attribute and associate it with everything else about you, it creates a **halo effect**. In hiring, this could be assuming a hot guy is also smart and a good hire, while an ugly fella is a schmo worthy of the ding pile. This bias—which is influenced by attractiveness, age, body type, race, and ethnicity, among others—is shown to disproportionately affect women and really hurts if you're overweight.[4]

So, grasshopper, find your superpower and learn how to exploit it:

- *Confirm Their Positive Beliefs.* **Confirmation bias** makes us focus on and remember things in a way that confirms our preconceptions. For example, if dudes believe women are not as driven to succeed, they'll find evidence to support this and punt on female candidates. Another widely held bias is that women are not as confident as men. This is bull.[5] Conversely, sometimes men believe that women are more compassionate and empathetic. This is an example of the **halo effect**. If you are a woman, use this to your advantage. Show them you're great at dealing with tough situations through calm understanding and steely focus. Use male bias against the bros!

---

[4]In 2017, Fairygodboss, an employer review site for women, conducted a study that found only 15.6 percent of hiring managers said they would consider hiring an obese woman, and 20 percent described her as "lazy." That same study revealed appearance biases against women of color, older women, and women who frown.

[5]According to a 2018 study by *Harvard Business Review*, women are not lower in confidence overall, but they do tend to *appear* less confident, due to how we *perceive* confidence to manifest.

- *Neuter the Negative Ones.* If you're a woman, gender stereotyping can really suck in a man's world. Consider if someone told you: "I asked my assistant to reschedule a client meeting because one of my bankers was unavailable." Would you automatically assume the banker and client were male and the assistant was female? If so, that's gender stereotyping bias at work. According to several studies, women's performance reviews contain nearly twice the number of "nice" or "warm" mentions as men's—not exactly words associated with leaders of world-beating companies. So what's a good woman to do? I believe it's important to not only play to your strengths, but also focus your energies on countering those stereotypes that are working against you. For instance, if you're a woman, you probably won't need to convince them you have empathy and can manage the juniors. Instead, focus your energies on proving you can be a badass negotiator and crush the family jewels of competitors without hesitation or regret.

Joanne Chen, general partner at Foundation Capital and former Jefferies banker, tries to establish credibility early. "I've found this is best accomplished by being more upfront and direct, admitting to weaknesses, but then showing your positives quickly," she counsels. "I feel that some women and minorities try to prove themselves so much and focus too much on perfection. Showing some vulnerability can actually neuter biases and make you look more credible and stronger."

As an Asian American, I certainly used what I believed others already thought were my attributes, but also surprised them with other qualities. They already thought I was good at math, but maybe not aggressive enough. I fit the **Model Minority Myth**: obedient, hard-working, and darn good at figuring how much to tip the waiter. So I focused on areas where I knew they'd think I was deficient. I tried to be boisterous and affable. I brought creative ideas and not just STEM ones. I showed I could be a party animal. Early in my career, I wore dorky glasses and was just missing the pocket protector from my ensemble. But once I showed that I was an unofficial beer-chugging champion in college, I suddenly became the life of the party. Find your inner party animal! Of course, don't do anything stupid just to prove a point, like smashing chairs or dancing naked in the street.

Herald Chen, former co-head of Technology at Kohlberg Kravis Roberts (KKR) and Goldman Sachs banker, has some similar advice. He told me that growing up in a steel town as the only Asian American forced him to figure out how to become one of the gang, to become "a little more gentrified than most." But Herald had a stark awakening when he got to the University of Pennsylvania and wanted to join a particularly entrenched school fraternity. During Rush Week, he wasn't invited back, but once the semester started, without an invite he just walked through the door of the fraternity house and made himself at home. "Eventually, when they saw I could drink beer faster than any of them, they let me in, and in due time, I became fraternity president."

- *Be a Walking Billboard.* When you're born with a facial deformity, you can't help but notice the way people look at you and think, "Stop staring, asshole!" But like a car crash, I knew they couldn't look away, so I used the scars in the middle of my face to my advantage. One of the unintended benefits of having so many cleft lip surgeries is people will remember the billboard plastered on your face. In my entire career, I don't recall anyone *not* remembering meeting me, but whenever I met people who could help advance my career, I tried my darndest to make it memorable beyond just my face. I'd always have at least one insightful thing to say at every meeting no matter how junior I was. Unless my boss told me, "Shut your trap," I'd be sure to chime in so that in conference rooms full of old white people, I'd always be remembered as "that Chinese guy with the scars who said something helpful."

   Apart from my defect, I did have one genetic talent. I could turn fat into muscle. I started to exercise and lift weights and, after a while, I was able to add major muscle to my 6-foot frame, bench press 325 pounds, and squat 500 pounds. Sometimes just the physicality of someone can change the way they think of you, and given that I was stronger than almost everyone in the office, my bulk helped break any preconceived notions based on race. It gave me gravitas when I entered a room and the confidence to stand up and make a point if I wanted to be heard. But going all Hulkamania and Heisenberg created an unintended consequence. In technology, there is a term known as *user interface*, or UI, which refers to the interaction layer between humans and machines. My UI sucked. I would intimidate some and appear downright hostile to others. Thus, I went out of my way to immediately disarm people by being overtly warm at initial meetings. High fives, back slaps, and even ass out hugs to strangers I met for the first time—all to counter my UI, which was better suited to frightening small children.

- *Pick Your Battles.* Sometimes you'll want to go on the offensive and make a point. When you see someone do something inappropriate, fight. A female MD told me she was lucky because she grew up with brothers and had always been comfortable around men. "Of course, when I was coming up the **corporate ladder**, I experienced a lot of inappropriate behavior, but I just endured it. Now that I'm in a leadership position, I don't tolerate it and I try to institute change." You need to know when to pick your battles. Time and place are important and if you blow your wad too early, it will haunt you forever. Remember King Pyrrhus of Epirus? It's been 2000 years and he will be forever known as the origin of the Pyrrhic Victory.

   You also need to learn when to grin and bear it. On Wall Street, and in fact in all of America, it's a challenge to be accepted in a predominately white, male world. Rick Heitzmann, founder of the venture capital firm FirstMark and former Houlihan Lokey banker, has a friend, an African American woman, who dreaded attending work dinners because she knew she'd feel uncomfortable as the only female and person of color. She was also usually a decade younger than most everyone else at these events, and she knew that all the talk would be about sports and fratty things, that they'd drink too much, and that steak would be the only entrée. "You retreat, you lose," Rick told me. His advice to his friend was to attend those dinners every time, assuring her that others would be there who didn't care about sports, didn't eat steak, and didn't drink to excess. "Although it may be uncomfortable," he told her, "it's important in building relationships."

• *Develop Empathy.* Dan Ariely coined **assortative mating** to define how less attractive people learn to view nonphysical attributes as more important than the physical. Growing up as a dorky, scarred blob, I learned to discover and study nonphysical attributes more closely and it made me more perceptive and empathetic. I developed a pretty good BS detector and learned the distinct aroma of feigned interest. Today, I can sniff if someone is really passionate about something or just going through the motions. The subtext behind what one says is often more important than the actual words, especially when it comes to the questions one asks. There is almost always a question behind the question and the faster you figure that out, the faster you'll answer the real question and build relationships and trust.

• *Learn to Forgive.* I also believe in the power of forgiveness. Oftentimes, colleagues will say or do things that are outright malicious and should not be tolerated. We once had an associate who called an African American assistant's child a "tar baby" and was summarily dismissed. There is no tolerance for that in the workforce, but sometimes words can be taken out of context. Case in point: When I was an associate, there was a Caucasian MD who was a great mentor and friend. We would often make fun of each other to liven up the mood. In 1994, a controversial book was published which showed that on a bell curve, Asian Americans demonstrated superior intellect.[6] We never took it seriously, but whenever he made fun of my ethnicity, which was often, I'd counter with "Where are *you* on the bell curve?" That would shut his pie hole right away. So always look to the intent of the speaker before jumping to conclusions because I've found that often people don't mean real harm.

Sreene Ranganathan, a member of Facebook's Corporate Development team and former Jefferies banker, said that on Wall Street he never encountered any racism toward him and found his bosses welcoming—as long as he could win their confidence by doing great work. "It's important to establish yourself quickly so you gain their respect. I did that. So they never treated me any differently than other bankers because of my race. They treated *everyone* equally badly."

----

[6]Richard Herrnstein and Charles Murray, *The Bell Curve: Intelligence and Class Structure in American Life* (1994).

- *Reset Your Own Mindset.* I truly believe that we can be victims of our own expectations. Unfortunately, that forms the basis for stereotypes. In *Predictably Irrational*, Dan Ariely cites an experiment where a math exam was given to two groups of Asian American women. Before the test, one group was asked questions regarding *gender-related* issues, whereas the second group was asked *race-related* questions. The second group did better than the first one and met the expectation that Asians are good at math. Dan argues that expectations can override our senses, partially blinding us from the truth. I took this to heart and made it a point early in my career to challenge myself to break the negative stereotypes and focus my energies on improving my gregariousness and salesmanship. Practicing pitches in front of a mirror, honing small talk at local bars, and watching *Glengarry Glen Ross* about a hundred times all helped make me the sales god I am today.

- *Remember, You're Only Human.* When I was younger, I was sullen and withdrawn, but the adaptability of the human condition is amazing. They even have a name for it: **hedonic adaptation.** No, this isn't the name of a billionaire tent at Burning Man, but a fancy word for our ability to wipe the crap off our face when it hits the fan. As examples, Gary Cohn overcame severe dyslexia and managed to become president of Goldman Sachs and served in the White House as director of the National Economic Council and chief economic advisor to POTUS. Stan O'Neal was grandson of a former slave and picked cotton and corn on his grandfather's fields. He became CEO of Merrill Lynch.

- *Change the Narrative.* Sometimes your handicap isn't your gender, race, or physicality, but rather your hometown, your economic status, or even the firm you represent. Wall Street is an incredibly brand-focused place. In fact, I would argue that brand is the *only* thing that truly differentiates firms. The dirty little secret is that as long as you're talking to one of the major firms, any of them can do your deal. But I learned early in my career at Jefferies that almost any disadvantage can be turned on its head if you're willing to change the narrative. For instance, with client prospects, acknowledging our comparably tiny size, we'd try to convince them we'd be scrappier and hungrier than the other firms. I saw firsthand at firms like Goldman Sachs an arrogance around *choosing* their clients and not stooping too low with others. So we made it clear that we would do *anything* for them. Of course, it worked more often than it didn't, otherwise I'd be writing another book entirely. It would be my manifesto about how to live a healthy life as a 300-pound COBOL programmer.

Word to My Peeps

Being Asian American in America is not easy. The best way to describe it is that we're the *forgotten minority*. We lack political power and suffer from the **Model Minority Myth** I mentioned earlier. Some of you may think it's great that everyone thinks we're polite, law-abiding people who became successful through innate talent, hard work, and rugged individualism. No help needed! Of course, the dark side is this ignores the huge number of Asian Americans who live in poverty,[7] will perpetually be treated as foreigners,[8] and will never get any help from the system. According to Harvard Business School, we're the least likely group in the United States to be promoted to management,[9] and recent revelations in elite university admission lawsuits[10] have shown that Asian Americans typically rank lowest in critical admissions criteria such as "personality." To winnow down the number it admits, Harvard uses subjective "personal" ratings, which traffics in stereotypes about Asian Americans being quiet and studious.

Wall Street plays from the same banjo. *Bloomberg Businessweek* reported that at Goldman Sachs, 27 percent of its U.S. professional workforce were Asian American, but only 11 percent of its U.S. executives and senior managers were. And Goldman has had the same number of Asian American executive officers as the number of dates you have had with supermodels: *zilch*. Even at Jefferies, we had many Asian Americans at the junior and mid-levels, but for many years, I was one of the only MDs of Asian American descent.

You can complain about how you got a raw deal and the world isn't fair, or you can say "Screw it!" and plough your own path. Better yet, you can become a disciple of this book and spread the word! If you're an Asian American man, no one will cry you a river. Your penis means you have a huge advantage over women, but your race means you get no lucky breaks and a lot of put-downs. Spencer Wang, former banker at Credit Suisse and Salomon Brothers and retired chief investment officer of Seasons Capital, thinks getting ahead is about building relationships and developing **emotional intelligence (EQ)**. Both can be learned, but there is a huge cultural element to it as well. "As an Asian male, I was taught never to show weakness," says Spencer. "We're the strong silent types and aren't encouraged to develop EQ." He thinks the first step is recognizing your EQ deficiency and then addressing it over time. "Unfortunately, many Asian Americans like myself are brought up believing there's only a right and a wrong, that the world is black and white. That's not true. To develop EQ, you have to learn to maneuver in the gray areas."

---

[7]According to the U.S. Census Bureau, in 2016 over 12 percent of Asian Americans live in poverty. In major metropolitan cities, poverty rates are much higher, approaching almost 20 percent in areas like New York City.

[8]My favorite question, which I still get asked to this day, is "Where are you originally from?" Planet Earth jackass!

[9]Buck Gee and Denise Peck, "Asian Americans Are the Least Likely Group in the U.S. to Be Promoted to Management," *Harvard Business Review*, May 31, 2018.

[10]Anemona Hartocollis, "The Affirmative Action Battle at Harvard Is Not Over," *New York Times*, Feb. 18, 2020.

Some of you will be disappointed reading this. The self-righteous among you might even call this pandering. I don't. I was broke and needed to support my family early in my career. So I call it survival. I have no regrets. You need to get *in* the game to *play* the game; you can sit on your high horse and pontificate about how you're different and that's great. But bear in mind that employers and clients don't always want Neapolitan.[11] They may want to start with vanilla, then work their way up to strawberry. So get *in* the game and *then* work your magic from within.

I'll give you one last pointer. It's all about trying. Michael Jordan, arguably the Greatest of All Time in basketball, had the following to say: "I've missed more than 9000 shots in my career. I've lost almost 300 games. Twenty-six times I've been trusted to take the game-winning shot and missed. I've failed over and over and over again in my life. And that is why I succeed."

People with disadvantages, disabilities, or handicaps are sometimes too afraid to try, but successful people try over and over again. So give it your all!

Key Takeaways

> - Hierarchies tend toward less diversity due to uncertainty of decision outcomes.
> - *Cultural inclusion* has improved, but management diversity has not.
> - Wall Street is still a white man's frat house because of *affinity bias* and the need for *relationship capital*.
> - Turn liabilities into assets by harnessing your superpowers.
> - Asian Americans suffer from the *Model Minority Myth*. The cavalry ain't coming.

---

[11]Ice cream that is a Holy Trinity of chocolate, strawberry and vanilla. See that magic number 3 again?

CHAPTER 16

Laziness as a Virtue

Maximize Your ROTI

U p to this point, you may have been thinking, how the heck did this guy work as hard as he claims for over 20 years? Why isn't he dead?

I'm going to give you my secret. I did labor 80 to 120 hours a week for over 20 years and it did take a toll on my life. But I was able to sustain that level of intensity because I have that one innate human attribute to guide me— laziness. It made me mindful of my **return on time invested** (**ROTI**) and encouraged me to create **smartcuts**, not *shortcuts,* to create the best work in the least amount of time.

Smartcutter Extraordinaire

For all of us, there comes a time when the work is piling up and there's liter-ally no end in sight. You know why? Because you're essentially a fixed asset and employers will always take as much as you can possibly give them. It's your job to self-regulate and learn how to say, "No." Well, maybe not exactly, "No." It's really "Yes, but . . . ." The "but" buys you more time or leads to "You need to duke it out with one of my other bosses to decide whose project is more important." Regardless, you should purge "No" from your vocabulary. Only "Yes" and "Yes, but . . ." because what you're really doing is learning how to work *smarter* and not necessarily *harder*.

Here are some tips on how to do that:

- *Focus on Big Decisions*. An extremely successful strategy I mastered to maximize my personal ROTI was to use my immense brain power on only the big decisions. I'd use *defaults* for small decisions, clearing my mind for big choices—especially the ones I couldn't change. As Michael Henkin, former senior managing director of Guggenheim Securities, would counsel me, "Focus your energies on the irreversible decisions." For example, I had no interest in starting my day staring into my closet, trying to decide what to wear. As long as it wasn't embarrassing, I couldn't care less what I wore to the office, so I generally dressed the same every day. At any given time, I owned only two suits, five shirts, and five ties which I mixed and matched so I didn't look like a total tool.

- *Develop Habits*. Changing behavior is notoriously difficult, but it helps to form good *habits*. Early on at Jefferies, I developed daily routines that optimized my productivity. Every weekday, and sometimes on the weekends, too, I'd wake up at 5 a.m. and get to the office as early as possible because I knew none of the senior bankers would ever schedule a meeting before 9 a.m. Of course, this line of attack could backfire on days when I stayed in the office until 2 or 3 a.m., but I learned to function without much sleep.

- *Stay Healthy*. At the same time, I knew that all work and no sleep was a prescription for disaster, so several days after work, pretty much whatever time it was, I'd pump out the anxiety from my high-pressure job at a 24 Hour Fitness. In retrospect, I think I may have succumbed to my own **belief bias**, but I definitely convinced myself I was doing good, so I felt good. Power of suggestion? Maybe.

- *Template Everything*. To save time at my job, I also created standard templates for all my work, which I adapted to whatever project I was working on:
  - ○ *LIUMEMO*. As I mentioned previously, this was my one-page summary of the dreaded **Public Information Books**, or **PIBs**. Eventually, I didn't even bother doing these PIBs because they were a gargantuan waste of time and no senior banker ever read them cover to cover. Nothing is more demoralizing to juniors than doing busy work and knowing it's just killing trees. I started putting these one-pagers together and eventually, with technology,

was able to automate its production using macros. None of the senior bankers were ever the wiser and were always astounded at how fast I could spit these out.

○ *LIUCOMPS*. One of the staples in the business is market comparables, or comps for short. They give a company a sense of their worth by summarizing the valuation of similar companies. In the old days you had to download the financials of these comps and assemble the analysis by hand, but over time, technology became my friend. Eventually I could get a rough-and-dirty version with a simple push of the button, and using the template, I could whip up a new one on a moment's notice. It made me a rock star to my bosses because it created a domino effect and made them look like Mick Jagger, too.

○ *LIUMOD*. The most dreaded words for a junior banker to hear was, "I'd like you to run *a few* scenarios." This inevitably meant a financial model with over 100 scenarios, of which 99 were complete garbage but were needed because the senior banker had no idea what to recommend to the client. I solved this by creating a model with every possibility already built into it. IPO, LBO, sale, acquisition, or merger in a recession, expansion, or apocalypse? Got it covered. By including every harebrained, *fakakta* idea a senior banker on crack could imagine, I saved myself time and sanity.

○ *LIUPITCH*. Pitch books are the weapon of choice for investment bankers. Without one, the banker might as well be buck naked because it's usually the tool by which he fills the whitespace of meeting time. In my early years, on a typical month I'd have to pump out dozens of these suckers so I created a standard template book with our credentials, market overview, and recommendations—all formatted perfectly so I could just drop in company-specific data. I linked it to Excel so my LIUMOD could vomit out tables that would auto-update in LIUPITCH. Why did this work? Because the dirty little secret in the business is that the recommendations are generally *always* the same! We just wanted the company to do *something, anything*, that would generate a huge fee.

My templates became famous around Jefferies and I held them close to the belt, although I can't deny, I wasn't above doling them out discriminately for favors. A LIUMEMO could be exchanged for someone doing my comps for me—by hand. A LIUMOD would get me a stooge to answer the phones at night *and* deliver my food to my cubicle. A LIUPITCH would be grounds for hand-delivering my books to an MD's home in the middle of the night. Everyone wins!

- *Save Time.* OK, this seems really stupid, but do you know how much time the average American spends on nonwork activities? Most people spend at least an hour commuting to and from work. Or they spend mindless hours doom-scrolling on Twitter, gawking on TMZ, or window shopping on Amazon. And don't even mention the time wasted chatting up the opposite sex in the futile hope they might actually find you attractive.

  The World Wide Web hadn't been introduced into offices until a year after I started, but once it was, it created a whole new set of time-wasting prob-lems. One day, soon after browsers were installed on our computers, one of my officemates had the look of death on his face. "Dude," he told me, "I think I'm going to get fired." He showed me an email from compliance that said he had accessed the following unauthorized sites. What followed was the longest index of porn sites I'd ever seen. Fortunately for him, it was the early days of the Internet and he got off with a slap on the wrist.

  So in your case, once you tally it all up, it's no wonder you can't get your crap done on time. I forced myself to check game scores only once an hour, but my biggest timesaving hack would have been living near the office. But, of course, I didn't. I drove. I lived in L.A. for God's sake!

- *Choose Wisely.* While you need to learn to say "No" by saying, "Yes, but . . . ," this may just delay the inevitable. After all, some MDs are bad at math, but they do know there are 168 hours in a week. That's a lot of time to get their crap done, so you'll eventually need to say "No" to some things and that's where you'll earn your stripes. Place a bet on yourself and use your noggin to pick only deals that are winners for the firm.

- *Cheat Code.* Of course, like in any game, there is a cheat code that gets you off scot-free, and it's the one tactic that every manager since the Neolithic Era has discovered to maximize their ROTI: *delegate!* The smartest way to protect your time and maintain your sanity is to delegate responsibilities to junior staff. Let's save that for later, but the spoiler alert is that there is no such thing as a **free lunch**. At least you now know how to turn your penchant for laziness into a virtue.

Key Takeaways

- Learn to optimize your ROTI—it's the most important measure of efficiency.
- Replace "No" with "Yes, but . . . "
- Create *smartcuts*, not *shortcuts*, and hack your way to success.
- Learn the ultimate cheat code: delegation!

CHAPTER 17

The Minion-Circle

Find Your Master's Master

S o you've managed to weasel your way through the door and toiled away doing all the basics to keep your job and stand out. Hopefully, you've picked up a few tricks and tactics from me and are ready to put them into action. But before you go all Tess McGill,[1] let's cover a few more.

By now you've realized that unless you're an aspiring author writing a zombie-theme romance novel for young adults in Hell, Michigan, you'll need to figure out how to work with other people to climb the proverbial **corporate ladder**.

As an aside, I've always wondered where this stupid term comes from. No one knows, but before the actual ladder was invented, I'm sure we used poles or just sat on each other's heads. So be grateful someone invented the phrase **corporate ladder**; otherwise, you'd say, "I'm climbing up the pole" or "Striving to sit on face," both of which could be mistaken for another of your favorite pastimes.

---

[1]Administrative assistant character played by Melanie Griffith in *Working Girl*, an Academy Award–nominated movie made over three decades ago. Tess lies and fakes her way up the corporate ladder by pretending to be her boss, an associate in the M&A Department of an investment bank. Another complete fantasy by Hollywood, not because of the lying and masquerading (if you've learned anything by now, it's that everyone does this to some degree), but no associate would be negotiating and recommending a deal to the CEO. It would be the equivalent of you masquerading as Dwight Schrute from *The Office* to sell Dunder Mifflin to Georgia-Pacific.

Your Master's Master

I've already stressed the importance of getting the lay of the land by studying your company's org chart and its *shadow org chart* to understand your company's different departments. Equally important is knowing who works for whom. Every well-structured company has a limit on direct reports, usually less than a dozen, so by working from the top down, you can figure out who lords over whom. Use your smarts to identify the seats of power, which aren't always in the corner offices. In fact, it's usually the empty ones to watch because their occupants, who are gone most of the time, are the people with real supremacy. They're likely either out somewhere kicking ass or reaping the benefits of their power, like diving in the Maldives or golfing at St. Andrews.

Unless you're under 10 years old, not many of us can get away with saying, "You're not the boss of me!" We all answer to someone who ultimately determines our corporate fate. They determine if we get to move up the ladder, sit pat, or get pushed off into the abyss.

If you've learned anything from me, you know that unless you're a hermit, the key to your success is getting people to do what you want and, ultimately, understanding their motivations. More often than not, this means discovering the secret goals of their master. Knowing your boss's boss will prevent you from getting caught flat-footed or, even worse, completely blindsided. Only by identifying your master's master will you be able to understand your boss's motivations for doing just about anything, and only then will you have the opportunity to be the best underling possible by helping your boss shine. Pledge fealty to your boss and go the extra mile! With a little patience, your boss's success will trickle down to you.

Master the Circle

There's always a pecking order. On Wall Street, the analyst works for the associate, who reports to the VP, who answers to the MD, who does whatever their CEO asks. There might be additional layers like SVPs and group heads, but you get the idea. Everyone has a boss because everyone answers to someone. Let me decipher it for you with this handy-dandy illustration:

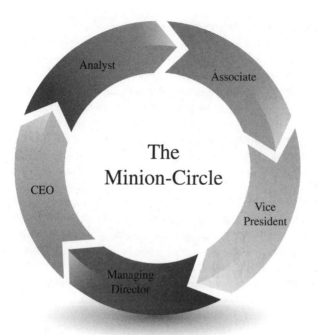

Now you may be thinking, that ain't a ladder; it's a circle! Congrats! You win the Captain Obvious Award. It's because even the CEO answers to someone, namely the company's stakeholders, which includes hordes of analysts, Reddit day-traders, Joe Blow shareholders like yourself, and every employee. You think that if a CEO did a crap job, the stakeholders wouldn't ultimately try to get them Marie-Antoinetted? Of course they would. CEOs of Wells Fargo, AIG, Deutsche Bank, Merrill Lynch, and many more have been sent to the glue factory by their boards, who answer to public shareholders. I call this the **Minion-Circle**. No matter who you are, you sit somewhere in this circle because even if you're sitting atop the corporate hierarchy, you still have someone above you whose ass you need to kiss.

I know whereof I speak. When I first joined Jefferies, in our small office there were already three "Davids," so we went by last names. Of course, given that I was the janitor, I had to have some embellishment or term of endearment that would signal my station in life. So in a nanosecond, instead of just "Liu," I was dubbed "Liu-Bitch." This was my moniker for the next four years.

Speaking as the anointed "bitch" in the office, knowing not only your position, but also your boss's position in the circle, will help you better understand their motivation. Who is your boss trying to please? What exactly did your boss get instructed to do? What is your boss's boss's plan for the minions beneath them?

When I was an analyst, I worked for some real pricks. One associate in particular would make me work around the clock and not let up. I thought he was a sadist who candle-waxed nipples. He would make me do 50 crazy scenarios and reprimand me if I questioned him. Eventually, I had a private tête-à-tête with his boss, the VP, and learned that this associate was vying for a promotion. To show he had the mettle for management, he was trying to prove that his taskmaster tactics of extracting every last ounce of blood from the analysts would yield the highest quality work. He would regularly claim that he spent a tremendous amount of his time training us and that without him, we wouldn't know our asses from our elbows.

Being a little immature, and not wanting to be a pawn in someone else's game, I hatched a plan. The associate trusted me implicitly and never checked my work, despite complaining to the VP how much time he had to spend double-checking it. One day I gave the associate a 100-page draft pitchbook, where every single page was blank. Sure enough, he gave the book directly to the VP without opening it and passed off the Herculean effort as his own. I later learned that the VP told the associate that the one thing he hated more than anything was a "passthrough"— someone who claimed others' work without adding value. The VP was wise to the associate's scam, thanks in no small part to my hints, and I was never staffed with that associate again. Thankfully, I had more than enough allies in the group that his vengeance didn't matter. Oh, and he didn't get the promotion.

Lauren Wu, former equity analyst and CFO of venture capital at J&W Seligman, worked as an associate at Merrill Lynch and spent all night working on merger models combining Samsonite with Smith & Wesson. Now, it doesn't take a rocket scientist to realize that guns and luggage have absolutely no synergy unless your customers are terrorists looking to get discounts on matching Tru-Frame Luggage and M&P Shield EZ Pistols. But she did it anyway. I bet her VP was told by his MD, who was told by the client, "Don't bring me obvious, bring me original!" That's usually how these clown shows get started. It's also how I'm sure we ended up with Harley Davidson Perfume, Cheetos Lip Balm, and Microsoft Bob.

Find Your Yoda

Once you've assessed the chain of command, it's critical to find a mentor who may not be your direct boss, but likes you, isn't an asshole, and understands your work. Many noble heroes have had a guru on their way to greatness: Luke had Yoda; Neo had Morpheus; Jesus had God.

Finding your own Yoda may be the single most important decision you make early in your career. Pledge allegiance to that person and that person's boss. Be sure to give up a business class seat for Yoda, and if you're dropping off presentations at their house and they ask you to play poker with them before heading back to the office at 11 p.m., do it! Volunteer for their poop patrol and do the crappy jobs no one else wants.

Think of your quest to find your Jedi master the same way you would get someone to fall in love with you—without the sex. If you're unsure who's who, follow the money. It's the yellow brick road to power. If that same person was involved in hiring you, be extra careful not to let them down. Make them proud. That way you'll be taking advantage of **choice supportive bias**. This is where you think positive things about a choice you've made, even if that choice has flaws. You may say positive things about the dog you just bought and ignore that he bites people. "You must have looked at Fido the wrong way!"

So make sure you develop mentors and stay close to the people who hired you or championed you in the past. They'll have a vested interest in your success because if you suck, *they're* to blame. This leverages the **endowment** or **IKEA effect** because your boss builds an emotional bond with you. You become *their* project just like that cheap armoire you built from IKEA.

Be mindful that you need to choose your Yoda wisely—especially if you are a woman. Ruth Porat, CFO of Google and former CFO of Morgan Stanley, warns that one of the biggest problems women have is that hard work for the *wrong* boss doesn't get noticed. "It may make that boss look terrific, but you get stuck," she points out.

So make sure Yoda's Yoda knows who you are, and once you've found your Yoda, make yourself memorable. Let them see you as either their charitable deed or their personal Mini-Me. Be the person they want around when they're stuck in the middle of nowhere. Laugh at their jokes, especially the dumb ones, all the while sucking their brain dry about how to get further around the **Minion-Circle**.

The Invisible Man Gets Fired

Maintaining visibility and communication up and down the food chain is critical. Make sure you never get cornholed or have your work subsumed by your boss—unless that's one of your explicit goals. And it should be. Remember, your boss is your guide and their success is critical to yours, although it never hurts to also make sure their superiors know your capabilities. That's not so hard to do. Make sure you worm your way into meetings where your boss is presenting the work to which you contributed. Say at least one insightful thing so your contribution is obvious. Make sure you aren't just known as "that junior banker in M&A." Build relationships with everyone and everywhere, from formal meetings, to coffees, to late-night karaoke.

But never forget that your immediate boss is your meal ticket. Don't press eject unless you come to the conclusion that they're the captain of the *Titanic*. If that happens, be sure to go scorched-earth and get the hell out of Dodge. Work for other bosses, appeal to the higher ups, and switch groups if needed. I knew my career wasn't going to be great if I focused on restructuring crappy consumer brands, so I made the switch to Technology. I thought this small thing called the Internet might be big one day. . . .

OK, Read the Prospectus

Remember when I told you to read the room and not the prospectus? It was a test to see how stupid you really are. If someone told you to down a bottle of sriracha, would you do it? SEC filings, research reports, shareholder blogs are all one click away if you know where to look. And what do they tell you? They answer all your questions. What's your CEO hearing from the company's stakeholders? What are shareholders demanding they do? What's the media saying they're screwing up? Which divisions are the research analysts telling them to jettison? How does your boss and your boss's boss fit into the company's future? Is your group the money machine or the black sheep?

You need to know all these answers so you don't get blindsided. Otherwise, one day your boss will come into your office and tell you that the whole division is being shut down and you now have to work at Bank of America as a teller.

One last note for those of you asking where it ends. There is one way to get out of the **Minion-Circle**. It's a long road, but it happens when you become financially independent, can fund your own ideas, and be the boss of your own company without any outside shareholders. You answer to no one and you don't give a rat's ass what others think of you. You can get there by dedicating decades of your life to a profession and squirreling away all your nuts, or you could just win the lottery. You choose.

Key Takeaways

- To understand human motivation, identify your master's master.
- Use your inner investigative skills and study your company's org chart and shadow org chart to figure out your place in the *Minion-Circle*.
- Read the prospectus. Know what your CEO's boss is saying and discover the source of your company's money machine.
- Choose your Yoda carefully. They're your downfield blocker.
- Win the lottery or stay in the Minion-Circle for life.

CHAPTER 18

Get the Last Word and Drop the Mic

Recency Bias at Work

W hen I was a kid and sassed back at my mother, she'd yell back, "Why do you always have to have the last word?!" I'd never leave an argument without declaring victory—even on my way to a time-out. I'm glad I did because it made me the man I am today. I made sure I'd always be remembered as a deal-making god by getting in the last word and dropping the mic.

Nobel Prize–Winning Shit

Nobel Prizes are given for bestowing upon humanity the greatest contributions to science, literature, and peace. But have you ever wondered who was its creator, Alfred Nobel? He created weapons and was the wartime equivalent of a crack dealer. But you know why we don't dwell on that? First, like many old rich people, he decided to turn a new leaf toward the end of his life to atone for his sins, and second, he made sure history remembered him not for the source of his stash cash, but rather for what he did with it. He didn't want to be remembered as the brainiac who invented *dynamite*, made piles of dough selling arms, and was left off the tree-hugging community's holiday card list. So what did he do? He gave his money to create the Nobel Prizes and, in effect, rewrote his own history. Ask anyone today what comes to mind when they hear the name Nobel and

I guarantee you they think of peace, love, and harmony, not blasted limbs and exploded torsos.

So why am I giving you this gory detail? It's because the tip I'm going to cover in this chapter was practiced by Nobel himself and is from Nobel Prize–winning Daniel Kahneman's concept of **Two Selves**. It's about **recency bias** and the **Peak-End Rule**. Simply put, it's about making sure you get the last word!

Just the Two of Us

Kahneman explained that human beings are made up of **Two Selves**: the *Experiencing Self* and the *Remembering Self*.[1] In a nutshell, the Experiencing Self lives your life while the Remembering Self evaluates your experiences, draws lessons from them, and decides your future. One lives in the present and the other keeps tally as chief historian. Kahneman discovered that the memory of an experience differs from how it happened. He proved this by showing that people who had a colonoscopy that was shorter in duration but ended with higher pain remembered the experience as far worse than those whose overall pain was longer but ended on a less severe note. He concluded that the Remembering Self was influenced by the *Peak-End* more than the overall length and amount of pain. I know it seems counterintuitive, but Kahneman won a Nobel Prize and you didn't. Personally, I've had a colonoscopy and the most painful experience was having a rubber glove jammed up my rectum and not the surgery itself. But that's just me. . . .

An example of these different selves might be how at the annual holiday party, your Experiencing Self wallowed in the corner of the Grand Ballroom of the Waldorf Astoria to avoid schmoozing with clients and colleagues, while your Remembering Self had you as the über socialite of the night. In this scenario, your Remembering Self was a tad delusional, to say the least, but both memories, real and not, got you thinking how to behave better next time.

You're probably thinking this sounds interesting when you're stuck at a client function or getting anal-probed, but what does it have to do with my workday? I'll tell you. We often go through painful episodes at work. Tempers flare when teammates point fingers at each other over missed deadlines. Subordinates and bosses come to loggerheads around performance evaluations and compensation. Someone leaves a half-eaten donut in the box. Work isn't all a bed of roses, and fighting and arguing are par for the course, but what do we do when the dust settles and we reach some type of resolution? Well, that's when I always tried to get the last word. I made sure I did whatever I could to salve any wounds and preserve the relationship. Remember, friends are worth more than enemies, and knowing that we all have Two Selves can work to your advantage.

[1] Daniel Kahneman, *Thinking, Fast and Slow* (Farrar, Straus and Giroux, 2011).

Deliver Shit Sandwiches in Person

Taking stock of these theories, I would always try to deliver bad news verbally and in person. We forget things all the time, particularly the older we get. Don't believe me? What did you have for dinner two nights ago? What day last year did you run out of toilet paper? On any given day, I can't even remember what I wore the previous day. At work, I wanted to make sure that any bad messages would be forgotten with time. Besides, people generally only remember their feelings, not the facts of conversations. I tried to keep it short and wrap it up with as much positivity as possible. My hope was that the message went down smoothly and by doing it in person, I was able to weave and bob and adjust based on the other party's reaction. So remember, a **Shit Sandwich** should always be hand-delivered.

Once the worst is over, there will no doubt be some ill feelings. Maybe the other party thinks you're irrational or too emotional. At this point, it's important to get the last word—in writing! Kahneman's Two Selves theory tells us that the way things end is the most important for our Remembering Self, so I always made sure my written version would be the clincher. Why? Remember the **TMZ Test**? Words are ephemeral, but the written word is forever. Yup, that's why you're still unemployed because your juvenile self wrote those idiotic posts on Facebook a decade ago for HR departments everywhere to see.

So if you've had a particularly bad experience with a boss, colleague, or client, be sure to be the final scribe. You want to make sure that you're the historian of your own story and paint events in the most favorable light for your future benefit.

We've all had bad experiences that needed readjustments and smoothing over. I always tried to structure fees based on *good, great,* and *over-the-moon* outcomes, meaning that if the outcome was only *good*, the fee would be modest. If *great*, it would be somewhere in the middle, and if *over-the-moon*, it would be considerable. This exploits people's **loss aversion**. A client's biggest fear is feeling they've lost something by forking over the fee in the lower-value outcomes they think wasn't earned.

A win-win I remember came when I achieved a stellar, over-the-moon outcome for a client. In this case, I achieved a fee three times what I would have received under our standard fee proposal, which this client had originally rejected. To be fair, if I had attained just a good outcome, our fee would have been below market for a firm of our stature. But after the fact, several VC board members were upset and wanted the CEO to chisel me into a million pieces. I wouldn't have it, and we were at a standoff. Both sides threatened litigation, and it got pretty nasty. After much penis-size comparisons, we ultimately settled on a compromise, which still represented a great fee for Jefferies, although not at an over-the-moon level.

After the dust settled, the CEO and I spoke by phone and he admitted being cajoled by his VCs into fighting us and told me he actually felt we earned our fee. I acknowledged that the over-the-moon fee might have been a little high, which is why we compromised, and we remained friends.

Then came my masterpiece moment. I sent the CEO a final email that expressed my resounding (and sincere) satisfaction that we had been able to reach a compromise, that it was going to be a great deal for him and the company, and most important, that our firm was so proud to have been involved. It was all true and needed to be said. He never acknowledged the email, but several years later he reached out and said he thought of me on another deal when he reread my email. So even though we almost came to blows in the heat of battle, many years later all was forgiven and he hired me again.

You may recognize that I gave you similar advice when we last discussed **recency bias**. It's why I told you to make sure your cover emails always ended on a good note. This is the tendency to weigh the latest information more heavily than older data. Thus, it's important to always end with emails or phone calls that recount history the way you want it to be remembered (i.e., you were the Savior). Especially when you have the hot hand, be sure to leverage it right away. Whenever we closed a deal, we'd send out a *tombstone*, or Wall Street's equivalent of an ad, to brag about our involvement. (I always thought a tombstone was appropriate because some poor junior banker probably died a little to make that deal happen.) These would inevitably lead to prospects wanting to talk about the deal and potentially hire us for future business.

When I didn't generate outcomes that made my client ecstatic (I know, shocker!), I always made sure I'd do a **post-mortem** where I'd explain why the outcome we reached was the best possibility and frame it as a success. We'd have a closing dinner celebration even though none of us really wanted it—a big party at a fancy restaurant, eating overpriced meat and overpriced wine. Then we'd shower them with gifts from Tiffany and by the end of the evening everyone would be butt-slapping each other like we had just won the Super Bowl.

If It Ain't Wrote, It Ain't True

One effective strategy to strengthen your standing as the dealmaker extraordinaire is to make sure you have the final word in writing. But *only* if it's praiseworthy. Anything bad should be verbal because written emails are forever, while the spoken word is in one ear and out the other.

No one writes letters anymore, so email is how you'll memorialize a narrative that matches what you want others to remember. When the project is all said and done, be sure to get clients, bosses, or colleagues to write emails to you for a job well done. These "thank-you notes" are your future currency—the stone tablets regaling your great deeds. Whenever I had a deal with even a mediocre outcome, I sent thank-you emails to the client (almost always after an enjoyable closing dinner) which would result in a return thank-you note with strong appreciation for my work . . . sometimes stronger than I deserved! I kept these for posterity—particularly in those situations where there were multiple senior bankers involved and I might need to jockey for credit at year-end bonus time. Some bankers get clients to write on their LinkedIn profile; I have a few of those myself. These work great because they're on the public record for all to see!

Talk to Yourself

There's lots of theory out there that sometimes talking to yourself helps. No, I'm not talking about babbling to yourself in the street with drool oozing down your mouth. I'm talking about psyching yourself up for the next pitch, speech, or deal. After a bad meeting or loss of a deal, it's easy to get down on yourself. It's called **negativity bias** and accounts for why we pay more attention or give more weight to the negative rather than the positive. It makes us take fewer risks when we should be doing the opposite, particularly at work. Research by Harvard Professor Teresa Amabile found that setbacks affected workers' happiness twice as much as progress, and you're therefore likely to remember and alter your decisions in the future based on this bias.

If a deal isn't going as well as you had hoped, reassure yourself that you've done all you can and it will work out for the better. Tell yourself not to dwell on the mistakes you made, but rather the progress you helped achieve. I took a few moments before every meeting to clear my mind, reassure myself that I could win the deal, and then go perform like a star. As Bing Crosby crooned, "Ac-cent-tchu-ate the positive, e-lim-i-nate the negative, latch on to the affirmative, don't mess with Mr. in-between."

Key Takeaways

- Defy your mother (or father) and get in the last word.
- Learn from Alfred Nobel. He wrote his own history.
- We're *Two Selves*. You're in a battle between your *Experiencing Self* and your *Remembering Self*.
- Recap events in the most favorable light and memorialize it in writing.
- Deliver *Shit Sandwiches* in person.
- Avoid *negativity bias* by practicing self-care and talking to yourself.
- Always, always end every interaction on a *positive note*.

CHAPTER 19

Get Paid Like a Player

Make F*ck-You Money

You're not working your butt off for the money, right? You're working for the dignity of a job well done, for the satisfaction of contributing to society, for, as Ralph Waldo Emerson said, "to be useful, to be honorable, to have made some difference that you have lived and lived well."

BS! Of course, you're working for the money. If you win the lottery, you're going to quit your job by simply ghosting your boss, then sitting on your ever-fattening ass eating bonbons watching *Animal Planet* from your château in France.

Now that we've gotten that straight, and even though you know you're never going to win the lottery, keep this one simple idea at the center of your brain: When the time comes to argue for compensation, it's a **zero-sum game**.

I'll say it again. It's a **zero-sum game.**

What's that mean for you? It means one more dollar in your pocket is one less dollar for your bosses, and no matter how many Porsches they have in their six-car garages, don't ever forget that greed has no bounds. Your coworker in the next cubicle would sell you down the river for an extra buck. Remember the old adage about the two folks in the woods who just need to outrun each other and not the bear? Same applies here. So come prepared. Convince your boss that you're the crème de la crème and that you deserve more than your fair share. Don't be bashful. You're a *luxury good* who deserves to be compensated for what you're worth.

But how much are you worth? Better question, how much can you ask for without your bosses breaking out into hysterics?

Like the purpose of that plastic in the middle of the pizza delivery box, the process of determining compensation is one of life's great mysteries. You really only get insight into how it works when you reach the upper echelons of your organization. But you're in luck. I'm going to let you peek behind the curtain.

Herded Like Cattle

For most firms, comp season begins with the annual review process. In investment banking, the bosses typically separate the performance review from the bonus discussions, claiming they don't want to needlessly distract you from absorbing their sage feedback. I've always assumed it's because they don't want employees to use positive evaluations against them if, despite glowing reviews, they give lousy bonuses.

Every firm is a little different, but in my experience, the process for reviewing junior bankers is like a reality TV show. All the bankers are herded into a room, or on a conference call, and the roundtable begins with each group reviewing the level below. The room starts with MDs, SVPs, VPs, and associates, and this group evaluates all the analysts. Once they're done, the associates depart and the MDs, SVPs, and VPs evaluate the associates. This process continues as each level is raked over the coals and then dismissed, until only the MDs are left. It always struck me as strange that some VP would be trashing some associate for not working his analysts to the bone and yet also faulting him for being a cantankerous jerk to the juniors. All the while I'm wondering, "Dang, I'd hate to think what they're going to say about me!"

These reviews are the warm-up to the main event—compensation! You may think the reviews don't matter, but they do. You know why? Because if you don't pass this first gauntlet, you might as well kiss that Maserati goodbye. Even if you get just a mediocre review, you're not going to get paid well. No one ever pays you if they can point to some way you screwed up. If you saw a brand-new car at the dealer's lot but it has a scratch, would you pay full boat?

On Wall Street, to get paid well, your firm has to do well. If your company isn't doing well, but you and your group are highly productive, you'll definitely get a few attaboys but you *still* might not get paid well. It took me a long time to figure this out, so I'll save you the heartache and break it down in a simple two-by-two matrix. If you're an MBA, you know these by heart because you've dropped a cool hundred grand or more to learn that everything at work can be distilled into one of these bad boys:

	Firm Has Bad Year	**Firm Has Good Year**
You Have Good Year	*Get Screwed*	***Get Paid***
You Have Bad Year	*Get Screwed*	*Get Screwed*

If you want to spare yourself the suspense of your job review, just look on this handy-dandy chart and find your box. *Hmm. . . .* I wonder if you'll get paid well this year?

Prep Your Negotiation

When I was an analyst, it was common knowledge that someone in our peer group regularly put together a spreadsheet that ranked his revenue productivity against the rest of us lowlifes. Everyone knew he was full of it and that he was as responsible for the revenue of the deals he listed as I was for deciding which icebergs to avoid on the *Titanic*. But there was nothing unethical with his tactics. He was just practicing what I'm preaching in this book by taking advantage of **recency bias**. No senior executive was going to double-back and check what the guy actually did on the ten deals he attached his name to. Most important, his tactic worked! He was always in the top quartile of compensation. You'll see how I know this later in this chapter, but for now, recall one of our most important lessons: *ABS—Always Be Selling*, in this case, yourself. Bret Pearlman, co-founder of Elevation Partners and former senior managing director at Blackstone, had it exactly right. "Your entire job," he was constantly telling people, "is one big interview for a promotion."

Before I get too deep into the weeds of how to get paid more than your worth, here are a few tidbits:

- You work for a profit-oriented organization. Charity comes from your parents.
- Every minute your bosses are evaluating how you are, or are not, adding value. Reflect on that the next time you pass on extra work or bring home a few extra kombuchas from the company fridge.
- A little *quid pro quo* can go a long way with your colleagues during comp season. You'll tell them your bonus, and they'll tell you something that hopefully isn't complete crap.
- Always aim to convince the powers that be that you're a great long-term bet; otherwise, you'll be at the head of the conga line at the RIF, or Reduction in Force, party. But you only need to worry if all the SVPs have been canned.
- Your company will pay you the least amount possible to keep you from walking. If you don't get what you want, leave. That's your only leverage.
- If you don't ask, you don't get!

Win the Zero-Sum Game

Senior executives never want you to think that the **zero-sum game** is at work and will go to great lengths to hide, obfuscate, and deny. Why? Because thinking about your pay from this perspective discourages teamwork. You'll come to realize it's not a win-win situation for everyone. It's me versus you. Recognizing this reality requires a mindset adjustment in order to put yourself on the winning side of the **zero-sum game.**

I'm sorry, but young people are naive about money, including my own kids, who assume we have a money tree growing in our backyard. I have no doubt that when I'm out of earshot, they call me "Bank-O-Dad." I could say the same thing about junior bankers. When they first drop from the metaphoric birth canal, it hasn't yet occurred to them that they actually *cost* the company money. When I tell their 20-something-year-old brains, "We're making a major investment in you by paying you six figures, health insurance including dental and toenail, a closely monitored expense account, and a fat 401k," a light bulb goes off in their heads. They suddenly start to realize, "Dang, I'm really expensive!"

Juniors also need to understand that at some point, they can get *too* expensive. It's your job to offset this possibility by *adding more value to the organization than you're costing*. Think of yourself as a **sunk cost** and use it to your advantage. Your company is already invested in you, so gain leverage by making it clear you're a *good* investment and not a lost cause. I'll say it more simply: They're spending money on you, but thanks to you, they're making money. That's your defense; make sure they know that.

So How Much Are You Worth?

Ah, so how much are you worth? That's easy. You're worth what someone is willing to pay you. It's no different than that pristine first edition of *Harry Potter and the Philosopher's Stone* you've had on your shelf since childhood or the Picasso lithograph you found in your parents' basement. It's worth what someone is willing to pay you for it, no more, no less. Sound familiar? It's the **Greater Fool Theory**. In this case, your employer is the fool.

Compensation, of course, is a bit more complicated, only because it's the ultimate barometer of how you're progressing in the organization—from their point of view, not yours. It's the scorecard that tells you if you're on track, so it's important to think of yourself as an asset and enumerate the multitude of ways you generate a positive return. The formula is simple: your added value divided by the cost to the organization. The results better be greater than one; otherwise, consider yourself on thin ice.

In the corporate world, the rich get richer, and as you scale to the top of the organization, the compensation can grow exponentially. And what's true for Corporate America is even more true for Wall Street. If you're an investment banker, the answer is you're worth A LOT . . . at least compared to most Americans. In 2019, the average salary (including bonuses) of securities industry employees in New York City was $406,700, five times higher than the average in the rest of the private sector.[1] Think these bankers generated five times the value?

---

[1] According to "The Securities Industry in New York City" report issued in October 2020 by the Office of the New York State Comptroller.

This formula can be used in any industry, although the magnitude of the dollars on Wall Street is ridiculous. When I began in 1993, my compensation was $76,000 annually, half salary, half bonus. Today, first-year analysts at Goldman Sachs, Wells Fargo, and UBS earn an average of $91,000, *plus* bonuses.[2] So while negotiating for top dollar is always important in any field, the remuneration scale in investment banking makes the stakes even higher, with enough cutthroat greed to ready the sharp objects of even your mildest opponent . . . I mean, colleague.

Of course, starting salaries pale when put next to the compensation of the top dogs. Remember Michael Milken, Drexel Burnham Lambert's head of high-yield securities who was convicted (then pardoned by Trump) for insider trading? Before he was put in handcuffs, his yearly bonus was approximately $550 million. How is that possible? It's because he represented what we call *the plug*—the one who grabs whatever is left over after he's signed off on everyone else's compensation—all to his advantage, of course.

OK, that was before the financial crisis, but even recent compensation figures won't have you sending canned food to the likes of Citigroup's Michael Corbat ($23 million), Bank of America Merrill Lynch's Brian Moynihan ($23 million), Goldman Sachs's Lloyd Blankfein ($24 million), Morgan Stanley's James Gorman ($27 million), or J.P. Morgan Chase's Jamie Dimon ($30 million).

Millionaire Paupers

All these lucky bastards have accumulated **f*ck-you money**, but even those who are one, two, or three echelons below them are paid many millions. For most of them, it's not enough. It's never enough. In the banking world, one reason the compensation negotiations get so heated is that it's common for people to spend more than they earn, regardless of how well they're compensated. The more they earn, the more they spend, and they make their situation worse by evaporating their entire salaries before year's end, then holding on for dear life until the arrival of their bonus check, which can be as much as twenty times their base salary.

You'd think this would encourage people to save during the year and wait for the big payoff at the end, but in many cases, it has the opposite effect. Bankers are notorious for **lifestyle creep**, spending their total compensation rather than just their monthly salary as they go. I'm talking about people making $2 million a year who are constantly broke because they're spending $2.5 million, so if the bonus they anticipated doesn't materialize, they're in even deeper do-do.

---

[2]https://www.businessinsider.com/salaries-first-year-investment-banking-analysts-make-2020-8

I know, I know . . . "Boo-hoo."

So how much compensation is enough for these big spenders? Trick question. It's never enough! Vacations at the Four Seasons in Bora Bora, private schools for their children, and a beach house in Montauk so they can bond with their family—and they deserve a treat for themselves, too—at least one Ferrari LaFerrari. No matter how far their dollar number goes up, up, up as they rise the ladder, the lament is always the same: "I can't possibly live on that!"

One time, I was sitting in the room when the Group Head was announcing to senior bankers their compensation. This one particular MD was a highflier and spent way beyond his means. We had him down for $2 million ($500,000 salary and $1.5 million bonus). When the Group Head delivered the good news, the MD went ballistic. "Are you freaking kidding me?" he screamed as his voice reached a crescendo. "You know how much money I've made for this firm? This is BS!"

When his math didn't add up, he turned to another tactic: begging. He couldn't live on $2 million a year, he pleaded, not with the government taking half in taxes, alimony for his ex, private school tuitions, and the balloon mortgage on his beachfront estate.

The Group Head very deliberately went through his productivity numbers and matter-of-factly explained why $2 million was fair. Once this MD knew his pity party wasn't going to lead anywhere, he shifted gears and made all nicey-nicey, hoping a little sugar might buy him a couple hundies. That didn't work, either, and he left the room with a nice, limp handshake.

But you know what? This guy was right. There was no way he could live on $2 million per year.

I learned a valuable lesson that day, one that I decided was too obvious for high-IQ rich boys to ever understand. My biggest takeaway was that I would never, ever be like this fool and run on empty. I vowed to save all my bonuses because I never wanted to be stuck in this job, in any job, that I didn't necessarily want, making millions a year and not being able to walk away with more than a shekel in my pocket. I made a lot of money in my years as an investment banker, but the only reason I was able to walk away in my early 40s was that even after I rose up the ranks, I lived in a modest home that wasn't Versailles, and while my partners drove Ferraris and 7 Series BMWs, I was perfectly happy cruising in my Honda S2000.

For crying out loud, live within your means.

Tap the Whisper Wire

What are you worth or, more important, what are your bosses willing to pay you? Particularly if you're nowhere near the C-suite (which you obviously aren't), it's in your court to find any legal and ethical means to ferret out the answer. Don't go into your comp discussion without plenty of information to support your case. Start by investigating what others in your same position are getting paid; otherwise, you're flying blind when negotiating your salary and other compensation. But how do you do that?

First, ask around. "You tell me yours, and I'll tell you mine." I call it tapping the **whisper wire**. Start with your friends at your own company, and since you followed my advice in Chapter 10, and you only have friends and very good friends, you can talk to everyone!

Next, study your company's public financials and reports. The operating word here is *public*. Jefferies had already gone public by the time I started working there, so I studied anything I could get my hands on until I had a clear understanding of how we made money, our margins, and how much they *should* be paying me. It never ceases to amaze me how few employees take the time to do this at any company. My knowledge gave me a huge advantage when it came time to know the upper limits of what I could ask for. If I knew what people like me cost the company, I could much more easily extrapolate what I was *worth* to the company. It also helped to research other investment banks to at least get a hint of what people were being paid at my level.

If you work for a private company, your task is more difficult. Back in the day, we would actually hire compensation specialists to give us data on what the Goldman Sachses of the world were paying their people, and we'd adjust ours within that range. Now with the Internet, a wealth of information can be found on job sites like Glassdoor, Salary.com, PayScale, Salary Expert, LinkedIn, and a host of others. Even the Bureau of Labor Statistics has interesting information. Oftentimes, however, the best sources are personal blogs and bulletin boards, which are more than happy to spill the beans about third-party data.

In other words, search and you shall find.

Word of mouth works, too. In many industries, every Tom, Dick, Harry, Susan, Jane, and Mary talks, and everyone knows who's making what and understands the hierarchy of compensation. This puts everyone on the same playing field, with a clear understanding of who's in the top percentile and whether you have a chance of reaching that rarefied air. Think about who you know. If your significant other, or even the sister of the friend of your significant other, works at a headhunting firm, ask for the key to the juiciest data. Remember, human beings love to gossip, and what's juicier than money?

Go Shop Yourself

The most hazardous, but sometimes most effective, way to get data or comps on others is to shop yourself. That's dangerous, of course. If your employer finds out, it may not exactly destroy your relationship, but it does change the nature of it. It exposes the elephant in the room that you're not besties from another teste, that your relationship is transactional, that you're not there for love, but for the love of money. You also might get fired, particularly if you're that Joe or Jill Schmo who they wanted to let go anyway. But if you're a rising star, it just might work to your advantage by creating competition and forcing your company's hand. But be careful. No threats; more like calm, friendly banter. Remember, your bosses will pay you only the bare minimum needed to keep you from jumping ship, so you need to find that happy (happy for you) medium.

Spencer Wang, former Credit Suisse and Salomon Brothers banker, told me how the first year after leaving investment banking for a great job at a hedge fund, he thought he got screwed on his bonus, which was a lot less than what he had been making and what he thought he deserved. He was pissed because he had made a career change, was getting yelled at every day, and felt underappreciated. He went to one of his bosses (who Spencer said is still the best tech investor he ever met), and he told him calmly and honestly that he was disappointed in his compensation. He also explained that he had an offer to return to banking as a research analyst, but he was hoping he wouldn't be forced to make the switch.

"My boss told me he saw a lot of potential in me and things would work out if I stuck around," Spencer said, "so I stayed and it was the best decision of my life." The next year Spencer was paid eight times what he had made the previous year.

Spencer thinks that each situation is different and requires reading your boss, taking stock of the situation, and applying the right amount of EQ. "You have to handle compensation very carefully, and go in knowing your goal. Don't overplay your hand if you aren't willing to leave. What I didn't realize at the time, I actually had a lot of leverage because they had invested in me and wanted to keep me. By being honest and straightforward, I gained my boss's respect and proved my loyalty. I did it in a way that my boss sympathized with."

Shopping myself worked for me once in my career. I had been an SVP for a little over a year. You might remember that I liken the SVP role to being stuck on the River Styx, the river in Greek mythology that forms a border between the underworld and the world of the living. I knew I had to get the hell out of that role as fast as possible or potentially end up in the SVP graveyard. Up to this point, I had received numerous inquiries from competing banks to see if I'd ever consider joining them and I had given them a resounding, "Hell, no!" But I finally decided to listen and received an unsolicited offer from one of them to join as an MD. I didn't keep it a secret, letting a few well-placed colleagues know that this option was available to me. And guess what happened? I was bumped up to the *big role*—managing director. I could have just continued on my current path, investing the customary three to four years required before being eligible for promotion, but I escaped after only a year and a half—but only because I shopped myself.

Don't play this card lightly. Make a distinction between threats and honest explanations; in fact, never do the former because then it becomes an ultimatum, and no one likes ultimatums. The firm isn't going to collapse without you no matter how valuable you think you are.

The lesson I took from these experiences is that if you're a good earner and you shop yourself, they're not going to fire you. But if you suck, they're going to make sure the door doesn't hit your ass on the way out. So unless you're very sure of your perceived value, don't bluff!

If all else really fails, you could try learning how to pick locks or hack the company's computers. These are terrible ideas, albeit effective. I know people who broke into HR offices Watergate-style to uncover compensation details. Whatever you learn will give you the inside track when your boss plays hardball, and revealing this information to your cohorts will be like dropping a bag of donuts in a fasting community. Pandemonium!

But seriously, you're better than that, and smart enough to use the tricks I've taught you or to find more creative ways to do your due dilly. Don't even lie, even if you know you're being handed a bunch of baloney. During one negotiation that became legend, one top dog told an MD, "If I pay you that, I'll be paying you more than I'm paying myself." Right, and alien space lasers are causing the California wildfires.

If you're in investment banking, you may want to revert to your Cro-Magnon self and be tempted to do something stupid to get paid. Don't! Insider trading and front running are the fool's way out. FBI wiretaps are everywhere. They're probably reading over your shoulder right now. They don't care about those porn sites you frequent on your work laptop, but they do care if you're screwing the little people, or at least they should.

Lean on Yoda

For junior staff, it's critical to find a mentor to advocate for why you should get paid. If you do your job well, your Yoda will be there for you when it's time for your compensation to be decided. Always think about your future; be long-term greedy.

Lauren Wu, former equity analyst and CFO of venture capital at J&W Seligman and Merrill Lynch banker, adds that doing the leg work early in finding and developing a mentor can pay dividends, especially for women, at compensation time. "Having a mentor who is familiar with the culture of the firm and the best strategies to get what you want is critical," she explains. "You don't have to reinvent the wheel because, ideally, your mentor can show you the path. Otherwise, you will be negotiating in the dark and will likely leave money on the table."

When I was an associate, there was an SVP who I didn't directly report to, but who really liked me. We had a great, casual relationship and I asked him, "Hey man, what are the top associates getting paid this year at Jefferies because I think I got screwed?" He was extraordinarily helpful, giving me the wink and the nod on the ranges, and signaling what I should be paid. Of course, whatever he needed from that day forward, I was his Chinese drug dealer—serving for life!

One of the defining moments early in my career occurred when I was still an analyst. Our Group Head was an early fan of my work and recruited me to assist him with our business planning. It helped that by this time I had proven myself to be an Excel God, and he was a closeted neophyte. I had also proven myself to be 100 percent trustworthy, an equally important attribute because bankers are constantly in possession of material information, and unless you want to live behind windows with bars, you really need to keep your trap shut.

In my case, the Group Head gave me insight into both departmental costs and the bonus pools. At first, it started with him sharing only high-level data, but as the department got bigger, it became more difficult for him to keep me out of the individual discussions about compensation. Eventually, I saw everyone's comp and would help him run all sorts of scenarios by modeling different outcomes according to costs, revenue, and profitability. He'd ask me to project the bonus pool if we hit particular revenue targets by year-end. Remember, this was extremely sensitive information, but there I was, essentially the janitor, helping the Big Guy play out different scenarios and determining everyone's pay.

I did this work for almost five years, through at least four bonus cycles. It gave me tremendous insight into the process that determines who gets what. We'd evaluate each banker's worth to the group, and he'd ask me key questions, like who wasn't making their goals, how many bodies reported to whom, and ultimately, who seemed replaceable.

This really got me thinking about my own compensation and what I was worth. As we did every comp cycle, one time we were going through names one-by-one and he was making small adjustments based on their reviews and the market comps. We finally got to my name and I saw the bonus number he had scheduled for me. It was pretty awesome; I had never seen that much money before in my life and could barely contain myself. But I didn't flinch a muscle. We both looked up at the same time without speaking a word. We glanced at each other, he gave me an almost imperceptible nod, and quietly said, "Add another $25K."

Let the Games Begin!

You thought the interview process was the "Big Show"? You ain't seen nothing yet. When the time comes to haggle for your compensation, that's the real deal. Going in, just remember there is always a little leeway, with a few quarters still left in the sofa. The key is to exude confidence and give off the sweet aroma of *success*. Make your peers, bosses, and clients all see dollar signs when they look into your eyes! Otherwise, prepare to get shafted.

Lauren Wu would make sure she knew exactly what her ROI was to the firm. "I'd prepare spreadsheets showing exactly the revenue I had generated and the value I delivered."

Gina King, partner at Supernode Global and former Jefferies SVP, would similarly come armed with market comparables and demonstrate to her bosses how they were actually getting a great ROI from her. "I'd show the breadth of duties I had versus others in the industry who had a narrower scope and less responsibility. This gave me the evidence to advocate for a much higher salary and role."

In negotiation, the *when* and the *where* are almost as important as the *what*. Particularly for you junior execs, the *optimal time* to discuss your bonus is *after* your bosses get their numbers. Your $100,000 ask will seem like small potatoes to their $1 million. Try to suss out what they might be getting, which will help determine their state of mind when you ask to get paid. If their results were good, you've got an excellent chance your higher-ups are likely to fight for you. If not, then you're on your own.

In general, I've found the best advice with regards to talking about money is the same as that supposedly given by gangster Al Capone with regards to voting: "Early and often."[3] In this case, that means starting well before the comp season. Here's a great lesson from Edward Fu, president of Happy Masks and former banker from Jefferies. After delivering great results, he'd go to his boss and say he's undercompensated and didn't want to be distracted thinking about his comp. "Don't make me think about it subconsciously!" he would signal. He would do this only when he knew he had momentum, and he never waited for comp season. The message he sent was clear: "I am going to do amazing things, but I need to be focused. Help me stay focused by paying me!"

If possible, try to have a preliminary talk with your boss about compensation in a social setting; it can be disarming and give you an advantage. Matthew D. Lieberman, a professor of neuroscience at UCLA, says that humans have two different *brain networks*, one for *social* activities and one for *nonsocial* ones.[4] When people use logic or reason, they engage a part of the brain you might call *book smarts*. When people try to understand another person's problems, they use a different aspect—the *social brain*. This means that if you discuss numbers in a social setting, it's more likely your boss will defer to his or her social brain and understand your needs from a personal rather than business perspective. So go out to dinner, drinks, or even high tea!

My go-to place was usually on a flight to some God-forsaken hellhole in the middle of nowhere where the only Chinese were likely the people running the local takeout or laundromat. I'd have my boss captive for at least four hours and we'd throw back a few highballs and wax poetic about work–life balance or lack thereof. Inevitably, the conversation would veer toward dedication to my career and the sale of my soul to the job. That's when I'd gently remind him that many a devil has come a-callin' and my soul doesn't come cheap.

When you're ready to meet your boss in the office face-to-face, it's best to have an open mind. You never know where the discussion might lead. Sometimes you get so fixated on a particular number that you can't see beyond your nose. You've fallen victim to the **anchoring effect**, where your original number is anchored in your subconscious and distorts any thinking that comes later, particularly during the actual negotiation.

---

[3] John Kobler, *Capone: The Life and World of Al Capone* (2003).
[4] Matthew D. Lieberman, *Social: Why Our Brains Are Wired to Connect* (Crown, 2013).

Also, there's got to be a strong element of trust between you and your negotiator. There is a bias called **hyperbolic discounting**. It's the tendency for people to want an immediate payoff rather than a larger gain at a later date. Most people would rather take $5 now instead of $7 in a week. You should play the long game. Organizations look at employees as either short- or long-term. Are you that person who your employer can envision at the company five or ten years in the future? Even if it isn't likely, the answer must always be "Yes!"

Be a Long-Term Short-Timer

Maybe one year your value to the firm stinks and you're not tracking the way management expected, but they see you as a future leader. Many industries are more long-term-focused than Wall Street because they're not necessarily transactional-based or market-driven. Silicon Valley is a great example because it often takes years to build a successful product. To make sense of all this, follow the money. If a company makes its revenue on a short-term basis, they're going to be very short-term in their expectations of you. If they make money on a long-term basis, they're likely to be more patient, with a longer-term outlook.

Frank Baxter, former CEO at Jefferies and later the U.S. ambassador to Uruguay, used a short-term perspective to his advantage. "Knowing human nature, I know you can never give anyone anything you might have to take away," he said. "When we had a tough year at Jefferies and I needed people to stay and not go elsewhere, I gave everyone a higher 20 percent override but told everyone it was for one year only. Nobody left that year even though they could have gotten jobs elsewhere."

The lesson here is that you've got to think about how you're perceived from both a short- *and* long-term perspective, and use this knowledge to *your* advantage. Remember, every day is evaluation day, so if you've been doing well, it's your opportunity to convince the organization that you're a good long-term bet. If by chance, you stunk up the farm this past year, it's even more important to reassure your higher-ups about your potential to generate money, or call attention to what you can do for them next year.

In the same way I advised you to do **pre-mortems** for projects and presentations, do the same for your negotiations. In this case, envision the good, the great, and the over-the-moon outcomes. Doing this will prevent you from getting caught up later in the **hindsight bias**, where you ask yourself how the hell did you get paid less than you had expected.

There's also another powerful force in play here—the omnipotent mathdom theory, the **mean reversion**. It states that everything goes back to the mean. That's also true for compensation. If you're in it for the long haul, you might get paid well one year, but eventually it all evens out. So choose your time to fight wisely. And don't forget what this chapter is all about: Bonuses are tied to the **zero-sum game**, where the compensation pool might not be as full this year as it will be the next. So be willing to make short-term sacrifices in remuneration for promises of more in the future. But get it in writing if you can!

On Your Mark, Get Set, GO!

So you've done your research and have your aces in your back pocket. Now you're ready to sit down and negotiate. Unless you and your boss are totally on the same page, chances are there is an information gap between what you think is fair and what the organization thinks is fair. Your goal is to bridge that gap either directly or passive-aggressively. You need to master this negotiation for yourself if you're ever going to get anywhere in life because if you can't fight for yourself, how can you fight for anyone or anything else?

There are entire books about negotiating, so I'm not going to waste your time. But here are some no-brainer tactics:

- *Listen* and use your EQ to read what your boss is thinking.
- If there's a huge information gap, eliminate the conflicts.
- Be credible in your accomplishments, creating the illusion of *scarcity* to get *maximum value* out of your work. But never lie, although half-truths are acceptable.
- Use interesting (and perhaps entertaining) analogies about yourself, like you're Warren Buffett Junior or the Young Bob Rubin.
- Try not to *split the difference*. Make Numero Uno happy (that's you, doofus).
- If your future looks bright, and it's an option, consider taking a lower salary (or fee) in exchange for steeper payouts.
- Add passion into the equation, though be cautious with anger.
- Do *not* keep your mouth shut in compensation discussions. On Wall Street and most everywhere else, you'll get eaten alive. Your boss will think you were overpaid and just pay you less next time. Always speak your mind because you earned that right. And always, always express disappointment.

On the last note, Paul Clausing, managing director at Fluential Partners and former Jefferies banker, said one year he was paid well and told his boss, "Thank you." His boss, who was also his mentor, turned to him and gave him two pieces of advice. First, his boss said, "Don't ever thank me. You earned every penny with blood, sweat, and tears." Then the mentor side of his boss gave him a second piece of advice: "And don't ever make it known how happy you are because that means we overpaid you."

All Money Is Money

Companies have shrewd financial minds (especially on Wall Street) working behind the scenes and have dreamt up all kinds of *fakakta* ways to pay employees. All money is money, right? Wrong! Not all money is green, and not all money is created equal. Especially in the financial wizardry labs of Wall Street, money could be trash.

Fortunately for you, I'm here to give you a simple primer on money so you don't get bamboozled.

Compensation	Description	The Calculus
Cash	Benjamins, moolah, dinero	The King. Most people would prefer to get paid in cash, which, of course, is best for illicit transactions where one doesn't want to leave any trace. Drugs, late-night antics, and dodging taxes are all typical uses. Unfortunately, chances are only drug dealers, pimps, and local Chinese restaurants take cash nowadays. Of course, cash is also suitable for snorting cocaine, but let's not go there.
Equity	Stock options, restricted stock	This is how the rich really get richer because they own the stock market. If you're long-term greedy, hunker down because you'll likely have to stick around for years to fully vest all of this. Sometimes, the equity can be restricted, which basically means with strings attached. But this isn't friends with benefits! Think of it as a post-nuptial agreement. You get hired, you get paid, but if you leave your significant other before she wants, she gets to keep the house, the car, the kids, and your balls on her mantelpiece!
Restricted Cash	Cash with strings	A glorious invention from the best minds on Wall Street. It has all the restrictions of restricted equity but none of the upside. The house wins again!
Benefits	Healthcare, insurance	You'll thank your lucky stars you have this when you slowly waste away in your cubicle.
Freebies	Drinks, food, transport	On Wall Street, the salad days of buffet lunches and unlimited expense accounts may be over, but there are still lots of freebies at the major banks. It may not seem like much, but free kombuchas and Lyft rides do add up!

My Super-Secret Negotiating Strategy

I've saved the best for last: my super-secret negotiating strategy for everything: Introduce a *third player*. It's something that always worked really well for me. That third player isn't a person; it's a morality element—playing fair.

It's a trump card I usually add at the end. Leading up to it, it's incumbent upon you to make sure your bosses know what you *think* you deserve and why. In preparation, highlight the deals or initiatives you worked on and any comps you can offer. Then, at the right moment, pounce with, "Pay me what you think is fair."

Bringing up fairness at the end of your negotiations can bridge that last mile. That's because once you've exhausted all the rational reasons for making your case, you're simply asking them to "do the right thing." This appeals to your boss's morality and self-worth. There's nothing like leveraging someone's love of themselves and feeling that they're morally superior to help your cause. Plus, no one wants to believe they're immoral, unjust, or an asshole.

Once I became the decider, I wanted to be on the right side of the moral code when compensating my employees for a job well done. There's always a little wiggle fund, and if it costs $10K to make someone happy, it's a "no brainer" in the context of the $100 million we were handing out in bonuses. Spencer Wang, a prominent veteran technology banker, called it a "Nuisance Reserve Fund." At Jefferies, we referred to it as "The Plug."

The Post-Mortem

Even if you got what you felt you deserved, always express at least a slight trace of disappointment. Walk out like a petulant child if you want, even if you're thinking, "Holy crap! I can't believe they're paying me this much to do monkey work!" Buy yourself something nice—but not too nice—then go back to work. Any euphoria will dissipate like Vicks VapoRub and you'll be left thinking, "Dang, another year of this. . . ."

On the other hand, if you think you got screwed, even if you're still wallowing in self-pity, don't get mad; get even. How? Generate some competition. Flaunt your wares. Show some leg. Make sure headhunters know you're ready to spread your wings at a moment's notice. Stop wasting your office hours on Tinder and focus on LinkedIn. Tinder can't get you a job, but a hot LinkedIn profile can get you a better one, get you more dough, and make you more appealing.

Key Takeaways

- Be on the winning side of the *zero-sum game*.
- Compensation is the ultimate barometer of how you're progressing in the organization.
- It's a business, not a charity; you'll be paid the least amount of money to keep you in your job.
- Beware of *lifestyle creep*.
- Use the *whisper wire* and only legal and ethical ways to find out your worth.
- Make sure your employer thinks you're in for the long-term.
- Lean on Yoda to advocate for you.
- All money is money—except not really.
- Use *pre-* and *post-mortems* to conquer your financial dreams. Bridge the information gap in negotiations.
- If at loggerheads, use my super-secret negotiation strategy: Make fairness your *third player*.

CHAPTER 20

Manage Your Way out of a Paper Bag

Get Others to Do Your Dirty Work

Investment bankers are renowned for being terrible managers. Belittling juniors, working them to exhaustion, and providing inadequate guidance are all par for the course. Wall Street, of course, doesn't have a monopoly on crappy bosses. Main Street is full of the same ineptitude. By now, you might be thinking that I must be one of them. In fact, almost everyone who has worked for me directly thought I was a pretty darn good manager and mentor. Don't believe me? Check out my public recommendations on LinkedIn or my website. Once you get over your disbelief, I'll share some of my secrets, including how to get those you're managing to labor hard, smart, and effectively while still maintaining comradery among your team.

Everyone knows that getting the other cave dwellers to do your bidding is among life's greatest challenges. This is especially true in the workplace, where the skills you need to get your team to pull a few all-nighters on a low probability pitch are the same as those your ancestors needed to encourage their Neanderthal brethren to lift the boulders while they feasted off the latest spoils in the nicest corner of the cave. Don't feel guilty. Every great master has a team to do the grunt work.

The joke (on you, of course) is that they don't teach what you *really* need to know in any school I've ever attended. Sure, there are entire university departments, HR training, and organizational psychology classes dedicated to the study of management. If you're working at a Fortune 500 company, leadership training of some sort may already have been foisted upon you, and if you've learned anything, it's exactly what many managers have learned by *not* attending them that really works. It can be summarized in the following quote, rumored to have come from Albert Einstein: "In theory, theory and practice are the same. In practice, they're not." Only by learning on the job do managers gain insight into what motivates their minions. Managers learn by trial and error, not with standardized formulas. Everyone is different so what works for a goose might not work for a gander. For those of you ready to take a nap, I'll lay my personalized advanced placement course in management on you in one short paragraph:

My management philosophy is centered around a very simple framework: the **Empowerment Model**.[1] My starting point with those who reported to me was to focus on their competence rather than their deficits, to support their resourcefulness rather than their weaknesses, and to help them develop skills rather than disparage them about their ignorance. I figured out what they were good at and where they were weak, and I helped them fill the gaps. But given that I'm human, and fear **loss aversion**, I expected the worst from people but hoped for the best. With time, I continued to lower my expectations because I got burned so many times by people underperforming that I was crispy on the outside.

Find Those Ticks

One of the most powerful ways to maximize your **return on time investment (ROTI)** is by motivating and mobilizing others to help *you* achieve *your* goals. Without the assistance of your team, you're just a single hired gun with no leverage on your own time. And time, even *you* know, is money.

As we've already established, getting humanoids to willingly do what you want is not as easy as it sounds. That's because fundamentally, no one wants to be told what to do. Just ask any four-year-old, although at any age, there is ample research showing that one of the key tenets of happiness is feeling that *you* are in control of your own destiny.[2] Being managed, of course, flies in opposition to this credence because, ultimately, you're doing what someone else wants you to do. That's what you're up against as a manager.

What's the solution? *Incentives.* For these to work, you need to know what motivates each member of your team. Yup, that's the key to good management. What makes your employees *tick*? What drives them? On Wall Street, like a lot of places, their motivation is pretty obvious—money and power, and money, and more money. In Silicon Valley, it might be the coolness of your project or the ease of access to free Philz coffee. In Hollywood, it could be rubbing shoulders with C-listers or getting social media ammo for your name-dropping escapades.

On Wall Street, knowing that investment bankers are naturally incented by wampum is the good news. The bad news is that because they're motivated by money, essentially everyone's a mercenary. And money is the most expensive way to incent someone. Attaboys, rah-rah speeches about changing the world, are way cheaper but not nearly as effective. But don't despair. You can use this clarity

---

[1]Roger K. Allen, PhD, is a leader in this field. https://www.rogerkallen.com/the-empowerment-model/
[2]According to a report by *The Journal of Personality and Social Psychology*, the number-one contributor to happiness is *autonomy*—defined as "the feeling that your life—its activities and habits—are self-chosen and self-endorsed." https://www.psychologytoday.com/us/blog/bouncing-back/201106/the-no-1-contributor-happiness

to your advantage. For example, as a manager, you can incent your team with the threat of *less* money and the lure of *more*. But know something about whence they came. Those from Wharton won't need anything from you aside from the money and an occasional lullaby singing their praises as the second coming of Gordon Gecko. As for the Stanford liberal arts major, not so much. They may be working on Wall Street because Daddy told them a museum curator job wouldn't cut muster when he's comparing parenting success with his bros at the local country club.

Despite what I said about the greedy wolves of Wall Street, you cannot assume to know what motivates each and every individual. Believe it or not, it's not always money. Well, maybe it *is* always about money, but it might be money *and* something else. Not knowing what that something else is constitutes an information gap which you, as manager, must fill by probing deeper. This is especially important if you think one of your direct reports is not giving it their all or resisting doing what you want them to do.

One banker who worked for me didn't seem particularly motivated, but when we sat down to discuss her career trajectory, she told me she had always wanted to work in China and was hoping I'd send her there. We had clients located in China, so I decided, "Sure, why not?" After spending my childhood years there, I certainly didn't want to move to China myself, but I could see the benefits of having someone on the ground. She became my lieutenant and worked tirelessly to help establish our presence there. Granting her the opportunity to achieve a particular career goal unleashed her capability and became a win-win for both of us.

In some businesses, there are myriad other incentives which drive human behavior—like making a mark on the world, improving the environment, helping children, or creating the best and most innovative product. You just have to figure out what motivates each particular person and leave it out there for them to grab after doing what you wanted them to do in the first place. But don't offer too many choices. Three is *bastante*. Decisions are pain points and can cause your strategy to backfire if a team member selects what you know is not the best option for you.

Decoy Your Way into Heaven

At the same time you want your people to do what they're told, you also want them *to feel like* they're *somewhat* in control. I had great success when I gave people choices about which deals to work on, although I often used the **decoy effect** to direct them toward the one I preferred. Anyone who purchases products online has been played by this tactic used by almost every Internet company.

You probably weren't aware of it (until reading this), but almost all choices are presented in three's: purchase options, shipping choices, and those hard-to-say-no add-ons. Why three? Because it's almost always the case that you're really being offered two choices. A third is introduced only to make one of them look better. And BINGO, that's the one you decide to take.

The **decoy effect** is a useful strategy not just for the Amazons of the world, but also as a manager. Everyone has good and bad clients. With my team, I'd always give them options on the deals they wanted to work on, but I'd usually have strings attached to make the *right* decision. If they wanted to work on this hot IPO, they'd need to crank out a bunch of marketing pitches. If they wanted me to fight for them during bonus season, they'd have to help me flog an M&A client that was harder to sell than haircuts at SantaCon. Often the most common requests from my team were around specific deals, conferences, and boondoggles. I'd willingly offer one or more if they did what I wanted and opted for a little bit of donkey work.

Let Them Eat Cake

In my world, to be a great manager, you have to give people agency, but with the important caveat that they have to *give* something to *get* something. If they want guidance, wisdom, or to be on a winning team to advance their career, what could *they* contribute? At the same time, as a manager, you also have to live up to your end of the bargain. That means you delegate and give people agency to take responsibility for their assignments. You've got to assume that they *want* to do a good job, not be freeloaders, and most important, live with the consequences of their own actions.

I used to give my team the freedom to spread their wings, but also just enough rope to hang themselves. When they'd say, "Hey, Dave, I think the client might be interested in this idea," I'd respond with, "Oh? Let's try it and see what happens." If they succeeded, great. I'd deserve Boss of the Week for letting them run with it and making a client happy. If not, I knew that by letting them fail, they'd learn an important lesson and no doubt do a better job the next time. Now, lest you think I'm a moron, I never let my team fail in front of a live client. I'd be there to rescue them if they were flailing or course-correct the discussion if it was trending into the sewer. It also gave me the higher ground if a similar impasse occurred in the future, as my underlings were less likely to question my judgment and more likely to acknowledge that maybe I wasn't ready to be put out to pasture. This method was way more effective than just saying, "I'm open to your opinion as long as we do it my way."

I know you won't be surprised that there's science behind this strategy. It's the **endowment effect** (also known as the **IKEA effect**), where people overvalue their own solutions and fail to appreciate the suggestions of others. While some execs go for the more traditional "Do as I say" method or its close cousin, "Unless we're in *Bizarro World*, I don't pay you to tell me what to do," I've found that allowing people to fail is more effective, particularly with those convinced they can do your job better than you. I could also be tough when I had to be. I never thought twice about telling a person outright that they had performed poorly, or that someone else could take their place, or that they had let the team down. My goal was always to get them to the point where they would ask themselves, "What would Dave do?"

Eliza Effing Doolittles

It was important to me that my people looked to me for answers not because I was a great person, but because I was smart, efficient, supportive, and fair. I needed my employees to *want* to work for me, and, because I led by example, for them to believe they could achieve things they couldn't have imagined when they were first hired. This is critical in competitive industries like Wall Street and management consulting where you're essentially up or out. People need to constantly punch above their weight to ensure career longevity. I wanted them to succeed and told them so, and more often than not, this resulted in a win-win for both of us.

This is the **Galatea effect** at work. No, it doesn't refer to the ivory statue carved a couple of thousand years ago by Pygmalion, the Cyprus king, but I'm impressed you know your Greek mythology. Actually, maybe it's related, since after falling in love with the statue, the goddess Aphrodite brings it to life and the happy couple marries. It's also called the **Pygmalion effect**, named after the George Bernard Shaw play, which became even more famous when it was turned into the musical *My Fair Lady*. This classic story is about Eliza Doolittle, a Cockney flower girl who takes speech lessons from a professor, Henry Higgins, so that she may pass as a lady. Higgins is an arrogant ass who treats women poorly and yet, in the musical at least, somehow still ends up with the girl. For you dudes out there, don't go fantasizing. It's set over a century ago.

At any rate, the **Galatea effect** is relevant to your career because it refers to situations in which a boss's positive expectations of you become self-fulfilling. For example, it's when that jerk associate gave me enough work to fill 140 hours but didn't really know if I could handle it. Dang, even I thought I might need last rites that week, but by pulling through, I proved to him, and myself, that I was freaking *Eliza Effing Doolittle*.

It's a mindscrew and it happens all the time in sports. When Joe Namath, New York Jets quarterback, famously guaranteed that his 18-point underdog team would win Super Bowl III, you really think he was 100 percent certain they could win? No, he had a great coach in Weeb Ewbank who believed in Joe and the team and probably deserved more credit than he got. In fact, it's like how I'll take full credit for your career success once you become a Master of the Universe after reading this book.

This is also a classic management device that works really well, especially for younger people who don't really know their ceiling. A cynic might think you're basically lying to kids. Guilty as charged! I had to overcome my own bias when I set my expectations low for young bankers and questioned whether they had it in them to complete a task above their pay grade. Of course, there was only upside for me. If they *did* succeed, I had not only identified future promotion material, but also got them to do more senior work at a lower compensation level. The house wins!

Sometimes, the rewards can be substantial. I had a VP who I wasn't sure would ever have the chops to make it to MD, let alone SVP. He had all the right fundamentals for his current level, but didn't appear to have the MD killer instinct needed to get clients to commit to pay handsomely for our services. I learned early in my career, "You don't ask; you don't get," and this VP definitely had a problem with directly asking for what he wanted. He was eager to prove himself, so I encouraged him to work on a prospect that was a real hard nut and was likely sucking our brains dry with no intention of ever hiring us. I told him, "If anyone can get this guy to hire a banker, I know it's you." My VP hounded the guy incessantly, giving him pro bono advice and feeding him fancy dinners. Finally, my VP wore him down and the prospect called to ask for an engagement letter. Today that VP is a very successful MD.

Another secret is to reward the *process* and not necessarily the *outcome*. In the banking world, a junior's life can be so miserable that it's important to praise early, publicly, and often while in the heat of battle—right after pulling an all-nighter, presenting at a pitch, or wrapping up a client meeting. This is especially important when your employees are trying something new or out of their comfort zone because it will encourage risk-taking. In the famous words of Waldo (Ralph Waldo Emerson, not that other guy), "Life is a journey, not a destination." The process is that journey.

Bret Pearlman learned from *his* mentor the importance of giving people the rah-rah speech and making them feel great. Anytime his team had worked around the clock, he would tell everyone to take their significant other to some outrageous restaurant, order a great bottle of wine, and send him the bill.

It's a Tragedy . . . of the Commons

It's a given that there's a pyramid in every organization, with each level leveraging the teams below them to do their work to make those at the top shine. Often, however, managers become greedy and overuse common resources, particularly in companies where employees have multiple bosses. This happens all the time in investment banking because you have a pool of juniors—analysts and associates—who work for multiple MDs, VPs, and SVPs. When I was at the worker bee level, for example, I didn't work for just one person. I was a commodity, tossed around by many masters, and it was to their advantage to work me to the bone because if they didn't, another senior banker would!

There's a name for this. It's called the **Tragedy of the Commons**, which is when every individual has an economic incentive to consume a resource but at the expense of every other individual. I believe the **Tragedy of the Commons** is one of the single biggest reasons junior bankers flame out on Wall Street. How can you not end up in a padded room when you have six different bosses asking you to perform six full-time jobs? Some people can't even do *one* job for *one* boss well.

I've seen it from both sides. From a manager's point-of-view, when I shared a pool of juniors, I empathized with their dilemma. Even though we had a system whereby a VP would be in charge of allocating resources like doling out food from a soup kitchen, MDs would always figure out a way to game the system by currying favor with the juniors. One MD would chum up to them by exclaiming, "Swinger! You're my guy!" and sprinkle in a few, "I love you, man!" Of course that endeared him to the naifs who all clamored to work for him, until one day he inadvertently left his office door open and was overheard saying to his five-year-old son, "Swinger! You're my guy! I love you, man!"

As for me, when the juniors chose their masters, I wanted them to ask themselves, "Who do I really want to work for? Who will best enhance my career? Who's my Yoda?" Yours truly. In addition, I'd play the empathy card. Before they pledged their allegiance to a senior banker, I wanted them to think, "Well, Dave's been *Groom of the Stool* so at least he knows what I'm going through." For you uneducated peasants, the *Groom* was the King's courtier who was responsible for helping the King with his toileting needs. It's unclear whether he actually had to wipe the King's ass, but at the very least, he needed to bring the bowl, towels, and other supplies to ensure the King had a good bowel movement. The analogy is apropos because like a junior banker, you do all the crap work for the MDs.

I've also experienced the **Tragedy of the Commons** as a commoner. *Prioritizing* who I was going to satisfy during my 16-hour workday was probably the most important thing I did to keep my sanity. Did that mean I was disappointing somebody? Absolutely, and it also made me enemies. Some senior bankers thought I was a lazy schmuck after *Matrix-bullet dodging* their request for me to work on their deals. I tried to avoid the truth, that I thought their deals sucked and that if I spent my time on them, my career would be dead in the water right after jumping into the pool. So I was always very careful to scope out the superstars. Of course, this had political repercussions if two senior bankers were fighting for my time, but I made it their problem by letting them duke it out themselves.

You're Yoda Now

Previously, I told you to *find* your Yoda. Now it's time for you to *be* Yoda. Become the mentor you either wished you had or, like I was, were *lucky* to have. Becoming a master trainer is easier said than done, however. For one thing, it necessitates a lot of inner reflection and identifying your blind spots. That's because most people in management are complete hypocrites. The biggest culprits are those who lead from a "Do as I say, not as I do" perspective. Nothing frustrates (and pisses off) junior staff more than having a senior person give them an assignment which he has no idea how to do himself. As an associate, I was staffed with a VP who was hired because of his industry relationships and had no background in investment banking. He asked me to put together a dozen scenarios highlighting all the ways we could do a **leveraged buyout (LBO)** of a target company. I responded, "You do know that this company can't support any debt?" He looked at me sheepishly and said, "Do it anyway." From that day forward, I avoided him like the plague. So be forewarned, acolytes have a keen eye and can see through their emperor's new clothes.

One of *my* most effective tools as a manager was always to lead by example. That's how everyone learns, which is why I never make my employees do something I wouldn't, or haven't already, done myself. A lot of managers *say* that's how they operate, but from my experience, it's usually hogwash.

As a parting thought, I remind myself of the words of Roman philosopher Seneca who said, "Treat your inferiors as you would be treated by your betters." Of course, he meant this in the context of his slaves, which is completely inappropriate given we're using Wall Street as an example. Right?

Better Than Sex

There are a lot of great third-party resources to assist you in shepherding your flock. I'm a big fan, for example, of Angela Duckworth, professor of psychology at Penn, author,[3] and CEO of Character Lab, a nonprofit she created to promulgate her science-based research to underscore how **grit** helps people (especially children) survive and succeed. I'm not referring to some porridge that looks like a dog's breakfast; I'm referring to your ability to take crap and soldier on. Duckworth reveals what she has found to be the secret behind *grit*: a unique combination of passion and persistence. Her roadmap to success can help you understand why that one junior is suddenly more passive aggressive than a Taylor Swift song or help identify why someone on your team went from Isaac Newton to Apple Newton.[4] Once you discover these root causes, you can whip your people into shape so they can help you achieve *your* goals.

Another author I'd suggest you look to for inspiration is Dale Carnegie, seriously old school. His classic mega-seller, *How to Win Friends & Influence People*, has sold more than 30 million copies worldwide. It's one of the few books that's required reading at Harvard Business School and has sold more copies than *The Joy of Sex*. It's helped me get back to first principles for everything from convincing a company to hire me to getting my youngest son to wash his hands after a Number One, Two, or Three.[5]

I know Carnegie's words of wisdom might seem elementary, but make no mistake, they are some great gems.[6] Here's my take:

---

[3]Angela Duckworth, *GRIT, The Power of Passion and Perseverance* (2016).

[4]Apple didn't always make cool stuff. This Personal Digital Assistant was introduced almost three decades ago and was a royal flop. It did lead to the creation of your bathroom buddy, the iPhone, so that's something to be thankful for.

[5]I bet some of you didn't know there is a Number Three? In fact, there are a Number Four and Five, but they aren't suitable for this book. That fact alone just got you your money's worth.

[6]Dale Carnegie, *How to Win Friends & Influence People* (1936).

- *Praise, Encourage, and Appreciate.* Author Mehmet Murat ildan says, "In the empire of desert, water is the king." Slogging away on Wall Street can at times feel like a desert wasteland, so showering compliments early and often can go a long way in getting your team from one watering hole to the next. In fact, if you really want it to linger, do this publicly for all to see.

- *Identify Mistakes.* Everyone makes mistakes, so if your subordinate commits one, identify it early and help correct it. If it happens again, then you have my permission to fire them.

- *Show You're Human.* It's easy for juniors to think of you as something less than human, particularly if you're a royal jerk. So don't be. Admit your own mistakes before critiquing theirs, but do this sparingly lest they think you're a moron. And ask questions instead of giving direct orders. Who knows, you might actually learn something.

- *Aim High and Save Face.* Use the **Galatea effect** and help them build a reputation. They might surprise you. If they come up short or screw up, don't depants them, especially in public. Let them save face.

- *Give Them Ownership.* This is a good tactic for not just subordinates, but also partners and bosses. Whenever possible, try to make the other person think it was their idea. Making them happy about doing something you suggested means you win!

Don't Be a B-Player

When I was an undergraduate at Penn, we studied one of history's worst industrial disasters that occurred at a Union Carbide pesticide factory in Bhopal, India. The case study made a huge impression on me. If you've never heard of it, in 1984 an enormous poisonous gas cloud from the plant leaked into the atmosphere. Some estimate that it killed 16,000 people and seriously impacted another 600,000, many with permanent disabilities. Thirty-seven years later, people on the ground are still suffering.

After extensive investigations, the primary blame was attributed to sloppy management and poor oversight. My own biggest takeaway was the danger of hiring B-level employees, because mediocre B-people hire C-people, who hire D-people, who then hire F-people. Union Carbide took this road to ruin to new heights. It had B-managers in the United States, who hired C-people in India, who trained others who over time became D-people. No wonder Union Carbide's engineers had no clue how to activate the simple safety devices that could have stopped poisonous elements from being released into the atmosphere. The solution was as simple as closing your refrigerator door after getting a snack.

That case study really impressed upon me that you can't expect people to do A-level work if you give short shrift to their training. At some point, it will catch up to you, and time after time I saw that it did on Wall Street.

Here are a few fat-finger specials that illustrate shocking levels of incompetence. In January 2017, Morgan Stanley paid $13 million to settle charges that it overbilled its advisory clients due to billing errors. In April 2016, Goldman Sachs screwed up a share count and shortchanged Tibco Software's shareholders by $100 million in a go-private transaction. In the summer of 2020, in what a federal judge called, "One of the biggest blunders in banking history," instead of wiring $8 million to Revlon's lenders, Citigroup accidentally sent almost a billion dollars. They admitted it was a clerical error, sued to get their money back, and lost. Revlon's lenders kept $500 million. And here you thought you were having a bad day.

Remember, you get what you give. GIGO—garbage in, garbage out, but you can turn it around and make it VIVO[7]—value in, value out. So please, please, please—take the time to train your employees to be their best, to be *your* best. For God's sake, be an A-manager who trains only A-level people.

Escape from Alcatraz

When I returned to Jefferies after business school, I started managing the people below me. How well I did at delegation and getting my team and others to cooperate was an attention grabber for promotion. But there's a weird contradiction in that statement, which can be explained by another social-scientific term, called the **prisoner's dilemma**.[8] It's a well-known game theory that explains why two rational human beings might not cooperate even if it's in their best interest to do so. It should help you understand why you might find resistance among your direct reports.

Imagine two people, Abbott and Costello, are arrested and placed in separate cells, unable to communicate with each other. They're charged with insider trading, but the prosecutors have only enough evidence to convict them of a lesser charge. The lawyers offer each scoundrel the same plea bargain: They can testify against the other and receive less jail time, or they can choose to remain silent.

There are four possible outcomes:

- If Abbott and Costello each betray the other, they both serve two years in prison.
- If Abbott betrays Costello but Costello remains silent, Abbott will be set free and Costello will serve three years.

---

[7]Conveniently, *vivo* in Spanish means "alive."
[8]The prisoner's dilemma was discovered by mathematicians Merrill Flood and Melvin Dresher while working at RAND in 1950. It was formalized and named by another mathematical genius, Albert W. Tucker.

- If Costello betrays Abbott but Abbott remains silent, Costello will be set free and Abbott will serve three years.
- If Abbott and Costello both remain silent, they will each serve one year in prison on the lesser charge.

On the surface, it appears that one betraying the other offers the greater possibility of the rat getting off scot-free. But another brilliant mathematician, Professor John Nash,[9] proffered another theory, eponymously called the **Nash equilibrium**. He said that to solve a perceived dilemma, you need to work together, so in the case of the prisoners, it would be better either for both of them to rat out the other and serve two years or not to say anything at all and serve only one.

What does this have to do with being an effective manager? Everything! The entire workplace is one big **prisoner's dilemma**, in that everyone is competing for a limited, and shrinking, number of positions as you go higher up the **corporate ladder**, and yet all of you have to work together in order to achieve success for the company. This is especially problematic in cyclical or dying industries, because not only is a united front needed to battle competitors, but also the overall pie, and available jobs, may be shrinking. This leads to infighting, subterfuge, and that favorite office pastime, the blame game.

Once I rose to a managerial position, I encountered my own version of the **prisoner's dilemma**. In one-on-one meetings, people would often complain about another member of my team. Someone would come into my office, close the door, and whine, "I can't get this done because such and such analyst is a few cents short of a penny." Or "The VP needs to get a real job—somewhere else." Before I wised up, I spent way too much time trying to determine who was telling the truth, until I learned that everyone lies—it's just a question of how much!

Thanks to John Nash, I found a solution. I told all my direct reports that there would be no more one-on-one complaints. If anyone had a problem, I would convene the team and we'd hash it out together—in public. Dissent and criticism would be encouraged, but only in a respectful manner. I reminded them we had a common goal: to make money. "I'll be judge, jury, and executioner," I said, but added, "If I find out you're BS-ing me, there will be hell to pay!"

Once you confront the **prisoner's dilemma** head on, the situation is never as clear-cut as either party thinks it is. There's always a gray area, although nobody ever admits that. No one says, "Yeah, I *am* kind of a moron." But the more you communicate openly and with empathy, the more you put people at ease and can bond over common obstacles and goals. Figuring this out had many positive benefits for me. First, I had happy teams who collaborated willingly. Second, we made a boatload of money. And third, I came off looking like Solomon.

---

[9]Nash was the subject of the Oscar-winning film, *A Beautiful Mind*, starring Russell Crowe as the Nobel Prize–winning genius who also struggled with mental illness.

Guanxi, Baby!

This chapter has been all about influencing your team so they feel creative, independent, and appreciated. But it's also important to know that *trust* is the currency of business.

The Chinese call it **Guanxi** (关系), having personal trust and a strong relationship with another person. It's often translated as *connections, relationships,* or *networks*. That's why it's common for Chinese businesspeople to conduct initial meetings in informal settings, like restaurants and karaoke bars, to create a foundation for their future wheeling and dealing. Of course, this might lead to nepotism and cronyism but those are very minor details. . . .

Now consider how to build **Guanxi** between you and your team. Of course, it's to your advantage to make them *like* you, but the imperative is to make sure they *trust* you. One of my SVPs recited a story to me that went viral among the junior ranks. An analyst was waiting at the elevator banks and when she spotted me said, "How are you doing?" I replied curtly, "Yes." In my defense, I was probably engrossed in an email about a billion-dollar merger or checking my fantasy football scores, but even now as I write this I'm thinking, "What a jackass!" But it didn't affect how much my team worked their tails off for me because they trusted that I could do the job even if I was a jerk—sometimes.

So likeability isn't a prerequisite, but you'll get more out of your team if they trust they've jumped on the right wagon to advance their career. They'll go the extra mile and are less likely to abandon you in a crisis. So always give your people clear direction and honest feedback. Be straightforward about their progress and specific about their negatives. How else will your peeps know their blind spots and be given the opportunity for improvement?

In industries where there is a lot of distrust, take a page from social psychologist David Yeager. His methodology, which he calls **wise feedback**, is great for giving feedback across racial divides where there can be enormous distrust.[10] I've found it's especially effective in the treacherous world of Wall Street. Whenever you give anyone constructive feedback, you preface it with the following:

"I'm giving you these comments because I have very high expectations and I know that you can reach them."

Why does this look familiar? Because it's the **Shit Sandwich**! My version would be prefaced with the following:

"OK, look, I know you can be great, but you better get your act together. Here's how. . . ."

See how much better that tastes?

Give feedback often and early so members of your team can improve, and along the way be sure to differentiate *good mistakes* from *bad* ones. *Good* is when they worked hard and it didn't happen; *bad* is when they got lucky and the deal still went

---

[10]David Scott Yeager, "Breaking the Cycle of Mistrust: Wise Interventions to Provide Critical Feedback Across the Racial Divide" (University of Texas at Austin, August 12, 2013).

through. And keep these frank tête-à-têtes outside the compensation discussions. If they don't assume your criticism will directly harm their compensation (which it might, of course), they won't be so defensive. Take a page from the Chinese and spring your critique in a place they least expect it, like at a Denny's, Starbucks, or a Rockets game, where they'll be most open to really hearing you.

Here are some final easy to-do's that will strengthen **Guanxi** between you and your team:

- *Reciprocate.* Be a back scratcher! Bribes work, but don't buy off people with trinkets. Save your powder for the really big stuff, like flying private on an IPO roadshow or dining at The French Laundry. Then you won't get lip when you ask them to jump on the Redeye to deliver books to a board meeting in New York.

- *Be Friends.* Friends don't leave others hanging, especially when a third all-nighter is needed to make the bakeoff deadline. They also don't let drunk MDs drive home after a closing dinner. Their significant other will thank you.

- *Use Reverse Psychology.* Make them think you've got the Midas touch, even if you don't, so they'll want to work on your deals. But play hard to get. If they think you're a superstar, there will be groupies banging down your door in no time.

- *Establish Rule of Law.* You may be buds with your team, but never let them forget who's the boss. It's a slippery slope from "Dave's super cool" to "Dave will be totally chill about the financial model not balancing." If you find yourself at the bottom of that slope, you only have yourself to blame.

- *Wield Your Power Wisely.* There will be times when you need to just say, "Because I said so." When that time comes, don't be afraid to wield Thor's hammer. Someone needs to spend all night getting that pitchbook ready and it's not going to be you.

Never forget that empowerment is the name of the game; coercion and micro-managing are not. It's all about creating an atmosphere of positive **Guanxi**. Of course, if all else fails, fear is always an option. You're the boss, after all.

Key Takeaways

- Manage using the *Empowerment Model*.
- Find out what makes your people tick. Build incentives around them.
- Give people agency, but use the *decoy effect* to get them to do what you want.
- Master the *Galatea effect* to mold your junior into Eliza Doolittle.
- Beware of the *Tragedy of the Commons* and be Yoda.
- Read a few books, learn from the masters, and don't be Union Carbide.
- *Guanxi* gets you everywhere, but, if all else fails, rule by fear.

PART 3

Winning Time

CHAPTER 21

Win the Game of Thrones

Get Promoted in a Dog-Eat-Dog World

Admit it . . . before you even entered the workforce, maybe while you were still riding around on training wheels, you imagined yourself in business nirvana, sitting in the executive suite behind a sleek desk with windows overlooking the world. With a touch of a button, you'd have more of everything—more compensation, more respect, more power, to say nothing of the most expensive laptop in the world, the Voodoo Envy H171. I assume it's called that because when you stick digital pins into your mortal corporate enemies, they bleed, and everyone is jealous of your psychic powers.

No worries. If you've followed my sage advice thus far, your promotion should be a foregone conclusion. That, of course, assumes you have taken to heart Shirley MacLaine's counsel that "Life is just one big performance." The transmigrating, Oscar-winning actress is correct. It's not about what you've *actually* done; it's what people *think* you've done that gets you closer to the top.

Harry Nelis, former Goldman Sachs banker and now partner at the venture capital firm Accel, explained it well when he told me, "The big takeaway is that those who project the most self-confidence tend to get promoted and paid the most. You can still keep your head down and work hard and not play the game, but you know what will happen? You're never going to get anything early. No early promotion, no early compensation, nothing."

Harry offers two different examples to make his point. Early in his career, he had two colleagues. One was a young professional who everyone knew from the watercooler talk was jonesing for a promotion. Very respectfully, he began asking around the office for tips about how to make it happen. He even dropped a bread-crumb or two that he had spoken to a friend at a competitor and knew his *Greater Fool* number.

At the same time, there was another colleague vying for the same position who was clearly a rock star, deserved to be promoted, but had never discussed it with anyone. "It was an interesting lesson for me," says Harry, "because the first person got promoted and even got a pay increase even though the nonpolitical one was more deserving."

You need to work hard and not be a dolt, of course, but Harry's point is that you need to be vocal and self-confident, and vocal about being self-confident—in a constructive, nonthreatening way.

Chris McGowan, former managing director at Madison Dearborn, former banker at Morgan Stanley, and now adjunct professor at the University of Chicago's Booth School of Business, agrees, saying that to be promoted to the top, you can't just be a closer. You can't expect people to read your mind. You need to constantly telegraph what you want and think you deserve. "You can't always expect other people to promote you or sing your praises," he explains.

Prepare for Battle Royale

Since we know there's very little elbow room at the summit, and you're fully aware that everybody is playing the same game of musical chairs, clearly a lot needs to work in your favor to land that prized promotion. Sometimes it might be a stroke of luck, like a senior exec retiring early, your deal winning Deal of the Year, or per-haps an MD accidentally sending you a sext which may come in handy later. While biding your time, you've got to position yourself in the right place to steal the flag and fight for that coveted seat. It's the *Game of Thrones*, with a ton of closed-door politics that everyone knows is played in the shadows.

Understanding the intense competition you're up against makes it even more important to look out for Number One, because no one else will. Sure, your orga-nization wants to get the right leaders running the right groups, but maybe they're hedging their bets. Everyone's replaceable, even the POTUS, so if you get abducted by aliens, there will always be another who can do your job. Even if your Yoda goes to bat for you, you can't be assured that some Mr. Magoo will see eye-to-eye with your mentor's selection. So it's all about what you do leading up to the moment you feel it's time to be promoted.

Some of you may be thinking, "I'm perfectly happy where I am" or "I'm risk averse. Besides, my coworkers are like family; we're not like those mercenary cutthroats on Wall Street." Well, Dorothy, you ain't in Kansas anymore. *All* businesses are under pressure to grow, and that means constantly improving and innovating. The only way to do that is to kill complacency. If you're one of those worker bees who thinks they can naively hide in their corner, you're in for a rude awakening. Refusing to play the game and not moving up the ladder can actually be the *riskier* move. One day, you may get a call from your boss where they say you're being replaced by a younger, cheaper, hungrier, better-looking model. So for the conservative among you, take heed. Standing pat may actually be your one-way ticket out of the game.

Strapping on your combat boots is even more crucial if you're not part of the majority class, because the battle will be even more fierce and you're going to have to try even harder. Just like in every other high-powered industry, I repeatedly saw women and people of color fail to land the promotions they deserved, and as a result, many high-quality people I knew left Wall Street demoralized.

As an outsider myself, while I may not have looked like an average member of the tribe, I sure could talk like one, dress like one, and act like one. My ace in the hole was an infinite amount of cynicism. I knew full well nobody was going to be looking out for me, and ironically, I'm convinced that's what enabled me to ascend. Like a six-footer looking to make the NBA, I had an unyielding mindset that I had to shoot an almost perfect game to reach the next job title I desired.

Specialize Your Way to Nirvana

To make yourself really valuable, and thus increase your potential for promotion, consider becoming an expert in something. It could be an industry subsector, a programming language, a type of trading, even a form of art. Anything to be **Unus** and stand apart from the mob. That's because if others see your talents as helpful to their own ambitions, they may carry you on their wings to glory. So if faced with the choice of becoming a black belt in a valued area, or being above average in many things, I choose the former. Not standing out in any way can be a recipe for expendability.

When you're an Asian with a disability, you can't half-ass your way to success. That's how I knew I had to specialize early and with finesse. I valued my advancements because tactically, titles define who you are, and if you don't get the one you've had your eyes on, where do you really stand? We're living in a world where people's worth, pecking order, and how much money they deserve is defined by their title. So make no mistake, I pursued job titles aggressively, and by age 33,

I was co-running the Digital Media and Internet Group at Jefferies as one of the youngest MDs in the firm's history. By that time, Jefferies was among the top dozen investment banks in the world, so that meant I was like a bouncer at an exclusive night club. I was among a dozen people anywhere making decisions about which Internet startups would go public or be flogged for a gazillion dollars.

We'd all fight for Facebook and Twitter, but also mine for gold wherever else we could find it. I was a frog in an already fast-growing pond, but I chose to hang out at a lily pad called Adtech, or advertising technology. In layman's terms, it's the core technology that powers ads online that entice you to buy products that only five seconds ago you *thought* you needed. It's highly technical, lucrative, and full of tech companies that have mastered the art of gathering data, which they sell to the highest bidder.

Other bankers were drawn to the consumer Internet sector where the sexy start-ups were germinating. Don't get me wrong. I like sexy as much as the next person, and I routinely worked with companies like Google and Yelp, but I also knew that if I wanted to develop a name for myself, I needed to offer something others did not. I needed to be **Unus**, so I focused on Adtech, and for a while I was one of the top bankers in that subsector, regularly beating out the Goldmans and the Stanleys of the world who had a better brand and a wider platform.

Some senior bankers at other firms couldn't tell the difference between Adtech and Aztec. They were great BS artists in a one-hour client pitch, but stretch that meeting by a minute longer and they'd turn into pumpkins faster than Cinderella's carriage. They'd be exposed to know only what some junior scrub compiled into a PIB for them the night before and understood less about Adtech than your average teenage web surfer. Like politicians, these competitors relied on second-, third-, or even fourth-hand opinions to make their case. Would you take advice from your second cousin living in the Appalachian Mountains on anything other than how to hunt for rats? I rest my case.

Even Rocket Ships Need Janitors

One of *my* biggest strokes of luck came before my career even started—choosing the right firm. I wish I could say I was a genius in making my decision, that I predicted this small investment bank was going to rise like a rocket ship in the next 20 years. In truth, I was mostly intrigued with the money. I was poor. My parents were poor. And when I got my offer, it was like, "Holy crap, that's a lot of dough!"

I was still an undergraduate at Penn and I kept quiet about how much I would be making. I didn't want my friends to be envious. My plan was foiled at graduation when my buddy sitting next to me pointed to a classmate sitting a few rows ahead of us who had taped $76,000 in white numbers on the top of his cap. Obnoxious, I know, but we were all obnoxious; we assumed that in 10 years, we'd be Masters of the Universe.

"Isn't that guy going to be working with you at Jefferies?" my friend asked me. "Yeah, I guess so," I admitted.

"And you're making the same salary?"

"Yup." I had been outed!

At the time, I thought this $76,000 dude had gone beyond the pale in obnoxiousness, but he was already practicing what I didn't yet know—Harry Nelis's advice to be the loudest voice in the room. Indeed, this former classmate had no problems ascending the ladder. He's one of the smartest people I've ever met, and today he's a senior partner at one of the largest private equity firms in the world, probably making a thousand times what he broadcasted on the top of his head a couple of decades earlier.

While the big bucks made it easy for me to choose Jefferies, I took a huge risk when I turned down job offers at the larger firms. Somehow I resisted our old friend, **zero-risk bias**, which is where we prefer the option that totally eliminates risk, ignoring that it also eliminates a greater upside. This plays to our desire to have complete control over a single, not particularly exciting, outcome, while resisting our other natural desire for more.

Instead, I stumbled inadvertently into the **behavioral economics** subgroup, **Prospect Theory**, which assumes that individuals make decisions based on perceived gains instead of perceived losses. Sometimes you just have to take the plunge, even if you hate the cold water.

Eric Schmidt, Google's ex-CEO, is famous for saying to prospective employees: "When you're offered a seat on a rocket ship, you don't ask, 'What seat?' You just climb aboard."

I used to give a variation of this to new analysts and associates looking to join my team. I'd explain how I had joined a rocket ship and how its growth propelled my career forward. But for the really ambitious among them, I'd tell them to first master the basics before trying to steal my job. "Even a rocket ship needs a janitor, so start scrubbing."

Feed the Money Machine

By the time you get even halfway up the corporate hierarchy, your focus has to be on doing whatever it takes to generate revenue. It's the lubricant that slides you further along your career and the only surefire way to get promoted. On Wall Street, that means getting your greedy little mitts on as many deals as possible. You're never too junior to start thinking this way, so here's the right mindset to have:

- *No Such Thing as Small Deals.* Tag along on the deals, or projects, that have the biggest fees. There is no such thing as small deals—just small *fees.*
- *Don't Go Down with the Ship.* If you're sailing in barren waters, don't be afraid to abandon ship and switch bosses, departments, or even firms. Forget chivalry.

Get in the lifeboat before the women and children grab those choice seats in money-gushing departments.

- *Become a Horseshoe.* **Parlay** initial success by becoming a lucky charm. We're all superstitious; otherwise, we wouldn't mind if someone said, "Bad luck today!" Bankers are notoriously so. Make your bosses think your mere presence will ensure a deal's success, and when it happens, you'll be the horseshoe everyone wants up their behind.

- *Pick Wisely.* A huge part of being successful is picking the right company, the right team, the right deal. Others may recall that you were on the deal but not that all you did was format the presentation. So choose your deals wisely. What's a good deal? One that closes!

How do you know if a prospect could be a gusher? At the junior levels, it's all about following your nose. Stick with the seniors who have a track record for getting deals done. They're easy to spot. They've been with the firm for years. Clients love them. They may have not just one, but two assistants because their phones are ringing off the hook.

What if you're already a senior banker trying to make MD? How do you choose? Well, it's figuring out not just which deals to do, but also which ones *not* to do. Some are just not meant to happen: the merger of one great company and one lousy one; the IPO of a business that feels more Ponzi than perfect. Over time, you learn what works and what doesn't. Here are a few simple hacks that I used to figure out where to dig for buried treasure:

- *Rising Tide Lifts All Boats.* You can certainly fish in ponds that are stagnant or drying up, but then all you're left with is mosquitos and dying fish. Some of these are obvious, like going for digital media rather than book publishing, but the true senior banker identifies not just the right pond to fish, but the exact spot that will yield the biggest catch. Spot the nascent green shoots and place a bet on yourself. It's always better to be early rather than late, so be the first to anchor your boat and pray the tide comes in.

- *Become a Data Junkie.* In this day and age, the data are out there. You just need to know where to look. When I was trying to figure out where to fish, I knew that growth would be where I would find the most opportunity, so I simply followed the money. I'd track where the smart VCs were placing their bets and where the brightest entrepreneurs were rolling their dice. I'd use LinkedIn and other job sites to see who was hiring small armies to build products of the future. From there, I'd determine who was making money hand over fist. If Yoda was a banker, he would say, "Growth is the path to deals. Growth leads to VC. VC leads to jobs. Jobs lead to products. Products lead to revenue. Revenue leads to deals."

- *Join the Clubs.* Private clubs and secret gatherings where backroom dealings and secret handshakes lead to mega-deals have been a staple of American business since the dawn of the Union. I'm not just talking about the clubs that are invitation-only that you've likely never heard of, like The Bohemian Club, The Family, or Young Presidents' Organization, but also private cabals where founders of hot companies swap tactics on how to build their empires. For example, we'd host an all-expenses-paid soirée at Pebble Beach, where CEOs and their spouses would be treated to a weekend of golf and spa treatments. Behind closed doors, we'd have guest speakers like the commissioner of Major League Baseball spill the beans on performance-enhancing drug use or leaders of the CIA explain how close we really got to World War Three. Of course, we'd sprinkle in a few "working sessions," but for the most part, it was an opportunity for CEOs to mingle, relax, and get a few holes in before heading back to the office. If a few of them got sauced and revealed their secret criteria for hiring bankers, consider that a happy coincidence.

- *Date Around.* Banking at the senior level is a sales job and sales is a numbers game. Given the long sales cycle and competitive nature of Wall Street, if you want to win deals, you need to date—a lot. I would make it a point to meet every Internet company multiple times a month. Information is the currency of investment bankers and the key to opening doors. In fact, the more I dated around, the more appealing I became. After a while, not only did I know which companies had real traction and which ones were full of hot air, I also knew which might be in play. I knew who just got an inbound call from Google, who was about to win a large deal with Apple, and who was under investigation by the DOJ. Once I became known as the pantomath of the sector, I became everyone's welcome guest to tea, and when the time came to consider raising money or selling their company, guess who they'd call? That Chinese guy who seemed to know everybody's business.

Getting promoted is directly correlated to taking big risks that handsomely reward the firm, as well as you, the instigator. But be forewarned that feeding your company's money machine can get more difficult over time. As a company matures, **risk aversion** can seep in, which can cramp your style faster than running in dry heat. When I first started at Jefferies, and for many years afterwards, we were a scrappy firm where our collective mission was to grow the business. Taking a risk on a crazy project or client tended to be a no-brainer because all we could think about was the potentially huge upside. At some point, however, a line was drawn, maybe eight or nine years into my tenure, when the deal-making became more about "protecting the franchise" than making the big score.

Here's a classic example. In 2001 when I was a VP, I got a call out of the blue from a VP at Google. Now, this executive didn't know me from a hole in the wall but had gotten my name from three board members at Google who knew me well. The

VP told me that one of Google's founders wanted to sell $1 million worth of stock to buy his first house and asked if Jefferies would be interested. But the VP told me there were several caveats. First, I would *not* get any financial information, because plenty of people had already expressed interest and they didn't really need us to say yes. Second, the valuation was non-negotiable, at $300 million, and we'd be buying common stock, which is riskier than preferred if the company should fail but would still pay nicely if the company took off.

Oh, and one other thing. I had 24 hours to make a decision.

I immediately called our CFO. After my spiel, he said to me, "Are you nuts? There's no way we would ever do this. We're not a casino. We're an investment bank."

In hindsight, I think this VP thought of me as a chump who could do a trade like this quickly, with no information, and no questions asked. What they didn't take into account was the more risk-averse Jefferies. So we passed, and the rest is history.

Keep Your Head on a Swivel

For my own promotion strategy, I not only satisfied the requirements of *my* job, but also the job of the boss one rung above me. Nothing was too small or embarrassing to ingratiate my way into the next level. As an analyst, I kissed the asses of the associates by picking up their takeout, taking middle seats at the back of the plane, and giving them the complimentary NBA tickets we'd get from our vendors. I also elbowed my way into that next level by doing *their* job as well as mine, even triple-checking their work, all the while allowing them to get credit for my work and at the same time letting the associates think *they* knew how to manage *me*. I volunteered to be part of as many deals as possible, often choosing ones that were risky and therefore scoffed at by others. Most important, I took care of Numero Uno by gaining a well-deserved reputation as the workaholic who could complete every assignment with speed and competence.

Analysts tend to burn out quickly, which is why the job is usually viewed as a short tour of typically two years. Like many others, I opted to save my sanity and escape from Alcatraz (aka Wall Street) with a brief stint at Harvard Business School. This is a common route for anyone looking to change careers, get some new drinking buddies, or screw off for a few years without their parents wondering why they suddenly need money again. But it's not easy. The handful of top business schools have a secret quota that prevents them from hiring too many people from any one firm, which means you're competing with the grunt in the next cubicle for the same very limited spots. We didn't, for example, share our application essays with each other. Not that it mattered. We all knew they were filled with similarly hyperbolic BS, like "During my 170-hour a week job, I was basically running the place and curing cancer!"

After Harvard I returned to Jefferies and knew I had to hone my nonexistent managerial skills. (At business school the only thing I learned how to manage was my blood alcohol content level.) So I had three immediate, very specific goals with regard to managing my coworkers:

- *Juniors*. To oversee these hooligans and make sure they goose-stepped to my every whim. After all, I needed to give the impression that I was running a tight ship and not some two-bit operation lest it spoil my chances for ascension.
- *Peers*. To protect myself from my peers who were equally enamored with the idea of more pay, power, and promotion. Shallow bastards!
- *Bosses*. And most of all, to manage my bosses who were vying to keep their own sweet gigs going by doing the least bang for the most buck.

Nobody really teaches you any of this in school, or at work for that matter, so you have to learn it on your own. You'd better exercise your neck muscles so you can train your head to be on a swivel—effectively managing the juniors below you, which is the job you're supposed to be doing; managing your peers so they don't outshine you; and managing upwards so it becomes obvious you are senior banker material. Once I made it to VP, my eyes were immediately on the next prize: SVP.

Like all senior roles right below partner, the SVP level on Wall Street is the most dangerous way station on Wall Street. You're expensive, so you have to start generating revenue while at the same time constantly keeping your eyes in front of you because the MDs are threatened by you and will do everything in their power to block your path to making them expendable.

Because I knew that my neck was most vulnerable at the SVP level, my main tactic as SVP was to move out of that position as fast as possible. The way I decided I could do that was by lobbying all the MDs who weren't my boss, showing them I was doing a great job, and most important, showing them that I deserved revenue credit for deals. Being a good recruiter, a team player, and an all-around nice person were table stakes to getting considered, but much like most things in life, all that really mattered was revenue. And the key to that was deals, deals, and more deals.

I used multiple techniques to impress upon the higher-ups that I was deserving. For one, remember that your psyche is split into **Two Selves**, the *Experiencing Self* who lives your life and the *Remembering Self* who is the evaluator of those experiences that decides your future. The *Experiencing Self* has a powerful tendency to assume that what you see is all there is. It's why we generally think beautiful people are friendly and less attractive people are not. It's why baseball scouts make mistakes by ignoring a *Moneyball* analysis because a player "looks real good." So I made sure I looked the part. I may not have been a great banker, but I could play a good one on TV.

I also exploited the *Remembering Self* by projecting my sincere belief that I had made a significant contribution to any deal I touched. In most cases, that was true, so I was also aware of the **halo effect**, understanding that the *overall impression* influences how we think and feel about a person's character. I made sure that on my year-end deal sheets, I'd clearly state the deals that I not only executed for my MDs, but also the ones where I played Man Friday. I wasn't stupid enough to think that I'd be paid for the ones I merely supported, but at least I gave the impression that I wasn't just out for myself, but vested in growing the overall pie.

Making My Own Destiny

Sourcing my own deals would be my ticket to promotion, so I started to cold call prospects. I segmented the market into four categories: *Corpses*, *Lepers*, *Crabs*, and *Nymphs*:

- *Corpses* were companies that were walking dead and likely didn't have much growth, but might be interested in hiring a banker to put them out of their misery.
- *Lepers* were those high-growth companies that were making money by siphoning personal information like Google or Facebook, but didn't have the heft or diversity to bury their money machine beneath mountains of do-gooding or "Do No Evil" mission statements.
- *Crabs* were hermit companies whose founders never met with bankers because they thought we represented the scum of the earth.
- *Nymphs* were those blindly sexy companies that every banker wanted but few could ever attain.

I became a telemarketer and went for volume, using every second I wasn't executing some other MD's deals to fish for my own prospects. At first, I got mostly responses of "Jefferies? Who?" or "Thanks, but unless you lend us a gazillion dollars, we're giving our business to J.P. Morgan" or "We're brand whores and we'd never sleep with you."

It was tough sledding, but slowly, I was a recipient of the old adage that you raise money when you don't need it. *Corpses* would need help to sell themselves and salvage whatever they had left. *Lepers* needed to find that one Greater Fool hiding in Outer Mongolia to invest in their company. *Crabs* decided maybe now was time to come out of their shell and monetize their life's work. And *Nymphs*, well many of them still told me I wasn't worthy of licking their toes, but I started to get enough nibbles to start building my own book of business.

Of course, winning the deal is only half the battle. You also need to sell your organization on approving and staffing it, so I also learned how to win internal approval. I did this by practicing my variation of the **Sinister Six Syndrome**, which you may recall is when foes call truce to defeat a common enemy. As I approached the upper echelons of management, there were parties who became aligned with me out of mutual self-interest. For instance, even though I was still just an SVP, I convinced my bosses that I'd give them full credit for the deals I did, thus neutering their fears that I was stealing food from their children.

Whatever level I was working—analyst, associate, VP, or MD—I played the part of the rung above me and helped my bosses *visualize* me doing a great job at the next level. How do you put this into practice? You might not yet be an MD (or any senior executive), but you can imagine, both in your mind and in action, that you're already in that position. In other words:

- If you're an analyst, do the associate's job.
- If you're an associate, do the VP's job.
- If you're a VP, do the SVP's job.
- If you're an SVP, do the MD's job.

Simple, right? But don't misunderstand me. You need to be a stork, not a pigeon. Do your boss's work, but *never, ever* make your boss do *your* work. Don't send them a partially completed assignment (it's like a half-eaten sandwich), and if you can't do exactly what they want, then send them multiple versions of what you *think* they want. Rather than make them send you the dreaded Jeff Bezos briefest of emails, "?" which is short for "WTF!?" give them solutions. Make life easier for them so that all they need to do from their beach cabana is send back one word: "OK."

If you take to heart what I said about risk, and if your bosses see what you have taken on—including some of *their* responsibilities—they'll see that promoting you will have a low risk of failure but a high potential for success. But recognize that your competition lurks everywhere. Remarkably, upward promotions can sometimes be viewed as *more* risky than external *lateral hires*, so prove otherwise and remind your bosses that the devil you know is better than the devil you don't.

They Don't Call It the *Art* of War for Nothing

When vying for the big promotion, just like when you were groveling for better compensation, do your research. Do the 1000 hours of work it takes to really know the market, how you fit into it, and what Greater Fools might be willing to do to hire you. Only then will you know what you deserve and maybe even gain leverage on your employer. But don't shoot yourself in the foot like one of my friends did. At one key point in his career, he was pissed off at the managing partners because he was one of four people waiting in line to be "Made Men as Partners," as he puts it. My friend concocted the idea for all of them to gang up on the managing partners, telling them "in bold and in underline" that making them wait for their promotion was total BS. The result was that because this Gang of Four tried to force their hands, the managing partners put them in the penalty box and made them wait even longer. "We ended up accused of being a meddlesome group of union types," my friend remembers. "It taught me a lesson that while you might think you have leverage, eight times out of ten you don't."

Rather than hand-to-hand combat, I was more likely to use the opposite tactic. Remember what I told you about negotiating for compensation when I suggested bringing in a third party named *fairness*? Yep, the same is true for getting a promotion. I would treat my boss as the *Almighty Father* but make *emotion* the third party in the negotiation trinity. I'd pray that He'd do me a solid by appealing to His altruism and make it clear that He held my future in His hands. Given the sacrifices of mind, body, and soul I had made for the job, I'd ask Him if he could live with Himself if He didn't give me that promotion.

Of course, emotion can still work if your deft moves reveal that your boss is in fact *Lucifer* and wouldn't give two cents about fairness. In that case, switch to the other unending well of motivation: *greed*. Make your bosses feel that you can maximize their own ROTI and get richer by promoting you. Swear fealty and show them that you'll go to Hades and back to win business—for them. When time comes to tally up the number of souls collected, credit will go to the *Prince of Darkness*. Facts don't matter much compared to the soft science of ego and self-love. If they won't do it for you, will they do it for themselves?

Paul Clausing, managing director at Fluential Partners and former Jefferies banker, thought he was working for Him but then quickly realized otherwise. He was a young eager beaver SVP and had struck gold when he found a prospect willing to hire the firm. However, when he returned from the hunt, an MD called him into his office. Like a dog pissing on a hydrant, this MD said to Paul matter of factly, "You do realize that this prospect is under my sector coverage?" As Paul squirmed, the MD told him, "That means any revenue you generate goes directly to this guy," and he pointed his two thumbs at himself. Paul could have said, "Screw you," but instead he showed his loyalty and replied, "Of course." Even though that demonstration of fealty would partly delay Paul's inevitable rise to MD, it earned him kudos from that MD during comp season and allowed Paul to bide his time until he was fully ready to go scorched earth.

Key Takeaways

- Life continues to be one big performance. Act like it.
- Don't ask; don't get. Be vocal about what you want.
- Standing pat and not playing the game can be the riskier play.
- Be *Unus*. Specialize and become an expert in something valuable.
- Even a rocket ship needs a janitor. To end big, you need to start small.
- Money is the lubricant for your career path and promotion.
- Build your own money machine.
- Beware of organizational *risk aversion*. It can cramp your style.
- Manage up, down, and all around. Keep your head on a swivel.
- Do the job above your pay grade.
- Figure out if your boss is the *Almighty* or *Lucifer*.

CHAPTER 22

Check Yourself at the Door

Career Checklist

Let's take a quick interlude and review how you're doing so far. Use this *Career Checklist* to see how you've fared:

☐ Took on risky assignments that have a good chance of making the firm boatloads of dough.

☐ So that your bosses only have one page to read, authored executive summaries using highlights, fonts, and enough formatting to make your kindergarten teacher proud.

☐ Triple-checked your way to zero defects and superstardom.

☐ Created templates to maximize your ROTI by using the same work seamlessly and interchangeably for many different projects.

☐ Delivered proposals and other requests from your boss faster than DoorDash delivers Thai food from across the street.

☐ Wrote succinct memos for higher-ups so that your boss can sound smart and still make the front nine.

☐ Created so many paper trails of your involvement in deals that you could win the office's Best Supporting Actor.

☐ Retold the history of painful deals by getting the last word in trails of emails that you've Hancocked.

☐ Persuaded satisfied clients to write testimonial emails, which you've also posted on LinkedIn, saying how great you were.

☐ Held your tongue so many times that even you believe your boss deserves the credit for your hard-earned work.

☐ Practiced your pitching technique with anyone who will listen, even your dog.

☐ Mimicked your boss's mannerisms, recommendations, tone, dress, and hobbies to the point where you can't tell the difference between them and you.

☐ Volunteered for poop patrol.

☐ Taken so many notes at meetings that you're known as Secretary of State(ments).

☐ If you failed at something, you covered your ass faster than a burp in a dust storm.

☐ Showed what a clear winner you are by proudly displaying your Lucite cubes commemorating all the deals you helped close.

☐ Extra credit if you made new Lucite cubes just for the hell of it.

☐ Extra, extra credit if you sent one to your parents to go with your *atta-kid* trophies for coming in fourth at the Middle School lacrosse championship.

☐ Maestro-ed your way to greatness by wowing your boss with your techno-prowess.

☐ Found your Yoda in the empty office on the third floor (points demoted if it was the janitor's closet).

☐ Accepted that decisions are pain points and have a regimen to eliminate them from your mind. Here are some possible strategies used by three of the greats:

  ☐ Steve Jobs: Wear same clothes every day.

  ☐ Tim Cook: Start every day with 5 a.m. workout.

  ☐ Me: Read, write, and work from 5 a.m. to 9 a.m. every day.

  ☐ Me: Eat the same thing every day for lunch at work. Variety is for dinner.

  ☐ Me: Have yesterday's tabs open when I launch my computer.

  ☐ Me: Exercise every night from 11 p.m. to midnight.

☐ Kissed the asses of people above you by getting them coffee, picking up their laundry, and sending flowers for their anniversaries.

☐ Faked it till you almost made it, where you are right now.

☐ Played hard to get with that offer from a competing company.

☐ Built a nice book of business with mostly Crabs, an occasional Nymph, a few Lepers, and hopefully no Corpses.

How'd you do? If you've checked at least 10 boxes, you're knocking on the door to the executive suite. If not, back to the salt mine!

CHAPTER 23

Mastering Your Sermon on the Mount

Group Selling

To this point, I've given you tips on how to negotiate one-on-one, particularly with regards to compensation, but mastering the art of selling to a group is just as important. You need to nail this skill to get employees to follow you off a cliff, bosses to anoint you worthy of premature promotion, partners to say "Yea" to your crappy deals, and boards to hire you over their cronies and progeny.

If you can't win over a group, you might as well kiss your career goodbye. No one ever gets very far unless they master this skill. So here is what to consider when convincing a group to approve your schemes or, at worst, not sabotage them:

- *Do Your Recon.* I told you to map the salt mine when you first started your career and I hope you didn't think it was a one-time thing. It applies at every stage, on every day, for every interaction—especially meetings. Before *any* internal gathering, I would buttonhole committee members and frame my pitch in a way to gain their support in the context of their self-interest. By now, your EQ should be approaching Oprah-level, so use it to determine in advance which managers might torpedo your deal. You'll have to back-channel one-on-one with every committee member to learn who might blow your suggestion out of the water and who will support it. To those who are on the fence and will be asking questions, provide the answers in advance, or promise they will be part of the pitch. This is the time to suss out people's issues and debate them there and then. By laying this kind of groundwork, your goal is to know the outcome before you walk into the meeting. Otherwise, as Sun Tzu warned in the fifth century BCE, "You've already lost."[1]

---

[1] Sun Tzu, *The Art of War.*

- *Unearth Motivations.* Make sure this reconnaissance gives you insight into people's motivation for supporting or nixing your deal. In my experience at Jefferies, 9 of every 10 deals brought to committee should have been easy sells because on the surface at least, everyone should have been unified in their goal to make money. Not necessarily so. I routinely brought multi-million-dollar fee opportunities to the table and knew that certain senior managers would be asking themselves, "Liu may make the firm a couple million bucks, but is this deal good for *me*?"

  You've got to get to know your colleagues and observe their behaviors. Become fully aware of their **heuristics**—those mental shortcuts that help you problem-solve and make judgments, often too-quick ones, which can result in irrational or inaccurate conclusions. Identify your prey. Who tends to be risk-averse? Who thinks all Internet companies are evil because spyware was downloaded onto his laptop when he was looking at naughty sites? Discern the *true* motivations of every participant and address them one-on-one. If someone is worried about the riskiness of a bond deal, comfort them that you aren't loading the firm's balance sheet with securitized nukes. If they wonder how acting as an advisor in a hostile M&A scenario will impact the firm's reputation, point out how Enron was advised by J.P. Morgan and they kept on trucking. If they're concerned how a busted IPO might impact the firm's institutional investors, remind them that Goldman called its clients "Muppets," and no one even blinked.

  Gina King, partner at Supernode Global and former Jefferies SVP, adds, "Either by trial and error or reputation, you can eventually determine everyone's motivations. You then need to figure out how by helping them, and by making it clear to them that their priorities are your priorities, you can help yourself."

- *Use Peer Pressure.* From our childhood days when we swallowed a bottle of Tabasco sauce on a dare, to now when we loaded up on Dogecoin because Elon Musk told us to, we're all subject to peer pressure. If harnessed correctly, it can do wonders for your career, particularly in a group setting.

  Peer pressure and social influences are enormously important in driving decisions by consensus. We all want to be part of the pack and it takes brass gonads to stand out from the crowd—particularly if you turn out to be wrong. The key is to orchestrate the meeting so that momentum builds in your favor until approval becomes a foregone conclusion.

  I always started the meeting with my deal's negatives because hell if I was going to let anyone be my devil's advocate! Critiques that start off as minor prods can quickly escalate into the group wanting to burn you at the stake. Addressing concerns at the outset allowed me to defuse them quickly and ensure they would be a distant memory by the time I rattled off the numerous positives. "The deal could blow up in our face if interest rates turned, but did I mention the firm could make 20 million buckaroos?" "I know the CEO was tried for insider trading, but he was never convicted. Did I mention we're going to make $20 million in fees?"

Thanks to a successful recon mission, I knew who my supporters were and pulled them into the fray by soliciting real-time feedback. "That completes my presentation. Lawrence, do you have any specific feedback on my deal?" Of course, no one needed to know that Lawrence lobbied me on his last deal which was a turd, but I supported him as a favor. Make sure you convert supporters into evangelists and use them to turn the tide in your favor.

- *Shrink the Pond.* In most group settings, majority rules. On Wall Street, to become a senior banker, you need to get deals done, and to get them done, you need approval from a committee of peers. By now you've done your prep and you should know if your upcoming meeting is destined for victory or failure. If, after incessant lobbying, **Guanxi**, and powers of persuasion, you're still looking at a loss, use your first-grade math skills. Shrink the pond and make the group smaller. This makes for decisions that are faster and better—for you. You can do this by getting proxy votes ahead of time or orchestrating people's time so that fewer fish show up. For instance, no one wants to attend meetings during family time, so be sure to schedule them when most appropriate for your supporters and least appropriate for your detractors. I would always try to schedule mine on a Friday afternoon. The fact that it coincided with tee times was purely kismet.

- *Neuter Your Enemies.* Among the senior banker ranks, there were a bunch of us young guns who were viewed as a threat by some of the established, old-school geriatric execs. We acted like we were already running the firm, and frankly, these "geris" didn't like it. It would activate their **reactive devaluation bias**, when an individual dismisses something out of hand because it comes from one person in particular. In fact, there was one curmudgeon who thought the Internet was a fad and went out of his way to say "No" to every deal I brought to the table.

Whenever in doubt, I always assumed the worst in people. My default goes back to a book I read as a young man which has never steered me wrong, called *The Lucifer Principle* by Howard Bloom. He says that "evil" is a by-product of nature's strategies for creation and is woven into our most basic biological fabric. That idea resonated with me because it never ceased to amaze me when people are surprised by the nefarious actions of others. When they were screwed out of a deal or cheated on pay, colleagues would say to me, "I can't believe he did that." C'mon, you think that if humans are capable of cheating on their spouses or killing someone for a side glance, they aren't capable of stiffing you on your bonus!?

Harry Nelis, former Goldman Sachs banker and now partner at the venture capital firm Accel, put it kindlier: "People aren't out to get you; they're out for themselves."

So, in any meeting, watch out for people speaking up whose only intention is to screw you and make themselves look good. You never know who that might be—a two-faced client, a conniving peer, even an insecure boss. As you're rising in the ranks, reading the room is critical to your survival.

- *Give 'Em Ownership.* Groups tend to be made up of professional non-smilers who may not say "No" but certainly won't give out a "Yes" as easily as you handed over $10 for movie theater popcorn. Individuals like to banter, swap ideas, and correct each other so that they appear smarter. I know this can be exhausting, but resist the temptation to yell, "Seriously, can you shut your pie hole for once?" and let them marinate. Your patience will pay off because it can defuse other insidious factors that can torpedo your cause, the **Not Invented Here (NIH) Syndrome** and its evil twin, **ownership bias**, where groups prefer their own ideas rather than those provided by others. They're the insecure slobs who backseat-drive every meeting. They need the best ideas to be theirs, *so let them!* Leave enough breadcrumbs that even a blind pigeon could find the trail. Once they latch onto your idea, be sure to say, "Jimbo, that is a great idea!" and shower them with compliments. Just make sure that when the battle is over and the dust settles, the powers-that-be know who made it happen. Demonstrating your prowess in overcoming all these obstacles might be the very thing that gets you noticed and hoisted onto the big chair.

- *Preach; You're a Preacher.* Another way to bolster your case to a group is to take advantage of **belief bias**, where people make faulty conclusions based on what they already believe to be true. For instance, one might conclude that all bankers are psychopaths, and all psychopaths are murderers, and therefore all bankers are murderers. This may sound absurd, but people do this all the time.

  When making a pitch, it's in your best interest to reinforce, not contradict, what the other party believes. For example, when the Internet market was raging, CNBC's daily broadcast demonstrated that any clown show could add a ".com" on the end of their name and go public. So when pitching the board of *any* company to go public, I knew I was speaking to a receptive audience purely focused on maximizing value. We knew they wanted to be valued based on traffic, rather than cash flow, because it yielded a higher valuation, so our presentation catered to their bias and focused only on the valuation metrics they cared about. Heck, the market was so hot, we could have valued them on the number of Herman Miller chairs in their office. It was like preaching to the choir. The crazy thing is, all we were doing was telling them what we all knew they wanted to hear.

- *Anchors Aweigh.* Even the most obstinate group can't fight human nature. Your audience is more likely to remember your words if you use *anchoring* to convince them and, most important, to prevent them from messaging on their phone or falling asleep.

How do you *anchor* yourself? In a literal sense, this means physically moving your body in order to stand in specific spots of the floor to make certain points. When discussing a company's past performance, I'd stand in one position, then move to another when discussing the present, and then another spot when talking about the future. If it was to a company's board, and I wanted to make a point that really hit home and got people's buy-in, I'd stand next to the Chairman of the Board. Hard to text when you should be looking in the chairman's direction. Or if I was trying to rile up an especially tall group of Neanderthal employees, I might stand on a chair, or even a table, to not only show my enthusiasm but also establish who was king of the hill. Think about how you can use physical gestures and tonal changes to highlight key aspects of your pitch. Practice in front of a mirror.

Another way to look at anchoring is through the lens of the **anchoring effect**, which is crucial to convincing anyone of anything. It's when a person making a decision relies too heavily on one piece of information. Anchoring bias will encourage you to hold onto a crappy stock that has lost value because you've *anchored* your estimate of its value to the price you paid for it rather than to its current fundamentals. Once in this trap, you'll illogically keep a stock in the hope it will return to its purchase price. We all know you're supposed to "buy low and sell high," but no one ever does it; we can't let go of the fact we overpaid. We look backward instead of forward.

- *Prime the Pump.* Another tip to assist you in convincing a group of people of pretty much anything is the **priming effect**. It's when an idea is triggered (either directly or indirectly) in the brain concerning something you want others to do in your favor. In other words, brainwashing!

I would use the **priming effect** in a variety of circumstances. I'd start every presentation or pitch with negatives. I'd show how the world ended for another company that *didn't* do what I'm about to tell them. How Goldman Sachs made enough dough to fund their partner's private jet fleet by doing a deal that we *rejected*. Or another deal that we *didn't* do helped Morgan Stanley beat its quarter and cover up a massive loss made by some fat-finger trade.

Then I'd move right to the positives. Before pitching a client on an IPO, I'd show how every public company in the sector had mouth-watering valuations. Before going into the details of a juicy acquisition target, I'd point out a competitor that bought some money-losing tech company and saw their stock pop 50 percent overnight. Or I'd create league tables showing how Jefferies was the #1 bank for doing any deal, at any time, on any planet, before pitching a board on why they'd be stupid not to hire us.

Chris McGowan, former managing director at Madison Dearborn, former banker at Morgan Stanley, and now adjunct professor at the University of Chicago's Booth School of Business, told me about a time when he primed a company's management team to win a particular deal. It was a mission-driven company, so Chris called everyone he knew who had experience with the organization and pumped them for information. He then wrote a five-page love letter to the management team about all the reasons he admired them, culling from what he had learned from the friends he had interviewed. "I was told my letter made a huge difference," he remembers. "It turned out it wasn't just about the money. They said no one else had taken the extra time and effort."

You can even use the **priming effect** to advance your career. On the morning of your promotion discussion, get your boss their favorite Starbucks order or accidentally leave a $100 bill near their desk. (Just kidding. That wouldn't even cover their dry-cleaning bill.) More realistically, during the weeks leading up to the discussion, drop hints about the deals you were involved with which were famously triumphant. Talk about your long hours and the models, proposals, and memos you created to seal them. Do this with everyone you know who has any kind of say in your future.

But also step back from the grind and get personal. "How was your weekend? Did you see that ball game? What else can I ask you that I really don't care about?" And remember I told you to take up their hobbies? If you've never actually gone golfing, tell them you want to learn. Offer to be their caddy. Make a point to have lunch every month or so with the senior executives most crucial to your promotion. It shows them you're interested, and we all know how much people love themselves. You know this by now as the ole **affinity bias**. Juan Alva, formerly of Goldman Sachs and now managing director of an alternative investment fund, suggests getting people to talk about their favorite subject: themselves. "Pump them with questions and take a genuine interest," he told me before warning, "but don't be a sociopath. It has to work for both sides."

On the other hand, Chris McGowan suggests asking your boss for advice even if you don't need it because it's a sign of respect and builds rapport. "A knucklehead next to me was always asking 'Daddy' a question, but it turns out for some bosses, that's exactly what they want."

Yes, the **priming effect** is elementary, but it's shocking how few people use it to their advantage.

Eye on the Prize

And so, my promotion-hungry friends, let me circle back to where we started: Think of this as war. The world of business, especially Wall Street, can be a cyclical place, and that means there are times of feast and famine, peace and combat. In the feast years, your bosses will be fawning over you to stay. They will offer the siren song of promotion, more pay, more responsibility, more of everything. But many tales have a flipside, and there may be times when no company will need new hires and will treat existing ones like the plague. Suddenly the fawning will turn to "What have you done for me lately?" When the winter is especially cold, there will be very few seats on the ladder. That's when you convince yourself things aren't so bad, that those late nights in the office are really times when you're molding yourself into a new and better person. But you'll probably also be *very* ready for promotion and do whatever you can to get that coveted role. Unfortunately, so will all your peers. So it will be a *Game of Thrones*, and you'll want to make sure you're the last person standing (or sitting).

Now I'm not recommending that you hire a hitman, but I am suggesting—no, strongly telling you—to treat your happy-hour coworkers as what they indeed are: competition. This is the time to reread *The Art of War* and apply lessons learned.

I promise you, however, that if you've scored great on the Career Checklist in Chapter 22, you're well on your way. But don't ever get complacent. One missed deadline, one formatting error in a pitchbook, one *reply all* of an inappropriate email, and it's back down you plummet! You're so close to the summit, you can smell the sweet aroma of success. Keep your eye on the prize, stay focused, and continue to climb.

Key Takeaways

- Master the art of selling to a group.
- Keep your eye on the prize.

CHAPTER 24

Congrats, You've Arrived

Now Get Back to Work!

Welcome! You've finally made it to the coveted spot at the top of the pyramid. On Wall Street, that's managing director, but on Main Street it's typically executive management. As managing director, you've mastered the skills I've preached. You may not be the Messiah (yet), but you have a gaggle of clients singing your praises and a cadre of disciples doing your bidding. You stand out in a sea of robotic bankers, give Oscar-winning performances at every interaction, and passed 10,000 hours of pitch practice years ago. You dodged every landmine along your career path, mastered every quirk of human nature, and are considered by everyone to be their BFF. You speak the *lingua franca* of Wall Street alpha dogs and covered up every one of your million blind spots. In fact, you turned every one of your bugs into features and you use your own time wisely. You're not only on good terms with your boss, but also your boss's boss and are getting paid handsomely. You're in the running for Boss-of-the-Decade and now you're officially a *Big Swinging Dog*.

Becoming a BSD

Big Swinging Dogs (BSDs)[1] are the Bigwigs. The Queen Bees. The Kingpins. The Boss Ladies. The Grand Pooh-bahs. These rainmakers rake in enormous fees to the firm and get paid for it. Becoming a *Big Swinging Dog* is the ultimate prize on Wall

---

[1] This is the PG version. *BSD—Big Swinging Dick*—was popularized in Michael Lewis's book *Liar's Poker* and has become the lexicon for becoming an MD, or top dog, at many Wall Street firms.

Street and can be the culmination of one's career. It's what every senior banker craves. Without it, you'd just be a Big Dog—read A-hole.

Every firm's promotion to MD is different. For me, it happened without much fanfare. When the day arrived, I got a congratulatory call from my boss, a corner office with panoramic views overlooking the San Francisco Bay Area, and new business cards with "Managing Director" etched on them. Nothing else—no cake, no dance party, just an email reminding me to log all of my client meetings and update a spreadsheet conveniently showing my current revenue for the year at a big fat *zero*.

Becoming a BSD isn't as much of a chucklehead party as it used to be. When I was a young intern at Goldman Sachs in 1992, one of the older VPs said to me, "This is a year when the crazies come out." He explained that Goldman was a private partnership with only partners—no MDs. Partners, of which there were fewer than 180 worldwide, ruled the roost and if you became one, it would be the equivalent of winning Willy Wonka's Golden Ticket a bazillion times over. Below them were an ocean of VPs, all vying to enter this elite club. This battle royale for partner occurred every two years and to be considered you needed to do something truly noteworthy. Leading up to promotions, VPs not only swung for the fences on big deal opportunities or giant trades but also lobbied all hours of the day. I was told that the backstabbing and politicking would put a U.S. congressional election to shame. VPs would get each other fired, steal credit on deals, take monster trading positions with the potential to capsize the firm, and flog "innovative" structures on unsuspecting clients.

Juan Alva, formerly of Goldman Sachs and now managing director of an alternative investment fund, explained that during his time at Goldman, perverse incentives seemed to permeate the firm. "One year there were two guys: one was clearly a Goldman lifer while the other lobbied hard and made it known that if he didn't get the nod, he'd leave. Even though they were equally productive, the lobbyist got the promotion and the lifer didn't. Word on the street was the lifer was screwed over because the firm knew he wasn't going anywhere, whereas the firm didn't want to lose the revenue of Mr. Machiavelli." Juan's story illustrates that sometimes the losers are those who are taken for granted and remain loyal through thick and thin.

Perks, Perks, and More Perks

When you become a BSD, you're now in an exclusive club where the rich get richer and you're showered with incomparable perks. Aside from the early tee times and that Maserati and McMansion you always dreamed of owning, you get to wine and dine clients at the Super Bowl, the U.S. Open, or Game Seven of the NBA Finals.

You stay at the Four Seasons and you eat at Planet Earth's finest. Just after you clinch a deal in Paris or Hong Kong, you take your family for a long ski weekend in Tahoe or on a diving trip to the Maldives or Bora Bora. You hobnob with billionaires and mingle with stars because you are one, and somehow you're able to finagle a 6 p.m. reservation the next day at n/naka. To hell with the 3-month waiting list; you can't be late to the Met Gala.

One of the first true signs that you're no longer a peon and that you have reached some modicum of success is knowing that your John Hancock now has the power to bind the firm. You can sign engagement letters, NDAs, and other legal documents. No one is going to auction your autograph as an NFT, but it does show your firm trusts you. Of course, if you did something stupid like buy swampland in Florida, I'm sure the firm's army of lawyers would figure out a way to claim you were mentally unfit at the time. Given your job, they wouldn't be half wrong.

As an MD, no one will be watching your clock or question why your lunch breaks are five hours long. You may disappear on Fridays for 36 holes and no one will question why you seem to be taking conference calls at a rave. You may be wondering how you suddenly went from inmate to guard, so I'll tell you why. You collect chits, or what scientists call **idiosyncrasy credit**. It's your ability to deviate from a group's expectations or how much you can screw off before your boss tells you to get in line. As you get higher in an organization and prove yourself, the less they need to watch you. Like that obedient inmate who never tries to escape, they let you roam around the prison grounds and take trips to the nearby village for ice cream because they know come lockdown, you'll return dutifully to your cell. For me, I had built up a ton of credit after 20 years. It got me complete independence, a few paid sabbaticals, and even a few deals jammed through committee—all because I had always delivered.

You'll have access to secret deals that only MDs get, like with hedge funds, Internet stocks, and professional sports franchises. G14 classified stuff. Everything just seems to coalesce around you, and you're a BSD. If you've played it right, you've become the banker who *owns* the relationship to every target in your sector. You're invited to the annual MD conference, where you and your peers are flown in from all over the world to hobnob not only with each other, but also with titans of industry, like Milken and Icahn. There are no reporters and no transcripts. Ideas are discussed. Deals are made. Everyone is selling, and there's something in it for all of you, including the goliaths.

Imagine the leverage of these titans. They don't do hundreds of deals a year; they do dozens, which means it's important for them to find the right ones, wherever they are in the world. You're yucking it up with these gods and several hundred of your peers, with the most expensive food and wine imaginable and being entertained by the likes of Streisand or Bono. The next time you find that hot software company, you'll have a direct hotline to these billionaires on their private shoe phones.

Oh, and did I mention the pay? Of course you didn't do this for the money, but if you did, it can be very rewarding. Becoming MD is an automatic invitation to the millionaire's club—often multimillionaire's club. So enjoy all the sins that money can buy. Plus if you work at a top white-shoe firm, you might get the ultimate prize any MD is seeking: the inbound call. This is when clients call you, not the other way around. Of course, they really want to do business with Goldman Sachs, not Mr. MD, but at least for you, it means less time on the road humping it and more time harvesting. Just practice saying, "Welcome to Goldman Sachs, may I take your order?"

Of course, everything I've said is *mostly* true. You've made it. Your life is great. You're awesome. Hell yeah, but now comes the catch.

No Rest for the Weary

You've spent most of your life toiling to get here and just want to kick your feet up and light up a stogie. For years, you saw how the MDs ahead of you did *bupkis*, showing up for the first client meeting, then doing the classic bait-and-switch, never to be seen again. You dreamt about that moment when you could fly in, grab credit, and show up only when they're doling out the bonus checks. All this time, you've asked yourself, "How do I get a gig like that?" Well, you're in for a rude awakening. You're far from done. In fact, now you're really on the treadmill. You need to keep producing every day or, in this world, someone will eat your lunch.

Juan Alva puts it more colorfully: "They tell you reaching the top is like a marathon, but when you cross the finish line, looking for the beer and pizza, some *putz* hands you a towel and tells you to keep running or you're out." Juan's point is it's really an *ultra* marathon and you need to keep delivering. You need to continue to be a stork—at least until the day you own the place.

Don't expect life to be easy. If you're an MD in investment banking, you have to generate fees for the firm, and lots of them. You're *expected* to be the Rainmaker—the God or Goddess who is living and breathing to broker deals and attract clients. You're a human money magnet for you and your firm. At the same time, you've got to manage all the people below you, as well as, for certain deals, some of your malcontent colleagues. Being an MD is like being a pro athlete: highly paid, short half-life, and someone always gunning for your seat on the team.

Life doesn't get any easier once you've risen to the top; you just get better at being able to handle it. So don't get complacent; this place of prestige isn't exactly Easy Street. You can't just sit on your laurels and take everything for granted. You've got to know your clients inside and out—when to go for a deal and when to walk. You've got to be an EQ master, balancing personal relationships and intuitively knowing when to delegate, when to swoop and step in, when to hire, and when to fire. And, of course, you've got to be Mr. or Ms. Swivel Neck, with eyes behind your head watching out for that unknown someone trying to push you off your game.

Also, just when you think, "I'm an MD and I'm the Man or Woman," they'll move the ball on you. A firm might add a "Senior MD" above "MD" to keep the savages wanting more. For instance, since my time at Goldman, they added "Managing Director" and "Partner Managing Director" (PMD) to their hierarchy. MDs are known internally as "MD-Lite," while PMDs are the real McCoy. It's like living in California versus Baja California. Big difference.

Another ugly truth is that what "is giveth can also be taketh." At firms like Goldman, with the PMD tier, you might make it to PMD, but don't uncork the champagne yet. You need to keep generating revenue and if you don't, the firm can *de-partner* you. You can still get into the building, but not the executive washroom. Just when you think you're set, you're on a treadmill set at level 10. Hopefully, you won't forget all the strategies that got you here and that will coalesce now that you've reached the top.

From where I sit, there are three superpowers that you need to be a good—no, a great—MD or any chieftain at any company. If singing, dancing, and acting are the Triple Threat of Broadway, these are the Triple Threats of Wall Street: the ability to develop *trusting relationships*, to *sell*, and to *negotiate*. If you don't master these, then one day the firm will send a notice to all your colleagues saying you've decided to "spend time with family." Of course, the question on everyone's mind will be "Which one?"

Trust Is the Coin of the Realm

By the time I was promoted to MD I had become the Bruce Lee of the Internet. Though I was no longer building models, I was still working 100 hours a week. I'd be in the office 14 hours a day, go home, have dinner with my kids, and put them to bed. At night I'd compile my target list for the days ahead and make calls to Asia pitching my wares. Then in the morning, I'd repeat the shtick with the Europeans. It was nonstop work. I was still 7-Eleven, but the tasks had changed. I was constantly researching. I needed to know everything that was going on within the Internet space. Which online ad companies needed an IPO to raise funds to fight Google? Which e-commerce companies were tasty morsels for Amazon? Which old-school content companies were going to get Blockbustered and needed to sell before getting demolished by Netflix?

Information was my currency, and even as the Google age arrived, that's not where what I needed could be found. At that point in history, no search engine was going to tell me that DVDs would be dead in a few years, that streaming would soon take over. I learned by talking to those who knew, so my personal contacts were crucial. Phone calls, wining and dining, attending networking boondoggles—that's where I'd find the most precious knowledge.

Selling in a Game of Inches

You may think that as an MD, or any senior executive, you've entered air so rarefied that they should bottle it up and sell it. Truth is, you have more in common with a used car salesman than you think. Salesmanship is the very essence of the investment banking business—of any business, really. But in the arena of Wall Street, it's truly a game of inches because you're competing against other BSDs. So here are a few tips to get that brain working:

- *Shut Up.* Don't sell past the close. Complex sales always involve **asymmetry of information**. Just like how we all know that Wall Street screws over the little people but not by how much, clients acknowledge they'll never really know how you work your magic. They don't know exactly how you're going to find that Greater Fool to buy their stock or overpay for their company, so once you have the sale, don't keep at it. You don't want clients asking themselves, "What do I not know? Am I the chump?"

- *Be Fast—Speed Wins.* There *are* a few things in life where it pays to wait, like your first sexual encounter, but not on Wall Street. Other BSDs are trying to eat your lunch, so speed makes a difference. If you see an opportunity, don't hesitate. If an issue arises, don't hide. Do tomorrow's work today.

- *Be Preemptive.* Few things are more intoxicating than getting a first look at something—that new house, a new movie, even this book. I've found that giving someone a preemptive opportunity almost always makes them lean forward. It works better than a straight auction because it appeals to the basis for all teenage angst: FOMO (fear of missing out). So FOMO your way to greatness by making the other side feel special, but be sure to slap an expiration date on it.

- *Build Relationships.* We all like to do business with people we like, so build long-term relationships. Develop **Guanxi**. Many of my clients were friends and people who I had called on for years, some for over a decade. Play the long game and know that one day, it will all pay off—hopefully. If it doesn't, stock up on voodoo dolls.

- *Call in Favors.* If any one of the dozen MDs kissing your ass can do your deal, who do you choose? The one you owe, of course! Cash in those favors, remind them of the hundreds of acquisition ideas, employee introductions, and fancy entertainment you provided for all those years. If that fails, remind them you have pictures.

- *Sell Ideas.* Everyone loves ideas! Clients may not act on them, but they'll appreciate the opportunity to give them a spin. Whenever I met with clients, even if it was just to shoot the breeze, I brought a book of ideas filled with at least a dozen companies. Most were downright stupid, but that one in a hundredth time when the client said, "Oh, that's interesting!" I heard the sweet sound of "*Ka-ching!*"

- *Get Emotional.* In the staid world of business, sometimes getting a little emotional or even acting a little crazy can differentiate you from the pack. Passion can convince a group, and anger can demonstrate social hierarchy like when your CEO swears worse than a drunken sailor. I've found that when I've done the unexpected, it's worked in my favor. One time, I was representing a client with a buyer who I felt was just taking us for a joyride. After numerous calls, I finally yelled, "We're done! You're just jerking us around!" and slammed the phone down. The following day, he called back and gave us a juicy offer.

There are caveats, of course, to selling, and you won't be surprised that there's a term for one of them: **Seersucker Illusion**. This is when people irrationally seek out and rely on experts. Bankers, for example, are called in as forecasters of the future. In fact, some MDs base their entire practice on giving good advice on what the market will do. "The market is wide open, so let's IPO now" or "The M&A market will close in a few months, so we should sell your business ASAP." Some go too far and predict future trends when, in truth, no one can do that. All it proves is that "For every seer there's a sucker."

Amateurs Negotiate Price; Pros Negotiate Terms

Negotiations never happen like they do in the movies. Hollywood's version is on fast-forward, so when the two sides have questions, they're quickly resolved. People shake on it and the deal is done. Like your life, reality is much more boring. It's like a tennis match in slow motion, with a series of back-and-forths. A lot takes place over the phone and by email, and what gets resolved in ten minutes on the silver screen, in real life is conducted over many weeks or months.

In the deal business, the first step in any agreement is the term sheet, a short document that highlights major issues, like price. Eventually that turns into what might be a thousand-page document, but it's at that early juncture when most senior people bail and head for the hills. The MD says, "My work here is done. Great job. Now my team will handle the minutiae." But that's *exactly* when you need to stick with it. It's the terms, stupid.

When the big guns vanish after concluding their work is finished, it's usually months or even years later when the client asks, "What the hell did we sign?" Particularly with complex negotiations, some BSDs either don't understand or don't care that it's not just about the price. Every negotiation has multiple facets, and ignoring all but the top-line efforts means you're ignoring deal points of value. Even the price can be impacted by the fine print, like whether payments are in cash, restricted stock, or toxic wastepaper. If you want to be a great MD, never forget that Lucifer was probably an awesome BSD. After all, he coined the expression, "The Devil Is in the Details."

A Different Kind of Matrix

The best way to manage any business is to have a portfolio with as many clients as possible. I kept them all straight using the **BCG Matrix**, aka the **Growth/Share Matrix**, created by the Boston Consulting Group in the 1970s. Whether you learned it in business school or preschool, indulge me for a minute as I give you a short refresher.

The **BCG Matrix** is a great way to manage your ROTI and is divided into four quadrants, based on market growth and relative market share:

- *Cash Cows.* These represent clients or products in which you don't have to invest a lot of time because they're gifts that keep on giving. They generate revenue year after year, so it's important to have a stable of these to cover your annual nut.

- *Dogs.* You can guess that these are ones not worth your precious time and need to be euthanized. Clearly BCG consultants are cat people.

- *Question Marks*, or who the hell knows? You can't know if they'll be successful, but one of them just might be a home run. Most start-ups sit in this bucket. You're not fishing wide enough if you don't have a bunch of these.

- *Stars*, or rocket ships. You'd sell your soul to be involved with these because they're the ones that ensure you get that fat bonus to pay for that third house.

You need your stable Cash Cows because they keep the lights on year after year, but also a few Stars. On Wall Street, searching for them is called *Elephant Hunting*. Along the way, say adios to the Dogs, but stay on top of the Question Marks. At any moment they could start to twinkle.

Practice, Practice, Practice

The way you rise in your career and in life is simple: practice, practice, practice. On Wall Street, you don't become a BSD by sitting on your duff. Before joining Jefferies, I had never made a public sales pitch; I knew I needed practice. As a junior, I treated every opportunity as improv, trying out my pitch on companies that would never do a deal and no one cared if I screwed up. Another way I practiced was at closing dinners to celebrate the completion of a deal. Everyone involved was invited, not only the client, but also the lawyers, accountants, and basically anyone who contributed—even the junior bankers who just printed books but weaseled their way onto the working group. Usually, we held the dinner at a 5-star restaurant like the Wayfare Tavern in San Francisco or Momofuku Ko in New York.

I'd volunteer to give essentially the "Best Man or Bridesmaid Speech." I'd make the content funny, but not offensive. Self-deprecating humor mocking one of the junior bankers was safe, but never the MD or the CEO. You didn't want to turn a low-risk endeavor into a high-wire act. When the evening wrapped, we'd typically give the client an expensive gift, often from Tiffany. Honestly, I think Wall Street (and adulterous husbands) keep that company in business because I can't for the life of me think who really needs $2,750 poker chips or a $10,000 chess set. Maybe that's why what worked even better was a gag gift, like a DIY vasectomy kit to the CEO whose top three C-level execs had four children each and complained about needing this deal to feed them.

Keep That Thinking Cap On

If you've reached MD, **cognitive biases**, whether you know it or not, have no doubt been instrumental in advancing your career. But now is not the time to forget them; they can also help you stay in the game by winning more business. Here are a few examples:

Cognitive Theory	Definition	Wall Street Application
Confirmation Bias	Tendency to search for, interpret, focus on, and remember information in a way that confirms one's preconceptions	Frame an opportunity the same as one previously done: "This Deal X is just like Deal Y, which you bought and loved."

Cognitive Theory	Definition	Wall Street Application
Groupthink	Psychological phenomenon in which the desire for harmony or conformity results in irrational or dysfunctional decision-making	Use to create "deal heat" and to convince arch-nemesis to compete for the same asset.
Irrational Escalation	Doubling-down based on a prior decision even when you know it was a bad one; also known as throwing good money after bad	It's why even when you own 500 shares of Lehman Brothers, you buy more; it can't possibly go lower.
Negativity Bias	Tendency to put more emphasis on negative experiences than positive ones	Convince buyers that not buying an asset can be catastrophic because a competitor will own it.
Overoptimism	Believing the world is a better place than it is, as when companies and stakeholders are naturally predisposed to think they can grow and expand	Frame all conversations with growth in mind. No one hires a Debbie Downer.
Pessimism	Opposite of the overoptimism bias (pessimists weigh negative consequences over positive ones)	If a company has been performing poorly, pitch concepts or projects as defensive (e.g., action is needed to make sure things don't get worse).
Post-Purchase Rationalization	After the fact, making ourselves believe a purchase was worth what we paid for it; a classic trick to validate a deal in the eyes of a buyer	Let the buyer know others were willing to pay more than they did. This way they don't feel like the Greatest Fool.
Reactance	Desire to do the opposite of what someone wants you to do to prove your freedom of choice; or reverse psychology used when pitching potential acquisitions to a buyer	"Oh, no, you don't want to buy that; the geniuses at Google are looking at it!"
Survivorship Bias	Concentrating on the people or things that "survived" some process and inadvertently overlooking those that didn't because of their lack of visibility; clearly demonstrated in how only successful stories are touted in the media	Don't ever discuss the deals that failed or didn't get completed. No one hires a loser.

Committed Enough to Be Committed

Once you've reached the top, you'll need to do whatever it takes to stay on top. There will always be more qualified people than spots available, and so the person who wins and stays in the game is the one who is most committed. I'm not talking about doing anything illegal, but you need to keep hunting and bringing home the bacon, otherwise one day the peasants will revolt and demand a new king.

In the never-ending quest for growth, you'll also need to jump higher. In a world of "what have you done for me lately," for every win, winning will become more difficult. For me, it was putting us on the map in the Internet sector. It's a high-profile category where a firm's brand can mean everything in getting you selected. As an up-and-coming firm, we didn't have the brand "sweatshirt" of other firms. I went hunting every day, 24-7, to find food to eat. After a decade of groveling, developing **Guanxi**, and doling out favors, I started to get the inbound call, albeit for table scraps, and just as I was hitting my stride, we had to push up market to grow our revenues to keep feeding the corporate beast. Co-manager roles needed to be lead-manager. Minimum-sized M&A deals went from $100 million to $300 million. It was a slog, but we did it largely by constantly outhustling other firms whose MDs were fat and happy.

For me, one ace in the hole was my willingness to meet client prospects anytime, anywhere, any place, just for the opportunity to convince them we were worthy of their business. One time after incessant pestering, I convinced the CEO of a red-hot company to listen to my pitch. He agreed to hear me out during a drive from Palo Alto to San Francisco—but not rush hour. So for a little under 45 minutes, I tap-danced as I explained why I would be the best banker to help him. Of course, once we got to San Francisco, he left me standing at the corner of Union Square wondering how the hell I was going to get back to the office.

I've taken countless flights when turbulence convinced me it would be my last, or helicopter rides where we were a gnat's hair away from crashing into the mountains, all in the quest for business. No matter the odds, I'd chase the opportunity, just like Jim Carrey's character in the film *Dumb and Dumber*. When his love interest tells him his chance of ending up with her is one out of a million, he responds, "So you're telling me there's a chance?"

I had been chasing one of the largest Chinese Internet companies for almost a decade, currying favor with the founders so they wouldn't think I was a complete shyster. Finally, I got a call from the CFO on a Monday in San Francisco. He said they were going to do a pre-IPO bakeoff, and in two days I would have a one-hour slot to pitch. I dropped everything, mobilized my team, and flew to Hong Kong. Of course, the CFO didn't show up and instead sent his VP of Finance, or Number Two, to meet with me—for 30 minutes. I spoke nonstop, then hopped onto a plane to London to help my colleagues with a European Internet IPO, circling the globe in less than 72 hours—all in a week's work hunting for truffles.

One last example shows I was willing to do *almost* anything to close a deal. I was working on a deal that needed a certain government's approval and was invited to meet at a palatial compound with flowing gardens and private rooms used for hosting foreign dignitaries. At 11 a.m., I was ushered into a luxurious room with oversized chaise lounges and a round table covered with bottles of distilled liquor. As I proceeded to get down to business, the party bureaucrat, who clearly had the fate of our deal in his hands, waved me off, poured me a shot, and demanded we toast to my safe arrival. As we swallowed this nasty excuse for gasoline, his face lit up like a Christmas tree.

After the first toast, the doors swung open and appetizers were served. The bureaucrat commanded another toast, this time to prosperity. Then came the first course and we toasted to long life. Then the second course and we toasted to happiness. This went on for hours and by the fifth course, my hosts were all beet red, mumbling incoherently. I thought at least this would be over shortly, until I saw one of them depart to an adjoining room. As I was nibbling at the fifth course, I could hear the retching sounds of vomiting. He returned, face flushed, but clearly ready for another round and once again, raised his glass.

One by one, each of my hosts used the adjoining vomitorium as I used every ounce of willpower to hold my lunch down, despite the fact I had enough alcohol in my system to spontaneously ignite. Finally, when lunch was mercifully over, my hosts, who could barely stand, said they'd follow-up with details on certain "payments" needed to approve the deal. (For the record, I never paid, and the deal was never consummated.) With one of my worst cases of alcohol poisoning, I returned to my hotel and passed out on the floor of my room.

The next day, as I was dry-heaving in the airport waiting for my flight home, I thought to myself, "I don't get paid enough for this shit."

You win some; you lose some. Congratulations on your promotion. Welcome to your reality. As author Robert Fritz says, "Reality is an acquired taste."

Key Takeaways

- Enjoy the perks of becoming a BSD. Your job is just getting started.
- Become a *Triple Threat*: Develop trusted relationships, and perfect your sales and negotiation skills. You're in the big leagues now.
- Don't ever forget that you're part of the *Seersucker Illusion*.
- Manage your ROTI by segmenting your business into *Cash Cows, Dogs, Question Marks*, and *Stars*.
- Keep honing those *cognitive bias* skills to win business.
- Do whatever it takes to keep the job. You've earned it.

PART 4

The Score

CHAPTER 25

Make a Deal with the Devil

A Very, Very Short Chapter on Ethics

Up to this point, I've been very clear about never doing anything illegal to get ahead. You know why? Because it's just good business sense. It's true that nowadays you could build a pitchbook, do a financial model, and even pitch a client using Zoom from your concrete cell at San Quentin, but so could a *gold farmer*[1] turned investment banker operating from China's Xinjiang Province. I guarantee that a Chinese gold farmer works harder, costs less, and is probably better at math than you, so keep your competitive advantage and stay out of jail.

Now I know the smartasses among you are thinking the law keeps changing so all I need is to be one step ahead. That's true. In the 1920s, investment banks and commercial banks could operate as one. They called it *synergy*. In the 1930s, it was deemed illegal and they called it *monopolistic*. Then, just like your jean shorts, it was *cool* again in 1999. So you're right, the law does change, but don't be stupid. Even if you know something is not illegal at this very moment, if it feels illicit and dirty, and not in a warm tingly underpants sorta way, then run it by the next test—the ethical one.

---

[1]A gold farmer is a game player who accumulates virtual money, or gold, which they sell for real cash to others. Even though it's banned in most online games, it's not in real life. The rich always pay to win!

What Would Christian Bale Do?

The ethical boundary can be a moving target. What exactly are ethics other than a set of moral rules that are shaped by society and change more than your underwear? Even General Douglas MacArthur proclaimed, "Rules are mostly made to be broken" (after he screwed up the Korean Peninsula). However, staying on the ethical straight and narrow can be the difference between being a pud or making it big. Since many on Wall Street already think of ethics as applicable to that other person on Wall Street[2]—the chump—what's an ambitious sod like you to do? You're likely tempted to think ethics are just stunting your growth, but shake off that notion. The world is a very small place, and your reputation precedes you everywhere you go. Before you act, think about whether it would pass the **TMZ Test**. If you're Christian, ask "WWJD" or "What would Jesus do?" If you're a Satanist, "What would Christian Bale do?"[3] Or closer to home, how will your shrink react when you tell them what you did?

Peer pressure can be massive. I never did anything unethical, but I heard of employees at other firms who committed insider trading,[4] broke into offices to steal corporate secrets, and built Ponzi schemes. And that's just the illegal stuff. Many others got ahead by spreading rumors to win deals, lying about other offers, and fudging numbers to "make the math work." I could have done some of this, but I never did.

Don't ever do anything to sell your soul even though others have to get ahead. It can get you fired or, even worse, arrested. Now a few of you may say, "But this is America, baby!" Impeached presidents, convicted financiers, and disgraced bankers have all lived to fight another day. True, the world is filled with comeback stories, and the media has **survivorship bias**. Redemption stories make for great page views. What doesn't? The countless untold stories about ex–Wall Streeters who died penniless, politicians who never got elected again after those dick pics, and insider traders who didn't get a movie deal with Martin Scorsese.

---

[2]"A Crisis of Culture: Valuing Ethics and Knowledge in Financial Services" is an Economist Intelligence Unit (EIU) report, sponsored by the CFA Institute in 2013. It found that 71 percent of investment bankers said that career progression would be tricky without being *flexible* over ethical standards.
[3]In his 2019 Golden Globe award acceptance speech, actor Christian Bale gave a shout-out to what he said was his inspiration in portraying the former vice president: "Thank you, Satan."
[4]Trading of a public company's securities based on material, nonpublic information about the company. This isn't illegal everywhere. In fact, in some countries it's viewed as a bullish sign that the insiders believe in the business!

For every Sage Kelly, a Jefferies MD who resigned after he was accused of participating in drug-filled foursomes with his wife and prospective clients[5] and now runs investment banking at Cantor Fitzgerald, there are countless others who didn't make it back. My graduating class at Harvard Business School became a rogues gallery of financial wrongdoers. Samir Barai pleaded guilty to insider trading and ruined his reputation. Adam Smith, an ex–Morgan Stanley employee, turned FBI informant and pleaded guilty to insider trading. Ifty Ahmed, an ex–Goldman Sachs banker, was ordered to pay over $100 million because of embezzlement and is currently on the lam in India. Finally, my ex–Jefferies partner Steve Bannon was charged with conspiracy to commit wire fraud and money laundering. Yes, yes, he's now a free man having been pardoned by ex-POTUS Donald Trump, but presidential pardons don't grow on trees.

The Joneses

The biggest morality test, particularly on Wall Street, is seeing the **Joneses** get rich and powerful around you. They will commit unethical, and even criminal, antics throughout their careers and be rewarded. Even so, don't be tempted. Hypocrisy is a fact of life and you'll see others get ahead by practicing from the altar of "Do as I say, not as I do," as they cheat their way to success.

You'll be tested at every stage of your career. Take this infamous tale of a second-year analyst at Morgan Stanley. This analyst got a lucrative expatriate package to work in the Hong Kong office toward the end of his two-year tour of duty. For his third year, he got a furnished apartment, a dedicated driver, and a big jump in remuneration compared to his U.S.-based colleagues. Then one weekend, as he was wrapping up his second year, a water pipe burst in the offices and sprayed some wrapped asbestos, contaminating the entire floor. Morgan Stanley instructed everyone not to return to the office and offered to reimburse anything lost.

This analyst claimed he lost a number of Ferragamos, Mont Blancs, and Hugo Boss suits, and without hesitation, Morgan Stanley cut him a check. A month later, this dude is out and about with his coworkers and brags about how he took the firm for over $12,000. Word got back to the powers that be and he was fired. He lost everything—the apartment, driver, and compensation. Many of this analyst's Morgan Stanley classmates have since become captains of the private equity industry. This moron could have been one of them.

---

[5]Emily Jane Fox, "Banker Once Accused of Drug-Filled Foursome Returns to Wall Street," *Vanity Fair*, March 14, 2016.

The biggest tests, of course, come when really big money is at stake. There are no silver bullets, but learn from Michael Henkin, former senior managing director of Guggenheim Securities. He was asked by a powerful client to pursue a course of action that he felt was unethical but would yield an enormous financial outcome for his client. Rather than acquiesce, or even resign, Michael agonized over the directive and ultimately told his client, "I can't do what you want, but I've come up with three other options. They require a lot more work, but will still get you the outcome you're seeking." The client accepted Michael's proposal and even thanked him for standing up to him when others simply caved. Michael didn't have to compromise his ethics because he went the extra mile and didn't take the easy way out.

Run to Mommy

Temptation and slippery slopes are everywhere. Cheating can be contagious, and big lies are really just snowballs of little ones. I stayed out of trouble my whole career largely by occasionally going back to basics. Just like preventing an electrical device from blowing, I would take the time to reground myself. I'd go home, talk to my mother, my wife, and other loved ones. They'll help you realize that oftentimes at work, you're surrounded by colleagues who may not fret over moral dilemmas the same way you would and after a while, end up not just drinking the Kool-Aid, but bathing in it.

I definitely could have made *a lot* more money being less ethical. I could have screwed clients on fees or lied to sabotage competitors. I could have retaliated against other firms' bankers who did all of this to me and worse. Even though the world isn't completely black or white, I've learned that there are really only a few shades of gray that separate them. Work is a game, and some people are much better at playing it than others, but I never wanted to win by breaking the rules. In the end, that had one tremendous benefit: I sleep well at night.

Key Takeaways

- Don't ever do anything illegal or unethical.
- Before you act, ask, "What would Christian Bale do?"
- Don't believe everything you read (unless it's this book), especially comeback stories of criminals and the immoral; the media drives *survivorship bias*.
- Screw the *Joneses* and accept that others may get further ahead by compromising.
- Sleep well at night.

CHAPTER 26

Parlay Your Way to Success

Social Proof Yourself

By now you should have mastered a few tricks and made your way far around the **Minion-Circle**. Take the next step and go from being just another hamster in the circle to ultimately controlling more of your destiny. How do you do that? By creating and enhancing your own brand. Unfortunately, your firm will not help make this happen because as your individual brand grows, their power over you (and ability to underpay you) begins to dwindle as you turn from being just another replaceable cog to potentially an irreplaceable piece of the franchise.

Become a Kardashian

How do you build your brand? Well, I doubt you can get an E! show where cameras follow you around the clock as you bitch to your siblings about the perfect toenail color, so for starters, here's some suggestions you can try at your company:

- *Build Your Client Base.* Creating a personal brand starts one client at a time. Make sure your clients know you by first, second, and last name. If you're a junior scrub, make sure they know who stayed up all night fixing typos, triple checking numbers, and getting the presentations to the meeting on time. The firm may be building its brand, but so should you. Then perhaps one day you can band together with your two good-for-nothing brothers or sisters, start a firm, and become rich and respected like Salomon and Lehman—or not.[1] The point is, you need to build an exclusive network of clients and you need to be on big deals. Unlike what you may have been told, size does matter. Even though on Wall Street there is no such thing as small deals, just small fees, bigger deals yield bigger fees, and money is the currency of fame on Wall Street.

- *Specialize.* You can't be just another crew-cut–, Ann Taylor–, or Brooks Brothers–wearing, good-person banker. They're a dime a dozen. Stand out and be known for something. Personally, I competed against a lot of Internet bankers, so I chose to focus on the subsector of online advertising technology. For a brief while, I was known as "Mr. Adtech." Another time, I privatized public companies and re-IPOed them on other exchanges. I coined a term called "re-potting" and was given the moniker "Mr. Repotter" by the media. I welcomed the fame, albeit fleeting, because it helped me stand out and win more business.

   Developing ninth-degree black belt skills in hypercompetitive industries is the key to becoming known and wanted. Michael Henkin, former senior managing director of Guggenheim Securities, advises, "We all have A, B, and C skills, but you need to soul search and determine your true talents and what is valuable for the job." He suggests you make yourself an A+ expert on your A− and B+ skills and not waste time trying to turn Cs into As. "It's better to have several A+ capabilities and compensate for your B or C skills by working with others who are A+ in those areas."

- *Be Selective.* As you become more senior, you'll have more control over where you focus your energy. When this happens, you'll need to learn when to fish or cut bait. Volunteer for high-profile assignments and schedule a colonoscopy during the dodgy ones. VCs are pretty good at this. They know that some of their companies are potentially superstars, but that others will die no matter what they do. Given that ROTI is the only thing that matters, some of the best investors learn how to focus only on the potential winners and broadcast their successes when the time comes.

   Case in point is Ram Shriram, a billionaire VC. He and I served on the board of a technology company that was struggling to find product-market fit and was dying a slow death. At the same time, he was involved in a start-up that was growing exponentially. Eventually Ram stopped coming to our board meetings and spent a lot more time at the other start-up. I couldn't blame him. That other company? Google.

---

[1]Salomon Brothers and Lehman Brothers were two major Wall Street firms founded by siblings. The former gave birth to a Treasury bond scandal in the 1990s, and Lehman Brothers went bankrupt in 2008 and became the poster child for Wall Street's contribution to the global financial crisis of 2007 to 2008.

- *Highlight Yourself.* No one likes a braggart—especially a humble braggart—but only *you* can talk eloquently about your achievements. Alternatively, your mom could come into the office and do it for you, but that would be just plain weird. So if you've achieved something good, make it known.

  Lest you think this is gauche, one of the top investment bankers in the industry who has nothing left to prove built a shrine to himself in his office. He had so many Lucites that he ran out of desk space and had a custom stand built to house them. You may wonder, "Why does he bother, given he's a Master of the Universe?" It's because when juniors come into his office and he barks out orders, no one ever questions him. They simply glance at his personal shrine and realize, "Holy crap. This guy has done more deals than I will ever do in my entire life, ten times over." So when he speaks, people listen.

Weapon of Mass Destruction

Most things in life get worse as we age. Your body, your brain, your tolerance for others, all depreciate with time. But your brand can *appreciate* if managed correctly. One way is to use the greatest weapon in business—the **parlay**, the art of snowballing initial wins into even bigger ones. It's how success begets success. Smart people do this all the time. They complete a great deal, broadcast it to the heavens, aim even higher, and then do an even bigger deal next time. In no time, they become known as the *King Midases* of their field. (In Greek mythology, King Midas was granted the power to turn everything he touched into gold by the gods. Of course, he croaked when he couldn't eat gold gyros, so always read the fine print!) Prospective partners seek them out like groupies because they believe lightning will strike twice. Parlaying success makes it easier to win future business, recruit top-tier talent, and it builds upon itself like a virtuous circle, eventually helping you unlock your freedom and escape your job—if that's what you really want.

After having some success, don't succumb to the temptation to take *every* deal that darkens your door. As your most precious asset, you need to protect your reputation and choose wisely. Just like the trips to your local bar, be aware of why someone might show interest in you. Some (or most) will only be interested because your Hermès bag or Patek Philippe watch screams, "I'm loaded!" At the same time, however, once you're famous internally, it's time to amplify your uniqueness and go public:

- *Breed Apostles.* Have others spread your word. Start with family and friends, but if you actually have something meaningful to contribute, others will soon echo your successes. Don't leave any stone unturned. One banker I know has two Lucites made for every deal he completes: one for his office and the other to send home to Mommy and Daddy. His parents are already his top shills so why not give them more ammo? At their independent living center when CNBC blasts the latest M&A deal, they can scream, "My BSD son did that deal, bitches!" You never know who's showing up at visiting hours; it could be an heir looking to hire an investment bank to sell the family business.

The more your name is spoken, the more likely it becomes a **self-fulfilling prophecy**. Just like when you bought that lime green Tesla and now it looks like everyone has one that color, you'll appear to be everywhere. This takes advantage of the **frequency illusion**. When I was selling a company, I'd encourage them to ramp up their PR machine to make them seem pervasive. Eventually, prospective buyers would notice the company's buzz and express their acquisition interest. In your job, this is why you need to ensure that when you hit major milestones, people take notice. The more they hear your name, the more likely they will consider you as someone to watch. Be the Kardashian of your industry. Yes, you may have some talent, but you're famous because you're famous. Be known as a heavy hitter, accumulate public testimonials, and **social proof** yourself to get leverage on your career.

Authenticity and fairness matter if you want others to preach your brand. Chris McGowan, former managing director at Madison Dearborn, former banker at Morgan Stanley, and now adjunct professor at the University of Chicago's Booth School of Business, advises, "If you want your reputation to grow, you need to be known as a fair person so people spread that knowledge about you. To do this, you need to give credit when it's due and fight for your people to get paid. Word gets around and this becomes your brand."

Edward Fu, president of Happy Masks and former Jefferies banker, says it takes skill to develop a following, but once you do, it can reap benefits: "I've found that in Corporate America, visibility is the key to promotion and compensation. To be good at that, you need to develop persuasion and presentation. Large group meetings are presentations, but so are even smaller meetings. Doing it well in both settings can bring a motor around your brand."

- *Leave Breadcrumbs.* Ultimately, you want to leave **behavioral residue**—not the blacklight type, but evidence that makes it appear as though you were involved in success. Tombstones celebrating recent deals are one form because in factories like Wall Street, you're only as good as your last deal. But individual deals can quickly become stale bread, so leave a mark in other ways. Write posts, develop thought pieces, establish best practices, or even launch your firm into new sectors. I helped build a good practice for Jefferies in arguably the highest profile category—the Internet—but I was known more for my tenure and staying at the same firm longer than the furniture.

- *Name Drop.* It's no secret many people think the powerful and famous hang out together. We assume LeBron James and Dwayne "The Rock" Johnson vacation on the same banana boat, or Warren Buffett and Elon Musk eat together at Smith & Wollensky to swap real estate ideas for Mars. But unless you're already a rock star, the next best thing is to make sure others *think* you know people who know people. Then you're guilty by association. Who you know can help your career grow exponentially. Because Jefferies hired many from the Drexel Burnham Lambert diaspora, I was frequently asked, "Do you know Michael Milken?" I didn't, but I got enough disappointing looks that I made it my mission to meet him. I finally chased him down at the Milken Institute's Global Conference and introduced myself. He looked at me as though I was the Chinese delivery takeout guy who got lost in the hallways—albeit better dressed. I'm sure to this day, he still wouldn't recognize me but at least if anyone asks if I know him, I can say I do—sort of, kind of.

- *Use the Media*. Who doesn't love porn? Especially success porn? The media loves winners. So be one. Talk about how you hatched a multi-billion-dollar merger at Chick-fil-A or got an IPO done the day before a financial Apocalypse. Leverage the power of repeated exposure and pray that something you say might actually go viral.

  Like a teenage girl, social media your brains out on TikTok, Snapchat, and the hottest site at the moment. Or like an old dude, post heavily on LinkedIn, Facebook, Twitter, Clubhouse, and whatever else your bros use to compare fly fishing trips. Post your latest and greatest projects and deals. Don't be shy. It's not a humble brag when you worked on a deal that made millions if not billions. It's only bragging if it's just you. The sherpas on Mount Everest never got crap for standing in those selfies taken by middle-aged desk jockeys. More likely, viewers looked at those pics and thought, "Wow, I wonder how that doucheberg got to base camp? He must have had an awesome sherpa!" Be the sherpa.

  Share your successes and hide your failures. Then, like everyone else, you'll be guilty of **self-enhancing transmission bias**. We all have failures but unless we're spreading *schadenfreude*, the media doesn't care. Ooze success, be confident, and live by the banker credo, "Often wrong, never in doubt."

- *Get PRed*. Some of the most powerful and famous people I know have PR firms working for them around the clock. You may be thinking, "What the heck do these people need PR for?" First, to protect their well-groomed reputations, and second, to keep it growing so they can continue to build their wealth and power. PR firms help them get speaking engagements, puff pieces, and talking head slots so they can wax poetic about topics ranging from how they grew their business effortlessly to their super-secret keys to success. Now, PR firms cost a pretty penny (thousands of dollars per month, which buys a lot of ramen), so unless you can afford it, you might have to recruit your unemployed siblings to help out.

  If you're a Wall Streeter, make sure journalists know you're available to talk about the state of the market. The great thing about financial journalism is there is always demand for experts in a field where no one really has any freaking clue what will happen next, so you can say just about anything and sound smart. You might even **parlay** it into speaking engagements where you can get paid thousands of bucks for saying the same thing over and over again. Jump on that gravy train.

- *Stay Front and Center.* If you're out of sight, you're out of mind. You need to keep that flywheel going. Even ex-presidents don't fade away. Wall Street is notorious for hiring ex-presidents like Bill Clinton and George Bush to speak at investor conferences for hundreds of thousands of dollars. Not a bad gig for an hour speech and a few selfies with some suits. Some have parlayed their fame into major coin even when they were losers. Al Gore, who was rumored to be worth less than $2 million when he lost to George Bush, subsequently joined the board of Apple. I highly doubt he knew much about running a sprawling consumer electronics empire, but the dude was one famous Number Two. He parlayed that into a net worth today of an estimated $300 million. I dunno about you, but I'd rather be him than POTUS. How's that for parlaying a loss into a win?

- *Incubate Before Ejecting.* It's important to realize that the sweatshirt you wear may change over time and the brand you wear isn't always transportable. We saw that a lot at Jefferies. We'd hire these muckety-mucks from top firms like Goldman and Morgan Stanley and once they got to our platform, they couldn't deliver a ham sandwich. They went from Iron Man to Tony Stark—sans brains. So grow your individual brand in the warm cocoon of your firm before you venture outside. Your time will come, and it could be glorious. Wall Street has many success stories of bankers who parlayed themselves into eponymous firms that made them wealthy. Bruce Wasserstein, Steve Schwarzman, and Ken Moelis all started as Wall Street schlubs at major firms, honed their craft, built their brands, and then started their own firms to become billionaires.

- *Write a Book.* Information travels under the guise of stories. If you have something valuable to say, it will eventually go viral. What better way to brag about your achievements than write a book? But please, write a humorous one with a snarky voice, not another boring business book with a disembodied narrator pontificating about strategery.

Have You Arrived?

How will you know if your success-porn career is taking off? You could look at your follower count, but that might just be a bunch of bots paid for by your PR firm. It will be obvious like porn—hard to describe, but you'll know it when you see it.

One true test of fame is if you get a nickname, ideally a good one, but even a bad one could be helpful in the vein of "At least I'm famous." My favorites include:

- Sidney Weinberg, CEO of Goldman Sachs: "Mr. Wall Street"
- David Solomon, CEO of Goldman Sachs: "DJ D-Sol"

- Warren Buffett, CEO of Berkshire Hathaway: "Oracle of Omaha"
- John Mack, CEO of Morgan Stanley: "Mack the Knife"
- Jamie Dimon, CEO of J.P. Morgan: "America's Least-Hated Banker"[2]
- Mike Milken, Head of Bond Trading at Drexel Burnham Lambert: "Junk Bond King"
- Dick Fuld, CEO of Lehman Brothers: "Gorilla of Wall Street," one of *Time*'s "25 People to Blame for the Financial Crisis," and *CNN*'s "Ten Most Wanted: Culprits of the Collapse"

Of course, the pièce de résistance is if you're portrayed in a movie. One of the films I've recommended, *Margin Call*, depicts a bank loosely based on Lehman Brothers. Jeremy Irons portrays "John Tuld." Get it? Tuld is what you get when you cross a Fuld and a turd. And you thought my jokes were bad.

As final proof that it doesn't matter what you actually do nearly as much as what you're known for, here's a personal story. In the aftermath of the global financial crisis, Congress was interrogating Wall Street executives for their role in the debacle. Dick Fuld was testifying and was getting grilled by politicians looking for a villain. As a powerful Wall Street investment banker and CEO of a collapsed firm, Dick was the perfect candidate. By 2010, I had been working on Wall Street for almost 18 years and my mother was watching the hearings. Like much of the country, she was wondering, "WTF happened?" Dick's testimony was filled with jargon and half-truths that even I couldn't decipher. At its conclusion, my mother asked me a simple question.

"Is this what you do!?"

To this day, when people ask her, "What did your son do on Wall Street?" she tells them I was an advisor—never an investment banker.

Key Takeaways

- Building your brand is the key to your freedom.
- *Parlay* every win, no matter how small.
- Breed apostles and leave *behavioral residue*.
- You've arrived if you get a baller nickname.
- If you work on Wall Street, tell people you're an advisor . . . and nothing like Dick Fuld.

---

[2]Name given by the *New York Times*. To be fair, coming from them, this is high praise.

CHAPTER 27

Money Can Buy Happiness

Duh!

Whoever said "Money can't buy happiness" must be rich as hell because I can tell you the opposite is definitely true: no money, no happiness. At the very least, money can sure buy a helluva good time, and unless you live on a commune and barter your way to prosperity, here are a few things to consider if you *do* have money.

Don't Be a Creep

Money equates to freedom, so accumulating wealth should be your objective unless you want to be a slave to your job for the rest of your life. It's hard to build wealth on W-2 income, but at least you have a fighting chance as a Wall Streeter. Why? Their cut is so much larger than the rest of America's.[1] But no matter how much you make, the trap most fall into is spending more than you actually have. If I make $1 million, I'm a millionaire, right? Wrong! First, you may keep half after Uncle Sam's *pizzo*.[2] Second, you'll have less because you're a spendthrift. People who make $100,000 often spend like they make $150,000, those who make $1 million spend like they make $1.5 million, and so on. So if you think of money as your ticket to freedom, which you should, spend wisely or it doesn't matter how much you make. If you spend more than you make, you're officially broke.

---

[1]According to CareerOneStop, the highest-paying industries in the United States are portfolio management, investment banking, and securities dealing, with average annual wages of over $275,000 in 2019.
[2]Protection money paid in the form of taxes. The word is derived from the Sicilian *pizzu*, which means "beak." It's harder to save money with Uncle Sam wetting their beak year in and year out.

Understand that the pay will not last. Let that marinate in your brain. At some point in the future—likely sooner than you think—the compensation will dry up. Every run comes to an end and so will the salad days of your career. Don't get caught in **lifestyle creep**. Like your receding hairline, it can sneak up on you. It starts with trading in that Honda for a BMW, then from your studio apartment to a four-bedroom house in the toniest part of town. Before you know it, you can't live on a million bucks a year. Or two, or three . . .

When Is Enough, Enough?

So if money can buy happiness, how much is enough? Of course, it depends. Every person's burn rate differs, but if you're looking for an answer, then look no further than the scientists. Researchers have shown that well-being does not increase above incomes of $85,000 per year.[3] They found that higher incomes do get the happy juices flowing, but it generally plateaus at that level. (Feel free to wire me every dollar you make above this amount. It may not make you happier, but what about me?) Intuitively, this holds water if you consider **Maslow's Hierarchy of Needs**. At the $85,000 level, you should be able to cover basic physiological needs, so any extra just helps you get bigger versions of everything and keeps you up with the **Joneses**.

It's notable that while the *starting* salary of many Wall Streeters actually *exceeds* this level, many people I know on Wall Street are deeply unhappy and simply work for more money. Wealth may give you the freedom to exert more control over your life and achieve greater happiness, but it can also be the thing that traps you in a constant state of misery.

Harvard psychologist Dan Gilbert clarifies the research on this subject by explaining that *more* money may not buy *more* happiness, but it provides an *opportunity* for happiness. He warns, however, that money "is an opportunity that people routinely squander because the things they *think* will make them happy often don't." Reflect on that the next time you buy that tenth handbag or second sports car.

Pursuing Happiness

There is no shortage of books and research papers promising you the secret to happiness. This isn't one of them; that is, unless your definition of happiness is being the Grand Pooh-bah with thousands of minions doing your bidding. If you're

---

[3]According to the *Proceedings of the National Academy of Sciences of the United States of America,* which drew on 1.7 million experience-sampling reports from 33,000-plus employed U.S. adults in 2020.

looking for another recommendation, try the Bible. After selling five billion copies, you'd think there must be at least one or two tricks in there to cure your funk.

If not the Bible, you may want to look at the **Grant Study**, which had a powerful impact on me. Conducted at Harvard Medical School, it tracked the lives of a group of Harvard grads until their 70s and 80s. Participants included a POTUS, John F. Kennedy; an editor of *The Washington Post,* Ben Bradlee; four men who ran for U.S. Senate; and a presidential Cabinet member. Classic underachievers. To me, the most fascinating elements of the study were the findings on what drives healthy aging. They found that those who had the best *mature adaptations* or defense mechanisms[4] against adversity fared the best. George Valliant, director of the program, explained, "The only thing that really matters in life are your relationships to other people. Happiness is love. . . . The short answer is L-O-V-E." Note that payola didn't make the list.

For the literate among you, this is old news. Two millennia ago, Aristotle's *Nicomachean Ethics* told us that human friendship is necessary in order to live a good life. So why aren't we all happy? This book's guru, Danny Kahneman, says there are three things that hinder happiness. Bear all three in mind the next time you're wallowing in self-pity:

- *Too Broadly Defined.* When one defines happiness across too wide a spectrum, it becomes meaningless. Figure out what it means to you and stick with it. For example, if you want a *happy ending*, make sure you know whether that means you want to watch a Pixar movie or visit your local massage parlor.
- *It's All Relative.* Kahneman defines happiness as "what I experience here and now," but he says that in reality, humans get wrapped up in social yardsticks. Brain science tells us that we care too much about keeping up with, and beating, the **Joneses**. Charlie Munger, vice chairman of Berkshire Hathaway and right-hand man to Warren Buffett, says staying cheerful is a wise thing to do and adds that to do that, you have to let go of negative feelings. Unless you forget the **Joneses** and focus on the now, you're on a one-way path to misery manor.

---

[4]The healthiest, or "mature," adaptations include altruism, humor, anticipation (looking ahead and planning for future discomfort), suppression (a conscious decision to postpone attention to an impulse or conflict, to be addressed in good time), and sublimation (finding outlets for feelings, like putting aggression into sport, or lust into courtship).

- *Focusing Illusion*. With David Schkade, Daniel Kahneman developed the **focusing illusion,** which occurs when we exaggerate the importance of one single factor related to our future happiness and overlook others that, in most cases, have a greater impact. Bear that in mind the next time you think the only reason you didn't get promoted was because you didn't wear your lucky suit to your review.

For those of you starting your career, or who are knee deep in it, take solace that the odds are in your favor that you'll feel better with time. Research has shown that happiness follows a U-shaped curve. It declines from our teenage years but starts to rise in our 50s.[5] Perhaps it's because the gap between our expectations and reality starts to close, or maybe because we know we'll be getting beaucoup discounts through our AARP membership. Whatever the reason, rest assured that your best days are ahead of you.

On the happiness trail, investment banking can create a siblinghood because of its shared, often painful, experience. After retiring, I found that even my most cutthroat colleagues are really quite tolerable outside of work. So given that nurturing meaningful relationships is a key to healthy aging, we all try to reminisce at reunions about the good times and, especially, the bad.

For myself, new pursuits that capture my interest and passion, like my family and writing this book, have kept me in good spirits. Because we're **Two Selves**, and our *Remembering Self* is often in conflict with our *Experiencing Self*, I wanted to memorialize major life moments since retiring from Jefferies. After my two boys were born, I started to record video montages. They document mostly the good, not the bad, because when I'm older, do I really want a permanent reminder of my kid's diaper exploding in my hands? This *Memory Box* has become my arbiter of truth. As I've aged, my memory is fogged by the chaos of parenting, and so I turn to it when in doubt. When my first son claimed he never liked rafting, I showed him a video where he gleefully exclaimed, "This is the best day ever!" When my second son disputed whether he had a birthday cake, we saw that he had two! The box has become an extension of our memories—only better because it doesn't forget and records only what it sees. We can fool ourselves, but not the Memory Box. Kahneman says happiness is *not* cumulative, and like the sign-off on the email that got you a job, or the wrap-up to every client interaction, how you remember your life story is how you judge your own happiness. Endings matter, so do what you can to make your recollections sing. Otherwise, what's the point of making all that dough?

---

[5]Jonathan Rauch, *The Happiness Curve: Why Life Gets Better After 50* (2019).

Key Takeaways

- Don't be a *lifestyle creep*.
- Note *Maslow's Hierarchy of Needs*. Cover the basics. The rest is gravy.
- Learn from the *Grant Study*. Love and relationships matter. Money doesn't.
- Don't stand in the way of your own happiness. Find new pursuits with passion.
- Remember the *Two Selves*. Build your Memory Box.

CHAPTER 28

Writing Checks Your Body Can't Cash

Mismanaging Your Life

You may think life is going to get more and more awesome for you now that you've achieved your career goals. You have more money to feed your habits. You have a better title to put on your Tinder profile and you have minions to boss around. But look into those sunken eyes of your peers. There is no **free lunch** in this world, and you'll realize that you're not only married to your job, you're melded to it. So consider yourself forewarned.

Be careful what you wish for. Rising to the top brings with it the **Winner's Curse**. Just like in an auction, the winner usually overpays to reach the top. In fact, to win, you have to overpay. You'll overpay in time, health, and family, but hopefully not your soul. Anyone playing the game faces this dilemma. To win, one must do more than anyone else, but doing more than anyone else is economically irrational.

Work and life are just one big game so don't take them too seriously. Even though being stoic is a prerequisite to surviving in high-intensity industries, you need to know when to cry, "Uncle." As you build your career, particularly on Wall Street, it's important to self-regulate because no one else will do it for you. Don't be that dog who gets a bowl of food put in front of it and doesn't know when to stop eating. Building careers are lifelong marathons, and your health is the only vehicle to get you to the top. So don't write checks your body can't cash and take care of life outside work or your story will be shorter than a *Dan Brown* chapter.

Resident of Fat City

In my analyst years, we didn't have a fixed stipend for food, so partly due to stress, I'd eat until I'd nearly burst. A couple bagels and cream cheese for breakfast, several helpings of fried rice or a couple hoagies for lunch, and a daily box of Pop-Tarts to tide me over between meals. Given how much crap I had to put up with during the day, for dinner I'd order everything on the takeout menu. It was no wonder that in my first year, I put the Freshman 15 to shame. I gained 30 pounds and my waistline ballooned to 40 inches. After four years of subsisting on ramen noodles in college, I was truly basking in Fat City.

Food was everywhere. I once worked on a deal for a chocolate company and every day while I was drafting their documents, the staff would bring in plates of freshly baked chocolates. I ate over a thousand bucks' worth of fresh chocolates and layered on 20 pounds in 20 days. I was a pig in mud.

But the joke was on me. I felt lethargic, suffered frequent headaches and dizzy spells, and experienced breathing and heart problems. I snuck away from the office and got a physical. The doctor said, "Son, you're a 20-year-old with the body of a 40-year-old." Today, I'd consider that a compliment, but back then I was insulted. He added, "I don't know what you do, but I suggest you find another line of work." Of course, that wasn't an option, so I course-corrected. Out were the Pop-Tarts and in were late-night exercise excursions. For dinner was fish and veggies, and out was my Joey Chestnut impersonation.[1] I tried to get six hours of sleep a night, but still drank half-dozen cups of coffee and half-dozen Diet Cokes all day. C'mon, I still had a job to do!

I also elicited the help of my colleagues, most of whom had become fat asses in their own right. We initiated a competition we called Project Gordo[2] in which we all put money into a pot and the person who lost the most weight by a certain date would get the winnings. Of course, with investment bankers, someone always had to take it too far. One banker ate just boiled cabbage for breakfast, lunch, and dinner for months and lost the weight equivalent of a small child. He won Project Gordo, but I'm not sure spending every waking moment doing the royal squat on the porcelain god was worth it.

---

[1] Joey Chestnut, nicknamed "Jaws," is an American competitive eater and is currently ranked #1 in the world by Major League Eating. He is best known for devouring 76 hot dogs and buns in 10 minutes to win the Mustard Yellow Belt at the famous Nathan's Hot Dog Eating Contest for the 13th time in 14 years.

[2] Bankers can't resist code-naming everything—even when it has nothing to do with business.

Spending Time in All the Wrong Places

Banker life is hectic and intense. Nervous breakdowns, even suicides, were common. You might have to whisk away to some hell hole at a moment's notice and cancel all your personal plans. When you're junior, you do whatever the MD tells you. You might get lucky and transfer to a regional office where the pace isn't as crazy. It would be the equivalent of being shipped off to Transylvania—not Transylvania, Romania, but Transylvania, North Carolina—where the climate is friendly and so are the people.

Even as an MD, you go wherever the client beckons. As an MD, I would routinely be on the road every weekday and come home on the weekend. I'd pitch an IPO in London, jet to New York City for an M&A negotiation, and wine and dine a client in Beijing, all in a single week. I had barely enough time for myself, let alone loved ones.

I knew I was getting to the end of my rope when I received a nice, black package from United Airlines. Inside was a personalized card, a couple of luggage tags, and a letter which read, "Dear Mr. Liu, It is my pleasure to congratulate you on achieving one million lifetime flight miles." I thought at the time, "That's nice of them." A few months later, I got a letter from American Airlines. It said, "Dear Mr. Liu, When an AAdvantage member has the rare distinction of earning 1,000,000 total program miles, it's our pleasure to celebrate that achievement." I thought, "Wow, that's a lot of miles." Then another million-mile welcome came from Delta Airlines.

I went through all of my statements and tallied up the total: *five million* miles. Just to put that into perspective, that would mean I'd likely flown at least one flight per week for ten years, or spent 10,000 hours in the air![3] You know what I could have done with that time? Yup, you guessed it—the Chinese Stan Lee.

If you do look for love, my suggestion is to find someone who understands your work and won't read you the riot act every time you have to go the extra mile to get ahead. I got lucky and married an ex–investment banker. She understood the lifestyle and the price of success. Many other MDs did not, and I saw it take a toll on their relationships and their happiness. Alternatively, you could simply accept that compromises need to be made. An extremely successful banker I know once said to me, "I'd never admit this publicly, but my work comes first, my kids second, and my wife third." Of course, he's divorced.

---

[3]Assuming a plane flies 500 mph, 5 million miles would take 10,000 hours, or almost 14 months.

The Work–Life Tradeoff Sham

Remember how I said there is no such thing as a free lunch? Unfortunately, the same applies to work–life balance. Because there are only 168 hours in a week, time is the ultimate **zero-sum game**. Something's gotta give. We fear loss more than value pleasure, but ask yourself, "What are you prepared to lose to gain?" Family or money? Title or spouse? You might defer payment, but everything has a cost sooner or later.

Hank Paulson, former chairman and CEO of Goldman Sachs and U.S. secretary of the Treasury, once said, "You can't ask the firm how many hours a week you're going to work. If you're working 50, how about 55 . . . 60 . . . how about 65? You have to learn to say no. You have to plan your own life. I know of many, many people who didn't quite get to their career goals, and they're happy. . . . I don't know anyone who says, 'Boy, I had a great career and I'm happy because I screwed up my life outside my career, my family life.'"

Speaking as a father, it only gets worse when you have kids. On average, three-quarters of the time you have with them will have been gone by the time they reach 12 years old,[4] almost all of it by the time they head to college. After you have children, the work–life tradeoff becomes impossible.

Ruth Porat, CFO of Google and former CFO of Morgan Stanley, says she hates the term *work–life balance*: "I think it's a setup, and a trap for all of us. I think what you want is a mix in your life that works. It's kind of like a kaleidoscope that would be really boring if it's just made of two even pieces of glass; you need to have it to mix and change."

Also, everyone's tradeoff is different, but Jack Hancock, a great friend who passed away in 2019, gave me some great advice. He was a major general in the U.S. Army, was a former EVP at Wells Fargo, and had numerous children and grandchildren. His advice was to move heaven and earth to be there for life's key moments, such as anniversaries, weddings, and birthdays, because toward the end of your life, those would be the only ones you and your loved ones would ultimately remember.

Default Yourself

By now, you should have realized that making choices is difficult because it means cutting off future options. By avoiding choices, we can avoid mistakes, but by making well-researched, long-term decisions ahead of time, you set yourself up for a greater likelihood of success.

---

[4]Ginny Yurich, "75% of the Time We Spend with Our Kids in Our Lifetime Will Be Spent by Age 12," *1000 Hours Outside* (2013).

I used *defaults* to manage my family life. I'd buy plane tickets for Thanksgiving and Christmas a year in advance so I could truthfully tell my boss I couldn't work on Christmas Day because I had plans to be home. I scheduled doctor's appointments months in advance so I could have my prostate checked rather than fix the fonts on a prospectus cover. Anything of key family importance, I'd put in my calendar years in advance and made sure not to miss them unless hell really was freezing over.

I also set up financial defaults to protect my future. If I wanted to make a change, I'd have to consciously choose to deviate from the defaults. I maxed out on 401(k) contributions and flex spending limits, tithed a fixed percentage of my salary, and never spent a single bonus check. I instructed my assistant that if I was ever traveling for personal reasons to fly me in economy. Of course, when it was for business, I flew like a baller and stayed at the Four Seasons. I may be cheap, but I'm not a fool!

To ensure my financial freedom, I set a goal to save a certain amount of money by the time I reached 40. This nest egg would allow me to walk away on my own terms without fear of not having enough once I left Wall Street. Many successful people I know have a similar attitude no matter how much money they made. I worked with a centi-millionaire who used to take extra drinks from the limo we'd rent for him and scoop up all the chocolates left on his hotel pillow. When we went on a roadshow, he would get irritated by all the uneaten chicken lunches laying wasted on the tables. One of my associates asked him, somewhat in jest, "Why are you so cheap?"

He answered without missing a beat, "So I will always be worth $100 million."

Key Takeaways

- Beware the *Winner's Curse* when you reach your career goals.
- Don't live in Fat City.
- Find someone who understands your career goals.
- Work–life is a *zero-sum game*.
- Set *defaults* to achieve your long-term life goals.
- Be a cheap bastard.

CHAPTER 29

It's Quitting Time

Exit the Stage

Business was good. In fact, it was great. My team was on a roll and we had invested almost 15 years building our presence in Silicon Valley. I had developed a strong personal brand in the Internet sector and I was finally getting the coveted inbound calls—less pounding the pavement in search of new deals and more harvesting the fruits of my labor.

However, I had the classic conundrum that faces a lot of executives. You want to leave on your own terms, when you're on top, but you're really hitting your stride and getting paid like a bull in heat. You tell yourself, "I could hold out for just another year," and then another, and another, until one day, life has passed you by. Your two sons have left the roost and are now married, your wife is hanging out with the gardener, and you're approaching 60 years old with the body of an 80-year-old.

For me, I never wanted to become one of the older bankers ahead of me: unhappy, bitter, and a stranger to their families. So I stuck with the plan to exit on my own terms, like Michael Jordan of the Chicago Bulls. I took his Gatorade commercial, "Be Like Mike," to heart. I didn't want to overstay my welcome.

Why We Stay

I've often wondered why people stay in crappy jobs. If it's for the money, I totally get it. For some, the word *enough* doesn't exist. Even though we learned that $85,000 per year—less than the starting compensation of many first-year analysts on Wall Street—should be enough to make you happy, for many, it isn't. **Lifestyle creep** sets in and they have only themselves to blame.

There are other reasons people stay. You might believe you're doing "God's work."[1] If so, I can't help you because unless you're an imam, priest, or rabbi, you're not actually doing God's work. Or it could be the **endowment effect** that makes you stay for years. You stuck with it even though you knew it wasn't the best place, but because it was your place. Or you suffer from the **sunk cost**[2] fallacy. You've invested so much that you can't possibly leave now—not when you're *only* twenty-five years away from that gold watch.

Psychologist Paul Farrell wrote, "During his speech at an annual dinner many years ago, our president joked, 'Working at Morgan Stanley is like making love to a gorilla. You don't stop when you want to, you stop when *she* wants to.'"[3]

I think the biggest and most insidious reason for staying is **relativity**. Dan Ariely says, "**Relativity** helps people make decisions, but it can also make them miserable. People compare their lives to those of others, leading to jealousy and envy."[4]

It's a vicious circle when we try to keep up with our friends and get trapped. My suggestion? Get new friends.

---

[1]Goldman Sachs created an investment vehicle to help a hedge fund client bet against the housing market in 2007. The Securities and Exchange Commission sued Goldman in 2010 for securities fraud and the firm eventually agreed to pay $550 million to settle the claims. At the time, Goldman's CEO, Lloyd Blankfein, said Goldman was doing "God's work."

[2]A *sunk cost* is any past cost that has already been paid and cannot be recovered.

[3]Paul B. Farrell, "7 Reasons Wall Street Bankers' Brains Act Bizarre," *Marketwatch*, July 26, 2012.

[4]Dan Ariely, *Predictably Irrational* (2008).

The Talk

I had already started to think about my exit when I turned 40. Some may call it a mid-life crisis, but I call it Dave 2.0. I thought about how I could help younger professionals, particularly the disadvantaged, and began considering writing what ultimately became this book. I even posted a short note at the time on my website:

Hard to believe that on this day 20 years ago, I joined my firm. A short stint turned into an amazing 20-year ride. Seems like only yesterday I sat at my cubicle with my landline (no cell phones), Pentium PC running Windows 3.1 (no browser), and HP-12C. No regrets but wish I could go back and give my younger self some advice:

1. *Master Excel. It will be the way companies will confuse investors for the next 100 years.*

2. *Remember those fancy dinners and limo rides when you were being recruited? Good. At least you'll have the memories.*

3. *When they offer you a pager, say, "No!" Trust me, the device may change but that dog leash is going to be with you forever.*

4. *Keep the faith. You'll eventually see your family and friends again . . . five years from now, in 1998.*

5. *Not everyone has nervous breakdowns in this job. Just the people in your Analyst class.*

6. *Don't worry about being in the building during the Northridge Earthquake. I hear the building is earthquake proof.*

7. *Stay away from those third servings at breakfast, lunch, afternoon tea, dinner, midnight snack, etc.*

8. *Buy clothes that are 2 sizes too big. You're going to ignore #7.*

9. *Tell people you're an advisor, not an i-banker. You may think it's cool now, but in about 20 years even your mother will tell her friends that you're a financial consultant.*

10. *Not all managing directors are jerks. Who knows, you may be one of them one day.*

11. *Can't wait to see what the next 20 years will bring. . . .*

When I finally told my boss I was going to retire from the firm, he paused and simply asked, "How old are you?" He was surprised that I was retiring at 41. I explained, "I joined over 20 years ago," to which he responded, "Wow, you've been here longer than the stains on the office carpet."

How to Leave

How you leave is just as important as how you start. Some choose to leave on principle, in a flaming blaze of glory. But this can backfire. In March 2012, Greg Smith, a former Goldman executive, wrote an op-ed for the *New York Times* titled "Why I Am Leaving Goldman Sachs" in which he ripped the firm's leadership for making client interests secondary to the firm's. Unfortunately, he came off as a hypocrite because he didn't seem to have a problem cashing his bonus checks for 12 years before quitting.

I never understood why some choose to make their departure personal. You joined a business, not a family. Perhaps there were times you felt wronged, but a company operates to achieve its business goals, first and foremost. I tend to subscribe to the words of Michael Corleone: "It's not personal, [Sonny]. It's strictly business."

Even if you're completely self-interested, it's always in your best interest to leave on good terms. You never know when you'll need a good reference or want to call on your old firm for help. After I resigned, I agreed to remain until the firm could find a replacement. Even after that, I stayed on as a strategic consultant so that the transition would be smooth. The world is a very small place and leaving on bad terms will only hurt you.

A few years after I left, I was worried that I had left prematurely and would be filled with regret. After all, the market continued to roar ahead and had I stayed, I would likely have continued to reach all-time highs in compensation. But when I heard my successor made even more money than I had, I immediately thought, "Good for him!" That's when I knew I was truly done!

Key Takeaways

- "Be Like Mike." Leave on top, on your own terms.
- Acknowledge why you don't leave and learn to live with it.
- Always leave on good terms.
- Have no regrets.

CHAPTER 30

The Afterlife

Now What?

The first time I got an inkling that I wasn't exactly in the Mother Teresa of professions was at a roadshow. These are in-person meetings where a company's management pitches itself to investors. Bankers attend these meetings primarily as chaperones, but investors generally don't like them in these meetings because even though they know we've coached management, they're hoping they can get the real skinny on the business by catching management with their pants down. I was in a meeting where one investor asked my CEO client, "Why are you hanging around with scum like him?" as he nodded in my direction. He added that I represented the worst of humankind, then paused. After some contemplation, he pointed his stubby finger at me and said, "Actually, he's a notch above pedophile."

It was early in my career and even if I believed I was doing God's work, there were many people who thought that being a Wall Street banker wasn't exactly an honorable profession. I could make the same argument for almost every profession except for those that actually save lives or souls. But despite my moral justification, it did make me wonder how long I wanted to stay just a gnat's hair above pedophile? Eventually, I'd need to answer the question, "What comes next?"

A very successful entrepreneur, who started multiple companies, once told me there are no such things as bad services or products, just bad distribution. In many respects, he's right. With almost eight billion people on the planet, a market must exist for your services or product no matter how inane. The key is finding it.

For those of you ready to exit stage left, don't despair if you're wondering what your life will be like after your current career. What could you possibly do as an ex-lawyer, -banker, -consultant, or -product manager? The good news is the functional skills you've honed are valuable to almost any business or organization. Moreover, you've mastered the skills needed to climb up the **corporate ladder** and those powers can be put to good use. The bad news is that if you came from a highly compensated industry, those fat bonus checks or stock grants may be a thing of the past. You'll need to recalibrate your lifestyle because the afterlife will likely not be as lucrative.

There's definitely life after a career on Wall Street. At Jefferies, Steve Bannon was a partner doing media banking and left to become a major politico who helped Donald Trump become POTUS. Sage Kelly resigned from Jefferies in disgrace but got a second tour of duty running Cantor Fitzgerald. Many of my ex-colleagues went on to become entrepreneurs and started investment banks and tech companies, and even more became titans of private equity and venture capital. As for me, I became an entrepreneur starting four companies and am an angel investor in over a dozen, several of which reached billion-dollar "unicorn" status. I finally have time to pursue my aspiration to be the Chinese Stan Lee and am trying my hand as an author, cartoonist, and filmmaker.

Be a Hero

Before we bid adieu, I leave you with one last story that hopefully will inspire you. Almost every major Hollywood blockbuster follows a formula known as the **Hero's Journey**, also known as the *monomyth*. It's a story that involves a hero who goes on an adventure, is victorious in a crisis, and comes home changed or transformed. Sound familiar? It should. It's the story of the stars of the world's greatest religions—Jesus, Moses, Mohammed, Buddha, among them. Some great movies too, like *The Matrix*, *Little Miss Sunshine*, and *Star Wars*. Frodo, Luke, Rey, Harry, Neo, and even Nemo have all been on this journey. They pursue meaningful lives by going on a journey where they use their unique talents to save themselves and ultimately others.

Now that I've spoiled every movie for you, the reason we love this formula is because it provides a good roadmap for how to live our lives. This book is my version of the **Hero's Journey**. The gift I bring to you is what I've learned the hard way so that it can be easier for you. So go on your own journey, learn something, and share it with others.

Key Takeaways

- It's never too late to remake yourself and try something new.
- Go on your own *Hero's Journey*.

Conclusion

Welcome to the end! If you've skipped to this page just to get the highlights, I'm proud of you, but no such luck. You'll still need to read the book to get the gist of my recommendations!

As I told you at the outset, this book was never going to be your one silver bullet to get you to the top. It's simply a book to teach you there are other ways to get ahead in your career that aren't taught at school or home.

As a gift to you, assuming you'll forget what you've read by the time you finish this paragraph, I've prepared a Career Codex that you can get by registering on my website.[1] This cheat sheet will help you remember the key tips, tricks, and science needed at every stage of your career. Feel free to rip these pages out, laminate them, and put them in your purse, wallet, or underwear for safe keeping.

I strongly believe that once you've achieved some success in life, it's important to give back. So a substantial portion of the net proceeds from this book will go toward charitable organizations that I support, specifically those dedicated to improving the lives of children born with a cleft lip or palate, Asian Americans, women, and other disadvantaged groups. I hope you'll join me in supporting these meaningful causes.

If you found my book helpful, enjoyable, or simply a great door stop, please help spread the word. If you have any questions or suggestions, feel free to reach me on my website at **www.liucrative.com**. If you didn't enjoy my book, keep it to yourself.

I'm so happy that you thought this was the best book you ever read and that it's the single biggest reason for your success. I hope that when you recall our fond times together, you'll remember this ancient Chinese proverb that does a great job of summarizing the game of work and life:

"If you must play, decide on three things at the start: the rules of the game, the stakes, and the quitting time."

Play strong; play smart; play well.

---

[1] www.liucrative.com

Glossary

Term	Meaning
Affinity Bias	Tendency to get along with others who are similar to you. It's why you enjoy the company of that lazy sloth who's always late and tries every get-rich-quick scheme.
Anchoring Effect	Tendency to over-rely on one data point when making a decision. Like when you assume I'm a jerk just because I write like one.
Assortative Mating	Pattern in which individuals with similarities mate with one another more frequently versus random pairings. Unfortunately, this explains your lack of success with the opposite sex.
Asymmetry of Information	Situations in which one party has more information than the other. Now you know why you always overpay for everything.
Attentional Bias	Tendency to pay attention to some things while simultaneously ignoring others. Cheeseburger, focaccia, chocolate cake, chicken curry, fried dumplings . . . hungry yet?
BCG Matrix (also known as the Growth/ Share Matrix)	Created by the Boston Consulting Group in the 1970s. It manages your ROTI by dividing prospects and clients into four quadrants based on market growth and relative market share.
Behavioral Economics	Study of psychological, cognitive, emotional, cultural, and social factors as they affect the decisions of individuals and institutions and how they vary from those implied by classical economic theory. It's the reason why Jeff Bezos is a gazillionaire and you're not.
Behavioral Residue	Remaining evidence of one's actions or involvement. Next time you leave a mess in your wake, tell them it's your creativity at work.
Belief Bias	Tendency to rely on one's beliefs, rather than logic, in reasoning. Now you know why no one listens to your arguments. They believe you're stupid.
Blind Spot Bias	Tendency to see oneself as less biased than others. No way!
Choice Supportive Bias	Tendency to remember one's choices as better than they were in actuality. That's why we're always right.
Clammy-Hand Test	Handshake test to determine one's propensity to lie or stretch the truth. Also perfect for spreading disease and pestilence.
Cleveland Airport Test	Test to determine if you would want to spend time with a person at a God-forsaken airport. Can easily be substituted for spending time with you trapped in an elevator.

Term	Meaning
Cognitive Bias	Deviation from the norm or rationality in judgment. It's why stupidity has company.
Cognitive Dissonance	When one holds contradictory beliefs, ideas, or values and experiences stress when their actions go against one or more of them. The reason why smart people do stupid things.
Confirmation Bias	Tendency to search for, interpret, focus on, and remember information in a way that confirms one's preconceived notions. For instance, I know everything I've written is 100 percent accurate so there really is no need for the citations.
Corporate Ladder	Describes the progression from entry-level positions to higher levels of seniority. A surprise is waiting at the top (see *Minion-Circle*).
Cultural Fit	Refers to when one's beliefs and behaviors are aligned with that of the company. Ever wonder how you and that nimrod in the other cubicle can both be a cultural fit?
Cultural Inclusion	Refers to reform that welcomes diversity in the workplace. What did you think this was? A frat house?
Curse of Knowledge	When an individual, communicating with others, unknowingly assumes that others have the capability to understand. My bad, the next edition of this book will be 100 percent cartoons.
Decoy Effect	Where you change one's preference by adding a third option. Now you know how you got supersized for only an extra dollar.
Dunbar's Number	Suggested limit to the number of people with whom one can maintain stable social relationships by British anthropologist Robin Dunbar. He proposed that humans can comfortably maintain 150 stable relationships. Sucks to be number 151.
Dysrationalia	Inability to think and behave rationally despite having reasonable levels of intelligence. A fancy word for stupid.
Emotional Intelligence (EQ)	Ability to recognize emotions in self and others, use emotional information to guide thinking and behavior, or adjust emotions to adapt to the environment. Inversely correlated with the "foot-in-mouth" disease plaguing much of your youth.
Empowerment Model	Framework used to focus on one's competence rather than deficits, to support resourcefulness rather than weaknesses, and to develop skills rather than disparage them. Of course, sometimes people can be hopeless, too.

Term	Meaning
Endowment Effect (also known as the IKEA Effect)	Tendency for one to demand much more to give up an object than they would be willing to pay to acquire it. Now you know why you can't part with that broken FARTFULL workbench you bought from IKEA.
Focusing Illusion	Magnifying the importance of something just because of one's increased attention on it. Misdirection technique used by magicians and your boss, especially at comp time.
Free Lunch	Situation in which no cost is incurred by one receiving goods or services. Like all those free services on Facebook and Google ;-).
Frequency Illusion	Tendency to notice something more often once it's been seen for the first time. No, not everyone is buying the lime-green Tesla.
F*ck-You Money	The amount of money needed to tell your employer to go f*ck themselves without any negative repercussions. Of course, this is a misnomer because we all love our jobs and would never say this to our bosses.
Galatea Effect (also known as the Pygmalion Effect)	When the belief in one's ability to perform actually impacts how they perform. It's how you got this far in life.
Grant Study	Over 75-year longitudinal study that is part of the Study of Adult Development at Harvard Medical School. The subjects were all male and of American nationality and evaluated at least every two years. The goal of the study was to identify predictors of healthy aging. Money was *not* one of them.
Greater Fool Theory	The price of an object is determined not by its intrinsic value, but rather by the demand of a specific consumer. Our economy remains healthy thanks to P. T. Barnum's phrase, "There's a sucker born every minute."
Grit	Passion and perseverance for long-term meaningful goals. Or ability to take crap and like it.
Groupthink	Occurs within groups where the desire for harmony or conformity results in an irrational or dysfunctional decision-making outcome. It's why you never use the Ask the Audience lifeline on the game show *Who Wants to Be a Millionaire.*
Guanxi	System of social networks and influence peddling that makes work so much easier.
Halo Effect	Tendency for one's traits to positively impact perceptions of one's other attributes. No, dudes, pasting a picture of Brad Pitt on your forehead won't make you more attractive.

Term	Meaning
Hedonic Adaptation	Tendency to quickly return to a relatively stable level of happiness despite major events or life changes. So if you win the lottery, feel free to send me your winnings since the happiness will wear off on you.
Hero's Journey	Common template of stories that involve a hero who goes on an adventure, is victorious in a quest, and comes home changed or transformed. Now you know the storyline of every Hollywood blockbuster.
Heuristics	Strategies based on prior experience with similar problems. These help you with everything from identifying good deals to stopping the toilet from overflowing.
Hindsight Bias	Tendency to see past events as predictable at the time those events occurred. You think you have the moral high ground to say, "I told you so," even if you didn't.
Hoogle	Being a physical embodiment of Google by helping one's boss discern the signal from the noise by distilling mountains of data. Of course, if you really were this, you'd be a trillionaire.
Hot-Cold Empathy Gap	Underestimating the influences of visceral drives on one's own attitudes, preferences, and behaviors. A good reason to have a cold shower before any major purchase.
Hyperbolic Discounting	Tendency to have a preference for immediate payoffs relative to later payoffs. Like the co-founder of Apple who sold his 10 percent stake for $2,300. Duh!
Idiosyncrasy Credit	It's one's ability to deviate from a group's expectations. It's why the old people tend to get away with bending the rules.
Illusory Superiority	Overestimating one's positive qualities and underestimating negative ones, relative to others. Now you know why you can't get a date.
Initial Impression Bias	Tendency to be biased by initial impressions. Of course, this worked in your favor when your significant other fell in love with you at first sight. Thank God they didn't do more due diligence!
Interviewer Illusion	Tendency of interviewers to overrate their ability to interview and choose the best candidate. Everyone who loves you is a genius and the ones who don't are idiots.
Irrational Escalation	Doubling-down based on a prior decision even when you know it was a bad one. Also known as throwing good money after bad.

Term	Meaning
Joneses	Neighbors who one tends to constantly compare oneself against. Of course, you might feel differently if you knew they were up to their eyeballs in debt and living a sham.
Lake Wobegon Effect	Tendency to overestimate one's capabilities; named in honor of a fictional town where everyone is above average. Must be the water.
Leveraged Buyout (LBO)	Acquiring a company by borrowing a substantial amount of money from third parties.
Lifestyle Creep	Occurs when more resources are spent toward increasing standards of living and former luxuries become perceived necessities. Contagious on Wall Street.
Loss Aversion	Perceived pain of giving up an object is greater than the pleasure associated with acquiring it. This is why you'll ride that loser stock right to zero.
Maslow's Hierarchy of Needs	A theory of motivation stating that five categories of human needs dictate an individual's behavior: physiological (food and clothing), safety (job security), love and belonging (friendship), esteem, and self-actualization.
Mean Reversion	Financial term for the assumption that a stock's price will tend to move to the average price over time. Remember this the next time you're on a roll and can't lose.
Minion-Circle	Variation on the corporate ladder because it assumes that everyone has a boss; everyone is someone else's minion.
Model Minority Myth	Typically used against Asian Americans, this refers to a minority group perceived as particularly successful, especially in a manner that contrasts with other minority groups. OK, you got us. We're all rich, obedient, workaholic, math geniuses.
Nash Equilibrium	Equilibrium reached when no individual participant can gain an advantage if the strategies of the others remain unchanged.
Negativity Bias	Tendency to put more emphasis on negative experiences than positive ones. It's why I hope for the best but expect the worst.
Not Invented Here Syndrome (NIH)	Tendency for one to avoid things they didn't create themselves. It's the only reason why you don't think this is the greatest book ever written.
Overconfidence	Excessive confidence in one's own answers to questions. You may not be as dumb as you think, but you're certainly not as smart.

Term	Meaning
Overoptimism	Believing the world is a better place than it is; our inability to accept the full breadth of how human nature leaves us vulnerable.
Ownership Bias	The tendency of groups to prefer their own ideas rather than those provided by others.
Paradox of Choice	Having too many options; rather than bringing happiness, causes more stress and stalls decision-making. See there is some upside to being poor.
Parlay	Snowballing initial wins into even bigger ones. It's how the rich get richer.
Peak-End Rule	Tendency to perceive not the sum of an entire experience but the average of how it was at its peak (e.g., pleasant or unpleasant) and how it ended. Happy endings all around!
Pessimism	The opposite of the overoptimism bias. Pessimists weigh negative consequences over positive ones.
Planning Fallacy	Tendency to underestimate one's own time to completion.
Post-Mortem	After a project is completed, determining what went wrong and could have been done better. This is the arena of second-guessers and Monday Morning quarterbacks.
Post-Purchase Rationalization	After the fact, making ourselves believe a purchase was worth what we paid for it. A classic trick to validate a deal in the eyes of a buyer.
Pre-Mortem	Imagining that a project has failed, then working backward to determine what could have led to its failure. We could be here all day with your projects.
Priming Effect	When one's exposure to something subconsciously influences their response. It's what makes you no different from Pavlov's dogs.
Prisoner's Dilemma	Explains why two rational people might not cooperate even though it's in their best interest to do so. Of course, it doesn't apply to your siblings who you'd gladly sell down the river for a dollar.
Prospect Theory	Describes how individuals assess their loss and gain perspective in an asymmetric manner. If faced with a risky choice leading to gains, individuals are risk-averse, preferring solutions that lead to a lower expected utility but with a higher certainty. If faced with a risky choice leading to losses, individuals are risk-seeking, preferring solutions that lead to a lower expected utility as long as it has the potential to avoid losses. Now you know why insurance companies are rich and lotteries are for fools.

Term	Meaning
Public Information Books (PIBs)	Gigantic documents containing every publicly available piece of information about a company, including annual reports, Wall Street analyst writeups, public 10-K and 10-Q filings, press clippings, etc. Makes good door stops.
Reactance	Desire to do the opposite of what someone wants you to do to prove your freedom of choice. Reverse psychology used when pitching potential acquisitions to a buyer.
Reactive Deval-uation Bias	Occurs when a proposal is devalued if it comes from an antagonist. It's why even if your archenemy has good advice, you ignore him as you drive off a cliff.
Recency Bias	Favoring recent events over past ones. This is why after one bad fantasy football game, you're ready to trade your best player.
Reciprocity Bias	Tendency to reciprocate actions others have done toward you. Favors make the world go round.
Relationship Capital	Sum of all relationships of all people within a firm. Whoever has the most, rules the roost.
Relativity	Coined by Dan Ariely, this is how people make decisions, but it also causes misery because they compare themselves to others. Those Joneses again!
Return on Investment (ROI)	Ratio between income and investment over time. The magic formula every finance jock uses to figure out if something is worth it.
Return on Time Invested (ROTI)	Ratio between output and time invested to generate that output over time. The best way to measure if you're just wasting your life away.
Risk Aversion	Tendency of people to prefer outcomes with low uncertainty to those outcomes with high uncertainty, even if the average outcome of the latter is equal to or higher in monetary value than the more certain outcome. Fancy word for being chicken.
Rule of Three	Principle that suggests that a trio of events or characters is more humorous, satisfying, or effective than other numbers. Sucks to be four.
Seersucker Illusion	When one irrationally seeks out and relies on experts.
Self-Enhancement Bias	Tendency to take all the credit for successes while giving little or no credit to other individuals or external factors. We all know bastards who practice this religiously.
Self-Enhancing Transmission Bias	Tendency to talk up ourselves and conveniently forget our mistakes. This is why we love ourselves so much. We're perfect!

Term	Meaning
Self-Fulfilling Prophecy	Phenomenon of someone predicting something and this prediction or expectation coming true simply because the person believes it will. I think I can, I think I can. . . .
Self-Serving Bias	Cognitive or perceptual process that is distorted by the need to maintain and enhance self-esteem, or the tendency to perceive oneself in an overly favorable manner. If not me, then who?
Shit Sandwich	Method of delivering bad news but in a more palatable form. Would you prefer just the shit?
Signal-to-Noise Ratio	Measure used in science and engineering that compares the level of a desired signal to the level of background noise. My formula for judging any junior's value-add and any Internet site worth bookmarking.
Sinister Six Syndrome	When enemies band together to achieve a common goal but then revert to adversaries once that goal is perceived to have been achieved. Amazing how they never learn.
Smartcuts	Smarter ways of doing things. This is why sometimes laziness wins.
Social Proof	Phenomenon where people follow actions of the masses because they think it must be the correct behavior. Get those likes and watch the money pour in.
Status Quo	Tendency to prefer that things stay the same. It's why even after reading this book, you're likely to just go back to your same ol' same ol'.
Sunk Cost	Cost that has already been incurred and cannot be recovered. Like what you spent buying this book.
Survivorship Bias	Concentrating on the people or things that survived some process and inadvertently overlooking those that didn't because of their lack of visibility. Why everyone seems to be über successful and getting filthy rich except you.
TMZ Test	Test to ensure that whatever one writes or posts is suitable for the front page of TMZ. Yes, I know it's a low bar.
Tragedy of the Commons	Situation in which individuals who have open access to a resource act in their own self-interest. It's why you work your juniors to the bone; if not you, then someone else will do it.

Term	Meaning
Two Selves	Created by Daniel Kahneman to describe how the brain works to create two selves. The *Experiencing Self* knows only the present moment, while the *Remembering Self* evaluates your experiences, draws lessons from them, and decides your future. Now you know why you're the only one who remembers you as a rock star in high school.
Unus	Latin for "one" and "only" and is the root of the word *unique*. Can easily be mistaken for another word sometimes used to describe your behavior.
Utility Theory	Explains economic behavior based on the premise that one ranks choices depending upon individual preferences or utility. It's why you would rather watch *Star Wars* and eat bonbons than hone your presentation skills like I told you.
Whisper Wire	"You tell me yours, and I'll tell you mine." Usually regarding compensation or bonus.
Winner's Curse	Phenomenon in which the winner of an auction is the bidder with the most optimistic evaluation of the asset and therefore will tend to overestimate and overpay. Now you know why so many rich and successful people are bitter old fools.
Wisdom of the Crowd	Collective opinion of a group of individuals rather than that of a single expert. It's why you always use the Ask the Audience lifeline on the game show *Who Wants to Be a Millionaire*.
Wise Feedback	Targeted, constructive feedback that conveys high expectations and thus reaches a more receptive audience. See *Shit Sandwich*.
Zero-Risk Bias	Tendency to prefer no risk even when alternative options produce greater overall reduction in risk. It's why you'll never dare to be great.
Zero-Sum Game	Situation in which each participant's gain or loss of utility is exactly balanced by the losses or gains of the utility of the other participants. Don't ever believe your bosses when they say what they pay you has no impact on what they pay themselves.

Index